natural michigan

A nature-lover's guide to 165 Michigan wildlife sanctuaries, nature preserves, wilderness areas, state parks and other natural attractions.

by

Tom Powers

Friede Publications

Natural Michigan

Friede Publications
2339 Venezia Drive
Davison, Michigan 48423

Printed in the United States of America

ISBN 0-9608588-6-5

Acknowledgments

A great debt of gratitude is owed to many people who helped a dream become reality:

Gary Barfknecht, for his unrepayable encouragement and help, and my wife, Barbara, who literally made this book possible.

And special thanks to a good friend, Dick Derenzy, who rode shotgun on my many forays and said he was just along for the ride but without whose help I would still be floundering around on some nameless two-track in northern Michigan.

And from all of us who enjoy the out-of-doors, a thank you to the Michigan Nature Association, the Nature Conservancy, the Little Traverse Conservancy and the countless other nature associations who are saving some of Michigan's most beautiful areas from condominiumization.

All photos are by the author unless otherwise noted.

Cover Photos: Jordan River Valley

Photo page *iii* : Pinckney Recreation Area

Explanation of Symbols

Hiking

Birdwatching

Camping

Picnicking

Scenic Attraction

Swimming

Introduction

This book was written for those of you who, like me, need to escape the daily rigors, tensions and hassles of modern life by taking an hour's walk through a quiet, peaceful woods; by leaving civilization behind on a several-day-long backpacking expedition; or by birdwatching, beachcombing or simply enjoying a Sunday picnic in a beautiful setting. No matter how you do it, the opportunity to experience nature's beauty, power, fragility, infinite complexities and sublime rhythms always offers a healing touch.

And we are blessed, for within the borders of our great state are almost numberless (though not always well-known) places at which to enjoy quiet, seclusion, unmatched natural beauty and an escape from the daily grind. *Natural Michigan* will introduce and guide you to more than 160 of these natural havens—parks, nature preserves, wildlife sanctuaries and wilderness areas ranging in size from less than 10 to more than 10,000 acres. Many, I hope, will be within an easy drive from your home; others will make fine weekend excursions or even outstanding vacation destinations.

And you don't have to be an expert naturalist (a Roger Tory Peterson or a John Muir) to enjoy nature at these areas. We all start out tripping over Petoskey Stones instead of finding them, are driven to distraction trying to identify birds, and couldn't on a bet pick out the one ironwood tree in a forest full of beeches. I still can't start a campfire without a blowtorch and will probably go to my grave without ever finding (even in a rock shop) a Lake Superior agate.

But it really doesn't matter because nature can be experienced and enjoyed on all levels of understanding. Seeing the sky blackened with migrating waterfowl at Fish Point on Saginaw Bay, standing alone on top of Pyramid Point at Sleeping Bear Dunes National Lakeshore, or passing quietly through the primeval Huron Swamp in Indian Springs Metropark will quicken the pulses and lift the hearts of experienced and uninitiated alike.

So don't let inexperience hold you back. Knowledge will come, and if you want to hasten the process, take along several field guides to identify those elusive birds, butterflies, insects, wildflowers and trees.

Then experience adventure, solace, privacy, breathtaking beauty and a renewal of the spirit in natural Michigan.

Tom Powers
Swartz Creek

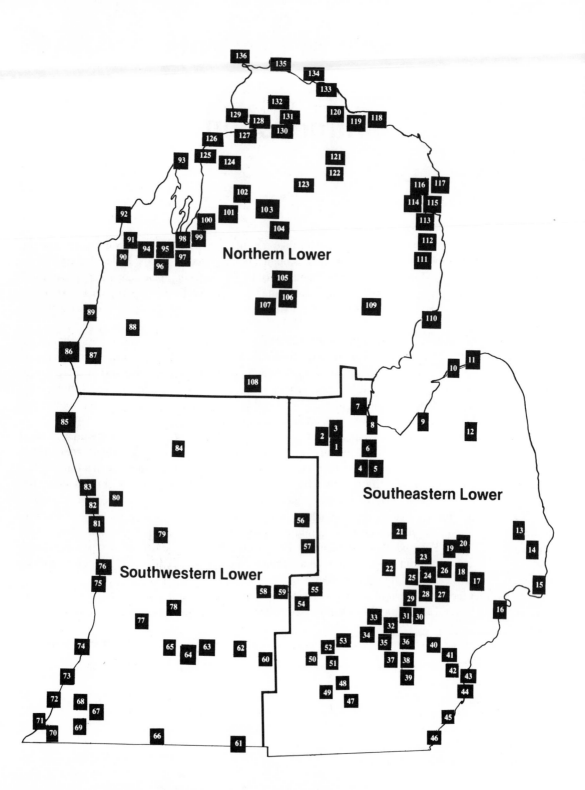

Northern Lower

Southeastern Lower

Southwestern Lower

Table of Contents

Lower Peninsula

(Continued on page viii)

CONTENTS
(Continued from page vii)

Northern Lower

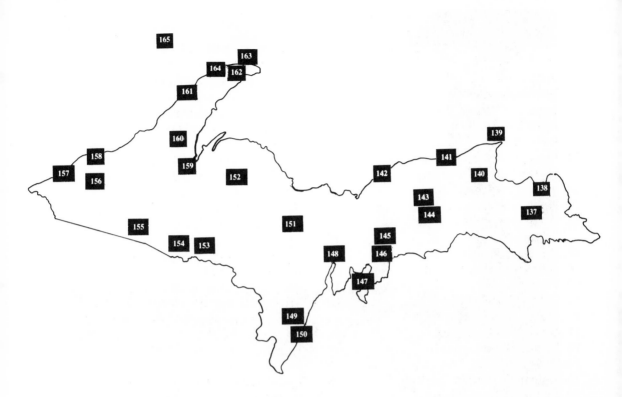

Upper Peninsula

Southeastern Lower Peninsula

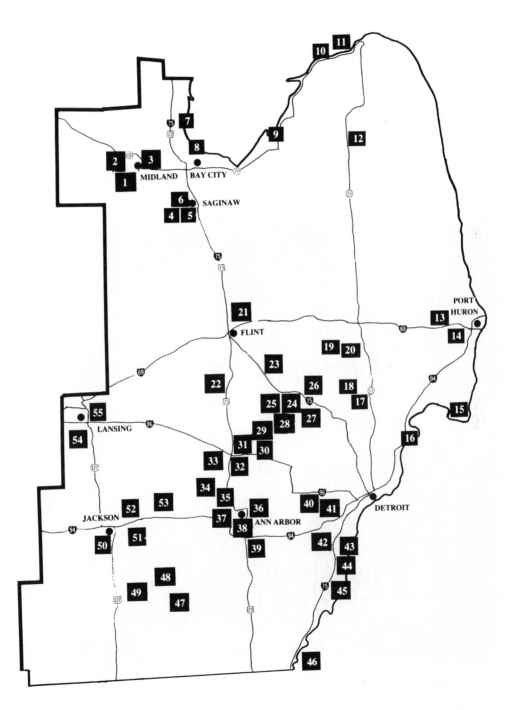

Maple River State Game Area (page 68)

1
BULLOCK CREEK NATURE SANCTUARY

If you like the freedom to find your own way and not travel the usual well-marked trail, you will enjoy Bullock Creek Nature Sanctuary. Except for a very faint path which enters from the east boundary but quickly disappears, no roads or groomed hiking trails scar this 80-acre parcel, and the owner and caretaker, the Michigan Nature Association, cautions that no one should walk this sanctuary without a compass.

But a careful exploration of this interesting and varied terrain usually will pay dividends. Michigan lily, tufted loosestrife, trillium, bloodroot, buttercup, violets and cardinal flower are just a few of the wildflowers you might see. This is also good birding area; grosbeaks, flycatchers, orioles and warblers are regular nesters. And, according to the M.N.A., most of the common Michigan mammals, including badger and beaver, roam the Bullock Creek area.

Bullock Creek itself cuts across the southeastern corner of the sanctuary, and sandy ridges—once part of the shoreline of ancient Saginaw Bay—alternate with low marshy areas throughout the property. All support a wide variety of plant life including burr oak, swamp white oak, hickory, basswood, cottonwood, red maple, black gum, white birch and sassafras. One substantial wet area in the center of the property supports a blueberry/cranberry marsh. You probably will encounter heavy brush and young woods as you enter the sanctuary, and prickly ash seems to be everywhere here, so wear heavy clothing.

County: Midland

City: Midland

Fees: None.

Schedule: Open year round.

Directions: From Business Route US-10/M-20 in downtown Midland, take Poseyville Road south; go six miles to Freeland Road; turn west (right) onto Freeland Road and go five miles to Five Mile Road; turn north (right) onto Five Mile Road and go .3 miles to a two-track on the west side of the road; pull off and park there.

Further Information:
Michigan Nature Association
P.O. Box 102
Avoca MI 48006

2 CHIPPEWA NATURE CENTER

The Chippewa Nature Center is the "Cadillac" of Michigan nature centers. In fact, the Center is "one of the finest—if not *the* finest—private nature center in the *world*," according to a vice-president of the National Audubon Society who visited in the 1970s. Since then, the Center has done even more to enhance that reputation.

The interpretive building alone is worth a visit. Midland's Alden B. Dow, the first Architect Laureate of Michigan, designed the structure, and his influence can certainly be seen and felt in this beautiful brick building, dedicated in 1975. The most striking feature is the Riverview Lounge, a 60-foot-long glass-walled room that is cantilevered over the Pine River. A fascinating and informative "hands-on" nature exhibit fills the Discovery Room, and a museum area features dioramas and displays of the natural and human history of the Saginaw Valley, including woodland Indian artifacts discovered during archeological digs on the Center's property. Other facilities inside Dow's creation include an auditorium, a library, classrooms and a gift shop.

But seclusion (you'll find it easy to forget that the city of Midland is just across the river), peace and beauty are the real hallmarks of Michigan's premier nature center. And to really experience, enjoy and appreciate the 1000-acre area, pick up a map at the interpretive center, then leave the building behind and take one or more

(Continued on page 5.)

Southeastern Lower Peninsula

CHIPPEWA NATURE CENTER
(Continued from page 4.)

of the 21 well-marked trails, totaling 14 miles, that wind through the Center's many and varied habitats. But don't plan to see it all in one day. You'll want to pay return visits to fully appreciate and explore the 700 acres of woodland, 50 acres of ponds, 110 acres of marsh, 300 acres of open field, plus three miles of river frontage along the Pine and Chippewa rivers and their confluence on the center's northern boundary.

A paved half-mile trail for the handicapped, the D.D. Arbury Trail, skirts the Pine River, passes a small pond and meanders through pine woods. Self-guiding tapes, available at the interpretive building, help the handicapped fully experience this trail.

Other attractions at Chippewa include a 16-acre arboretum, established in 1970 with the goal of displaying all of the approximately 300 species of shrubs and trees native to Michigan. Two carefully and accurately restored buildings, the 1870 Homestead Farm and the Maple Sugar House, are very popular with classroom visitors. Both are also open to the public.

A Natural Science Lecture series, mini-courses on natural history and ornithology, and a variety of programs for children are just a few of the reasons the National Park Service has cited the Chippewa Nature Center for its outstanding educational accomplishments and designated it as a National Environmental Study Area.

County: Midland

City: Midland

**Fees: Members—Free.
Non-members—Adults, 75 cents;
children, 25 cents.**

**Schedule: Monday through Friday,
8:00 a.m.-5:00 p.m.; Saturday, 9:00
a.m.-5:00 p.m.; Sundays and most
holidays, 1:00 p.m.-5:00 p.m.;
Closed Thanksgiving and Christmas**

**Directions: From US-10 Business
Route in Midland, take Cronkright
Street west and cross the bridge to
Poseyville Road; follow Poseyville
Road to Ashby Road; turn right,
onto Ashby Road and drive to Badour Road; turn right, onto Badour
Road, and follow it to its end at the
nature-center entrance.**

**Further Information:
Chippewa Nature Center
400 S. Badour Rd. Route 9
Midland MI 48640**

---

3 DOW GARDENS

A wealthy industrialist's home garden has grown to become one of Michigan's most beautiful tourist attractions.

In 1899, Herbert H. Dow, founder of the Dow Chemical Company, began Dow Gardens as a hobby in what essentially was his backyard: 10 acres of sandy soil covered by jack pine. Dow approached his hobby seriously. He corresponded with Luther Burbank and other leading horticulturists of his era and, during his lifetime,

(Continued on page 6.)

DOW GARDENS
(Continued from page 5.)

planted 5,000 fruit trees, including 40 varieties of plums.

After Herbert Dow's death in 1930, his family, through the Hubert H. and Grace A. Dow Foundation, not only cared for but expanded the gardens to its present 50 acres of trees, shrubs, flowering plants, streams, ponds, waterfalls, small foot bridges, paths and greenhouse.

Paved paths—including a recently completed Sensory Trail for the handicapped or young elementary students—lead through this place of natural beauty and charm, but visitors are encouraged to walk anywhere, including on the grass.

No matter where you walk, you can't help but be impressed with the spectacular variety and number of plantings. Each year, for example, Dow Gardens' staff plants some 20,000 annuals representing more than 200 species. A collection of over 90 different kinds of flowering crab apple trees reflects Herbert Dow's original interest in fruit trees. In mid-May when these crab apples—along with dogwood, lilacs, rhododendrons, azaleas and vibirnum—all burst into bloom, the show is dazzling. All plant materials in Dow Gardens are identified for visitors by both common and scientific names.

Because the varied habitat is good for both feeding and nesting, Dow Gardens is also a good birdwatching area.

Calendar of Outstanding Displays

January-February: Witchazel
March: Spring bulbs
April: Magnolia, spring bulbs
May: Crab apples, spring bulbs, rhododendrons, azaleas, viburnum, lilacs
June: Rhododendrons, azaleas, perennials, viburnum, lilacs
July: Vegetable gardens, rhododendrons, azaleas, perennials
September: Perennials
October: Fall color, perennials
November: Fall color

County: Midland

City: Midland

Fees: None.

Schedule: Open daily, 10:00 a.m.-Sunset.
Closed Thanksgiving, Christmas and New Year's Day.

Directions: From US-10 north of Midland, exit on Eastman Road; go two miles south to the corner of St. Andrews Street and Eastman Road. Park at the southwest corner of the intersection at the Midland Center for the Performing Arts and enter the gardens at the south end of parking lot.

Further Information:
Dow Gardens
1018 W. Main St.
Midland MI 48640

Green Point Nature Center (page 10)

Jonathan Woods (page 22)

4

SHIAWASSEE
NATIONAL WILDLIFE REFUGE

A staggering number of birds visit the Shiawassee National Wildlife Refuge every spring and fall. Twenty-five thousand Canadian geese (including Snow and Blue geese) 50,000 ducks (including Mallards, Teal, Wigeons, Mergansers, and Black, Pintail and Wood ducks), and 7,000 Whistling Swans, for example, annually stop over here. A bird checklist, available at the headquarters, lists 192 species—including hawks, shorebirds, warblers and sparrows—that frequent or nest in the 9,000-acre area. An additional 14 species are listed as rare or accidental visitors. Most summers a pair of Bald Eagles nest in the refuge, as do up to 200 pairs of Great Blue Heron.

Peak migration times for waterfowl are March, April, and September through November. Many,

however, arrive as early as February on their way north and pass through on their return journey as late as December. The earlier you arrive in the spring, the better your chances are of seeing large concentrations.

Located at the confluence of six rivers that drain one-sixth of the Lower Peninsula and form the Saginaw River, the area has always been a gathering place for waterfowl. To preserve and protect them from the rapidly encroaching and surrounding heavy agricultural and industrial development, the U.S. Fish and Wildlife Service formally established the Shiawassee National Wildlife Refuge in 1953.

The hand of man is still very much evident in preserving and maintaining this haven. Diked pools are mechanically flooded to add to the natural habitat of bayous, flood plains, shallow marshes, bottomland hardwoods, and grasses. And local farmers—who raise corn, wheat, barley and soybeans on 3,000 acres of refuge land—by agreement leave a third of their crops standing as food for the wildlife.

The same conditions that attract hordes of birds also appeal to other wildlife. It's rare, for

County: Saginaw

City: Saginaw

Fees: None.

Schedule: Open year round, Dawn-Dusk.

Directions: Five miles south of Saginaw on M-13, watch for directional signs. Turn west onto Curtis Road and go one mile to the headquarters or four miles to the trailhead.

Further Information:
Shiawassee National Wildlife Refuge
6975 Mower Rd., RR #1
Saginaw MI 48601

(Continued on page 9.)

5   PRICE NATURE CENTER

A beech/maple forest, untouched for over 200 years, plus a creek, open fields and a small area of wetlands make up the 173-acre Price Nature Center.

The best way to explore the area is to pick up self-guiding maps and helpful brochures at the information center at the park's entrance, then hike three trails totaling 3.5 miles. Hikers taking the White Oak Trail, named for a nearly 300-year-old tree that towers over the trailhead, have the option of walking a short .8-mile or slightly longer one-mile loop through the heart of the park. A trail shelter marks the halfway point of the longer loop.

An elevated boardwalk along the Cottonwood Trail, which branches off the White Oak Trail, crosses the park's wetlands. Portions of this mile-long trail pass through stands of cottonwood and, as on the White Oak Trail, a shelter has been constructed at the halfway point. An observation platform a few hundred yards up a .7-mile-long extension of the Cottonwood Trail, known as the Deer Run Trail, is an excellent spot to search for wildlife along the forest edges. Also along Deer Run on spring evenings, woodcocks can sometimes be seen in their courtship-display flights.

Cross-country skiers and showshoers are wel-

County: Saginaw

City: Saginaw

Fees: None.

Schedule: Open year round, 8:00 a.m.-9:00 p.m.

Directions: Go approximately five miles south of the Saginaw City limits on M-13, then turn east onto Curtis Road; go one mile east to Sheridan Road; turn north (left) onto Sheridan Road and go about 400 yards to the park's entrance at 6685 Sheridan Road.

Further Information:
Price Nature Center
Saginaw County Parks & Recreation Commission
County Governmental Center
Saginaw MI 48602

---

come on all trails in the winter.

Other facilities within the park, operated by the Saginaw County Parks and Recreation Commission, include picnic grounds, a play area and public restrooms.

SHIAWASSEE NATIONAL WILDLIFE REFUGE

(Continued from page 8.)

example, not to see white-tailed deer, muskrats and woodchucks during a hike. Red fox and raccoons are also common but not so easily spotted. And though you probably won't see the reclusive beaver, many conically cut saplings and small stumps along the bayous and ponds confirms its presence here.

You can walk into the area even during spring flooding on trails built atop the dikes. (Even the dikes, however, have been under water in some early springs.) At the halfway point of the five-mile-long main trail, an observation tower overlooks two of the flooded pools. Both good birding and scenery also come from a shorter 1.5-mile loop along the inner dike system. The trailhead for both loops is about 200 yards north of the parking lot, and an informative guide and maps are available there.

---

6 GREEN POINT NATURE CENTER

Hikers who arrive at the Green Point Nature Center in the spring might discover a feature unique to this 76-acre park: Because it lies in the flood plain of the Tittabawassee River, its entire trail system is occasionally under water. Though you can't hike during those brief spring periods, you still can observe the center's interesting ecosystem from the comfort of an interpretive building constructed well above the highest flood level. While inside, also take a look at the exhibits, which include natural history displays, live animals, a working beehive and a wildlife feeding station.

Green Point is home to a variety of animal (including a large number of mosquitoes during the summer, so bring insect repellent) and plant life. Like the yearly flooding of the Nile River in Egypt, which farmers count on to enrich the soil with annual deposits of new sediments, the floodings at Green Point Nature Center not only ensure a very nutrient-rich soil for vegetation, but also largely determine what kinds of plants grow here. Plants that can stand wet conditions thrive at Green Point. Common trees such as white pine and paper birch, on the other hand, are absent because they cannot tolerate standing for long periods in two-foot-deep water.

Green Point is also home to the Saginaw Valley Audubon Society and for good reason. The Shiawassee National Wildlife Refuge is located just across the river to the south and no doubt contributes to the 133 species of birds that appear on a checklist available at the interpretive building. For best birding, visit during spring and fall migrations.

Seven trails, totaling 2.5 miles, are as varied as the habitat—which includes two ponds, a marsh, open fields, a young forest, and riverbanks—they wander through. The Woodland Trail, for example, is a short self-guided interpretive nature walk. An excellent view of the marsh's wildlife comes from a wildlife blind along another path. Maps are available at the interpretive building, and during the winter months, the trails are open for cross-country skiing.

Green Point Nature Center, operated by the City of Saginaw Department of Parks and Recreation, also hosts a wide variety of nature classes and special events.

County: Saginaw

City: Saginaw

Fees: None.

Schedule: Hiking trails—Open year round.
Interpretive building—Open Monday through Saturday, 8:00 a.m.-5:00 p.m.

Directions: On M-46 three blocks west of the Saginaw River in Saginaw, turn south onto South Michigan Avenue; go 1.5 miles on South Michigan Avenue, which heads southwest, to Maple Street; turn south (left) onto Maple Street and go a half mile to the entrance at 3010 Maple Street.

Further Information:
Green Point Nature Center
City Hall
Saginaw MI 48601

7 NAYAQUING POINT WILDLIFE AREA

The Nayaquing Point Wildlife Area is nearly in the center of a long chain of great birdwatching spots that ring Saginaw Bay in a stretch from Port Crescent State Park to Tawas Point State Park. The exceedingly flat landscape of diked and ditched farm fields, plus marshland, lagoons and the open waters of Saginaw Bay make this an excellent area to observe both shorebirds and waterfowl. Spring and fall migrations are the best time. But in addition to the many migrates that pass through, several species stay here to breed, so birdwatchers are usually rewarded at any time of year. Among the sandpipers, ducks, gulls, hawks and terns, the lucky observer might spot a Dunlin, a Black-bellied Plover, a Tundra Swan or a Black Skimmer.

Parking areas at the end of both Kitchen and Tower Beach roads lead to the area's extensive dike system. You can walk for several miles along these dikes and, in the company of songbirds that continually flit through the bordering thickets, enjoy the sights of gulls soaring overhead, terns hovering then plunging into ditches to retrieve fish, and several different species of heron silently fishing from the dike edges.

Other parking areas are located along both Erickson and Goggins roads.

County: Bay

City: Bay City

Fees: None.

Schedule: Open year round, but there is no point trying to watch birds or even hike during the waterfowl hunting season.

Directions: From US-23/I-75 north of Bay City, take exit 173 (Lindwood Road); go east on Linwood Road approximately 1.5 miles to M-13; turn north (left) onto M-13 and go three miles to Kitchen Road; turn east (right) onto Kitchen Road and drive 1.5 miles to the wildlife area.

Further Information:
Nayaquing Point Wildlife Area
1570 Tower Beach Rd.
Linwood MI 48634

8

TOBICO MARSH STATE GAME AREA
and
BAY CITY STATE PARK

Tobico Marsh State Game Area was designated as a national natural landmark in 1976 and
for good reason. The 2,000-acre site—which in-

County: Bay

City: Bay City

**Fees: Bay City State Park—$2.00 daily
vehicle permit or $10.00 annual ve-
hicle permit valid in all state parks.
Tobico Marsh State Game Area—
None.**

**Schedule: State game area—No posted
hours.
State Park—Open year round, 8:00
a.m.-10:00 p.m.
Nature center—Open June through
August, Noon-5:00 p.m.**

**Directions: From I-75 north of Bay
City, exit on Beaver Road (168);
drive east on Beaver Road approxi-
mately five miles just past M-247
(Euclid Avenue) to the Bay City
State Park entrance. To get to
Tobico Marsh, turn north from
Beaver Road onto M-247 (Euclid
Avenue); take the first road to the
left and follow it to the entrance.**

**Further Information:
Bay City State Park
Bay City MI 48706**

cludes a 1,109-acre refuge, Tobico Lagoon,
hardwood forests and an extensive marsh—lives
up to its classification as an area of "exceptional
value to illustrate the nation's natural heritage."
Once the hunting grounds of Sauk and Chippewa
Indians—who called the area *Pe To Be Goong*,
meaning "little lake by the big one"—Tobico
Marsh and its adjacent neighbor to the south,
Bay City State Park, today are a haven to wildlife
and to people who enjoy the out-of-doors.

Tobico Marsh attracts thousands of waterfowl
and shorebirds. Prime birdwatching opportunities, especially during spring and fall migrations,
come from trails leading through the area. Several birds rare in Michigan—including the
Ruddy Duck, Yellow-headed Blackbird and Redhead Duck—nest in the marsh.

A wide variety of other Michigan flora and
fauna, including many rare wildflowers and
shrubs, thrive in the area, and deer, muskrat,
mink and beaver are among the mammals commonly seen here.

The best way to enjoy Tobico Marsh is to walk
the trail with two loops which circle through the
refuge. A one-mile loop leads to a panoramic
view of the lagoon from one of the preserve's
two 30-foot towers. This short trail also winds
through a hardwood forest to another excellent
look at the lagoon and marsh, this one from a
dam and weir. A longer three-mile loop follows
an old two-track to the second observation tower

(Continued on page 13.)

9 FISH POINT WILDLIFE AREA

Every spring and fall, migrating waterfowl nearly blacken the skies over the Fish Point Wildlife Area. Another reason this state game area and refuge, on Saginaw Bay just west of Sebewaing, has earned its reputation as one of

County: Tuscola

City: Sebewaing

Fees: None.

Schedule: Trail open April 1 through October 1.

Directions: From the center of Unionville, drive three miles west on M-25 to Ringle Road; turn north (right) onto Ringle Road and go approximately three miles to the headquarters. Parking and the nature trail is .6 miles north of the headquarters building.

the state's premier birding spots is that you don't even have to leave your car to enjoy and marvel at the staggering number of birds. In fact, remaining in your vehicle often is an advantage. A slow-moving car does not alarm birds here, whereas walking along the road usually produces the opposite results.

Ringle Road, which marks the western edge of the refuge, is an outstanding spot to observe shorebirds and waterfowl from a moving vehicle at close range. A variety of species communally congregate in a marshy area which hugs the roadside, plus geese and ducks swoop overhead before landing in the open waters a few hundred yards away. The shallow waters of Saginaw Bay adjacent to Fish Point provide other good spots, which are accessible from several roads joining the two areas.

But you don't have to stay in your car to enjoy the area. A 1.1-mile nature trail, cosponsored by the Saginaw Bay Chapter of the Michigan Duck Hunters Association and the DNR, begins at a

(Continued on page 14.)

TOBICO MARSH and BAY CITY STATE PARK

(Continued from page 12.)

and a nearby boardwalk built on the marsh's edge.

The driveway to the parking area is gated and locked, and anyone entering Tobico Marsh should obtain permission and a key at the Jennison Nature Center at Bay City State Park. Or, after obtaining permission to enter, you can park on the road's shoulder near the entrance and walk around the gate.

Jennison Nature Center itself is a focal point for many natural activities. Prearranged nature

walks to Tobico Marsh, less than half a mile north, begin at the converted single-family home, and a large collection of mounted birds and nature exhibits fill several rooms inside. Braille interpretive signs guide visually handicapped visitors from the Center along a short, paved, fenced path named the Chickadee Trail.

Bay City State Park has no other officially designated nature trails, but casual walkers have worn several paths, including one which circles a small lagoon.

Facilities at the 196-acre state park, located on Saginaw Bay within sight of Bay City, include 263 modern campsites, a swimming beach and a picnic area.

10   SLEEPER STATE PARK

More than four miles of hiking trails network the large, relatively unused southern section of this extremely popular state park located on Saginaw Bay.

All trails begin at the camping area, 280 wooded sites split into two sections lying just south of M-25. The Mile Circle Trail, for example, connects the campground's two wings via a loop through deep woods. The Outdoor Center Beach Trail branches south from the Mile Circle Trail, then connects to an unnamed two-mile loop that circles through the western area of the heavily wooded land.

A self-guiding pamphlet, available at park

> County: **Huron**
>
> City: **Caseville**
>
> Fees: **$2.00 daily vehicle permit or $10.00 annual permit sticker valid in all state parks.**
>
> Schedule: **Open year round.**
>
> Directions: **Go four miles east of Caseville on M-25.**
>
> Further Information:
> **Sleeper State Park**
> **Caseville MI 48725**

headquarters, identifies special points of interest and explains the natural setting along the Ridges Nature Trail. The one-mile walk starts at the west wing of the campground, briefly follows, then leaves the Mile Circle Trail to travel wooded sand ridges that marked the shoreline of Saginaw Bay during prehistoric times. The thickly forested ridges alternate with damp or water-filled troughs teeming with water-loving plants and wildflowers.

All trails are open for cross-country skiing in the winter.

Facilities north of M-25, which divides Sleeper State Park's 1,003 acres into two unequal parts, include a beach and picnic grounds.

FISH POINT WILDLIFE AREA
(Continued from page 13.)

parking area .6 miles north of the headquarters building, follows a dike bordering the Wisconsin Drain, which marks the southern boundary of the refuge, then circles through a cattail marsh.

Waterfowl commonly seen at Fish Point include geese, ducks, grebes and cormorants. Pintails, Redheads, Canvasbacks, Blue- and Green-winged Teal and Northern Shovelers

make up most of the duck population, but the area also holds good chances for spotting rare Tundra Swans, Surf Scoters and Oldsquaw Ducks. Shorebirds and songbirds are also plentiful through the area.

Fish Point Wildlife Area, begun with small purchases of land by the state in the 1950s, today totals over 2,000 diked, ditched and flooded acres divided almost equally between refuge and game area.

11 PORT CRESCENT STATE PARK

Rare dune grasses, a sand so fine it was used in smelting factories, beautiful hiking trails, two miles of beach, acres of rolling dunes and quiet woodland all add up to one of lower Michigan's most attractive parks. And 665-acre Port Crescent State Park—which stretches for two miles along the shoreline of Saginaw Bay on the site of a ghost town from which it gets its name—is also a nature lover's delight. Wildflowers and birdlife, for example, thrive in the wetlands that border the river here. And throughout the park, birdwatchers can spot waterfowl, songbirds, and shorebirds, including the relatively rare Piping Plover.

The Pinnebog River, which flows from south to north as it empties into Saginaw Bay, neatly divides the park into almost equal halves. On the west side of the river, picnic grounds, a large pavilion, beautiful sandy beaches and several hundred acres of low-lying Huron dunes that reach to the waterline make up the day-use area. There are no marked trails in this half of the park, but it is still a great place to beachcomb, explore or just plain wander. Visitors in wheelchairs can enjoy a beautiful view of the bay by taking one of several paved paths from the parking area a short distance to the pavilion, then crossing the sand on a boardwalk.

On the east side of the river, a 181-space campground now occupies the site of a ghost town whose remains are marked only by a few brick-chimney tombstones. An historic display, including photographs, near the campground entrance brings to life the town of Port Crescent that once thrived here.

Also on the east side of the river, a triangle formed by the river, the beach and an old river channel encloses a 2.5-mile marked hiking and cross-country ski trail. The trail—accessible ei-

ther from the west end of the campground or from a bridge (closed to motor traffic) located directly opposite the west end of Port Crescent Road on M-25—has two loops which wander through wooded dunes, border the Pinnebog River and follow the coastline.

County: Huron

City: Port Austin

Fees: $2.00 daily vehicle permit or $10.00 annual vehicle permit valid in all state parks.

Schedule: Open year round.

Directions: Go five miles west of Port Austin on M-25.

Further Information:
Port Austin State Park
1775 Port Austin Rd.
Port Austin MI 48467

12
SANILAC PETROGLYPHS STATE PARK

Here, in sandstone outcroppings near the south fork of the north branch of the Cass River in Michigan's Thumb, aboriginal artists left the only prehistoric rock carvings found in Michigan. Experts estimate that, at least 1,000 years ago, Michigan's early human inhabitants carved the wildlife figures, hunting scenes and animal tracks as part of a hunting ritual or to record dreams and visions experienced during religious ceremonies. A large 40-by-20-foot low sandstone outcropping about 1,000 feet from the parking area displays the main group of figures, and about two miles of trails lead to other carvings throughout the 240-acre park.

A locked entrance gate protects the fragile work of the ancient artists from vandals or wear from the footsteps of too many casual visitors. A key is available at a nearby house along with a reminder to please not walk on the carvings as every step imperceptibly shortens their life. To further preserve the petroglyphs from weather and foot traffic, the main outcropping is fenced and sheltered by a roof. And, there are no restrooms, picnic areas or camping at the park.

(Continued on page 17.)

Southeastern Lower Peninsula

13   PINE RIVER NATURE SANCTUARY

Soon after it had acquired this 17.5-acre parcel in 1963, the Michigan Nature Association conducted a 24-hour bird count and found 65 species within their tiny preserve. Ruffled Grouse, Whip-poor-wills, Wood Ducks and Great Horned Owls, for example, regularly nest in the sanctuary, and warblers and songbirds are regular visitors along the river, especially in the spring.

Plant life, too, thrives in this peaceful, secluded section of central St. Clair County. A beech/maple/hemlock forest—with a scattering of white pine, black cherry, hickory, cottonwood and witch hazel—cover a varied terrain made up of rolling hills, riverbanks, flood plain and low ravines. Several interesting species of fern as well as a profusion of spring wildflowers make annual appearances within the sanctuary .

A mile-long trail, which begins at the rear of the parking area in the northwest corner of the property, meanders across the upland forest, dips into a ravine, then officially ends at the banks of the Pine River. During normal water levels, however, hikers can ford the stream if they wish and explore a small area of the park on the opposite bank.

> **County: St. Clair**
>
> **City: Emmett**
>
> **Fees: None.**
>
> **Schedule: No posted hours.**
>
> **Directions: From Emmett on old M-21, drive 6.5 miles east to Cribbins Road; turn north (left) onto Cribbins Road and go 1.5 miles to the park entrance and parking area on the east side of the road.**
>
> **Further Information:**
> **Michigan Nature Association**
> **P.O. Box 102**
> **Avoca MI 48006**

SANILAC PETROGLYPHS STATE PARK
(Continued from page 16.)

The quiet beauty and solitude of the Cass River—especially at the back of the park where large maples and other hardwoods arch across the steam—provides the perfect setting to contemplate the strange and fascinating record left by people who passed through Michigan hundreds of years before the new world was discovered.

> **County: Sanilac**
>
> **City: New Greenleaf**
>
> **Fees: None.**
>
> **Schedule: Open year round.**
>
> **Directions: From the junction of M-53 and M-81 in the northwest corner of Sanilac County, drive four miles north on M-53 to Bay City-Forestville Road; turn east (right) onto Bay City-Forestville Road and drive four miles to Germania Road; turn south (right) onto Germania Road and drive approximately a half mile to the park entrance.**
>
> **Further Information:**
> **State of Michigan**
> **Department of Natural Resources**
> **Parks Division**
> **Box 30028**
> **Lansing MI 48909**

14

ST. CLAIR WOODS NATURE SANCTUARY

The Detroit Audubon Society and the Michigan Nature Association have combined four parcels of land, ranging in size from 7.5 to 75 acres, to create this 141-acre shelter for plants and animals, plus a place of peace, quiet and beauty for man. Maple, oak and birch—plus impressive stands of hemlock scattered throughout the south-central part—covers the property. The area also hosts ferns, shrubs and wildflowers, including three different types of trilliums (white, red, and painted), cardinal flowers, Indian pipes and Michigan lily. Warblers, vireos, flycatchers, owls, and Wood Ducks are among the many birds that nest in the sanctuary.

Though no formal trails run through the 41-acre Elmer P. Jasper Woods, a section owned by the M.N.A., guests are encouraged to leave a sand road which runs along the area's eastern edge and wander into the woods. Abutting Jasper Woods on its eastern edge is a 75-acre parcel owned by the Detroit Audubon Society. There, a 1.5-mile trail, which begins on the sand road, gradually heads south through imposing hemlock groves to a small stream.

County: St. Clair

City: Port Huron

Fees: None.

Schedule: Open year round.

Directions: From I-69 west of Port Huron exit on Wadhams Road and go south one mile to Griswold Road; turn west (right) onto Griswold Road and go two miles to Dunlap Road; turn south (left) onto Dunlap Road and go a short distance to an M.N.A. sign and parking.

Further Information:
Michigan Nature Association
P.O. Box 102
Avoca MI 48006

15 ALGONAC STATE PARK

At Algonac State Park, patches of original Michigan prairie remain undisturbed just a few hundred feet from one of the world's busiest shipping channels. Here at the gateway for shipping to lakes Huron, Michigan and Superior, little more than M-29 separates the park from the St. Clair River, and you feel like you can reach out and touch the freighters, iron-ore carriers and other ships—many bearing international markings—that pass by during the busy shipping

(Continued on page 19.)

ALGONAC STATE PARK

(Continued from page 18.)

season.

Stretching back from the highway, the 1,023-acre park is covered by a sometimes-dense mixed hardwood forest. Scattered around the property are four small remnants of the original prairie that was once abundant not only in this area but throughout southern Michigan. Though totaling only 62 acres, these plots, according to an identification program by the Michigan Natural Areas Council, support nearly 300 types of plants and grasses, many of them unique and rare.

Three nature trails wind through the back of the park and across three of the four prairie sections. To penetrate farthest into the park's interior, take a trail that begins at the west end of the trap-range parking lot. This estimated mile-long trail, which crosses the Marine City Drainage Canal, also circles through the largest of the prairie remnants.

The park's 281-site campground—an open, grassy, lightly shaded area next to the highway—offers little privacy. However, spectacular views of the parade of boats and ships come from there as well as from the park's large picnic area and playground. Other facilities here include a trap range, an archery range and an organization campground.

County: St. Clair

City: Algonac

Fees: **$2.00 daily vehicle permit or a $10.00 annual vehicle permit valid in all state parks.**

Schedule: **Open year round.**

Directions: **The park is located on M-29 just north of Algonac.**

Further Information:
**Algonac State Park
8730 N. River Rd.
Algonac MI 48001**

16   METRO BEACH METROPARK

What's a park that's located on the fringes of the state's largest metropolitan area, whose 3000-foot-long stretch of sand—the world's largest manmade beach—attracts a staggering number of swimmers and sunbathers on sizzling summer days, and whose parking lot is larger than many other Michigan parks doing in a book titled, *Natural Michigan*?

Because in spite of the crowds, commotion and acres of asphalt, the park, located on the shores of Lake St. Clair, is one of the two or three best birding spots in the state. Extensive marshes, open water and woods away from the man-made attractions plus the park's location on a major bird migration route are reasons that 260 species—some in large concentrations and 80 of which have nested here—have been spotted in Metro Beach Metropark.

The park is equally good for both waterfowl and shorebirds and is one of the best places in the state to see warblers during their spring migration. A short list of the diverse and interesting species you might spot here includes: Red-throated Loon, Red-necked Grebe, Tundra Swan, Snowy Owl, Oldsquaw Duck, Ruddy Duck, Osprey, Water Pipit, Loggerhead Shrike, Prothonotory Warbler, Northern Parula Warbler, Cerulean Warbler, Lapland Longspur, Virginia

(Continued on page 20.)

METRO BEACH METROPARK
(Continued from page 19.)

Rail, Yellow-billed Cuckoo, and Glaucous, California, Iceland and Franklin gulls.

For such a relatively short walk, a .75-mile nature trail that circles south along the western edge of the parking lot through woods, thickets and marsh and by a pond always holds great potential for seeing a large number of birds. Other prime areas for birdwatching include the park's two boat basins, a picnic area on Huron Point, the entrance drive that cuts through the south marsh, and the service drive in back of the nature trail. Birding is also good at the north marsh, but the only way into that area is by boat or canoe.

Helpful literature—including lists of birds, fish, plants, wildflowers and wildlife common to the park and a flyer describing the ecosystem of the marsh—are available at park headquarters, at the southern edge of the huge parking area. The park's staff also conducts a wide range of nature programs throughout the year. For topics and schedules, write the address below.

Other attractions include a grass-covered, tree-shaded picnic area that extends into Lake St. Clair on a small picturesque peninsula. You can work off your lunch, if need be, on a fitness hiking trail that circles the grounds. Shorefishermen congregate on the eastern tip of this peninsula, and sailboarders cruise along the western side. You can get to the peninsula's point either by walking or by taking a trackless train from the parking lot.

Unique to Metro Beach is the Voyageur Canoe, an exact replica of the type of canoes early fur traders and explorers used to journey throughout the Great Lakes area. The 34-foot-long craft, which is available for group charters, makes hour-long trips from the North Marina into the 213-acre north marsh section of the park.

Other diverse Metro Beach Metropark facilities, services and activities—not all of which are usually associated with the Huron-Clinton Metro Parks system or any state or local parks, for that matter—include two marinas, a putt-putt golf course, a tot lot, a huge swimming pool, a bath house, a roller skating rink, an 18-hole par-three golf course, basketball courts, a dance area, and tennis courts.

Winter visitors can cross-country ski, ice skate and ice fish.

County: Macomb

City: Mt. Clemens

Fees: $2.00 daily vehicle permit or $7.00 annual permit valid in all Huron-Clinton Metroparks.

Schedule: Opens year round at 8:00 a.m.

Directions: From I-94 south of Mt. Clemens, take the Metropolitan Parkway east to the park entrance.

Further Information:
Metro Beach Metropark
P.O. Box 1037
Mt. Clemens MI 48043

---

17 STONY CREEK METROPARK

Centered by a man-made lake, 750-acre Stony Creek Metropark is an excellent place to study nature and enjoy the out-of-doors.

The focal point for natural activities is a Nature Center, located in the northern part of the park. Maps to three self-guided nature trails, ranging from .5 to 2.5 miles in length, are available at the Nature Center building. These paths, which total 4.25 miles, wind alongside Stony Creek (which flows south to Stony Creek Lake), climb morainal hills, and pass through hardwood forests, open fields and marshes. Interpretive signs mark points of interest. A wildflower checklist, also available at the building, numbers an impressive 180 varieties, and a similar list for bird species numbers 170. The Nature Center building houses exhibits and displays, including a bird-feeding station. Nature programs and workshops are also held at the Center.

South of the natural area, a variety of facilities and attractions—including eight picnic areas, two swimming beaches, a boat-launching site (south shore), a boat-rental concession (north shore) and an 18-hole golf course (west shore)—encircle Stony Creek Lake, created by the damming of the creek from which it gets its name. All are connected by a scenic (especially during fall color) 10-mile paved road that circles the lake. A nearly 10-mile-long paved hiking/bike trail also follows the lakeshore.

Fishing is good in Stony Creek Lake for pike, walleyes, smallmouth bass and panfish. Shore-fishing is permitted except north of 28 Mile Road, which separates the nature-study area from the other facilities.

Cross-country skiers, ice fishermen and sledders can enjoy the park in the winter.

County: Macomb

City: Rochester

Fees: $2.00 daily vehicle permit or $7.00 annual permit valid in all Metroparks.

Schedule: Park—Open year round, 7:00 a.m.-10:00 p.m.
Nature trails—Open May through September, 8:00 a.m.- 9:00 p.m.; October through April, 8:00 a.m.- 9:00 p.m.
Nature Center Building—Summer: Monday through Friday, 10:00 a.m.-5:00 p.m.; School Year: Monday through Friday, 1:00 p.m.-5:00 p.m.; Weekends Year Round: 10:00 a.m-5:00 p.m.

Directions: To reach the Nature Center, take M-53 north of Utica to 26 Mile Road; go west approximately 1.5 miles to Mound Road; turn north (right) onto Mound Road and go approximately 3.5 miles to Inwood Road; turn west (left) onto Inwood Road and drive a half mile to the entrance.
To reach the picnic and beach area, take M-53 six miles north of Utica to take 26 Mile Road; go west on 26 Mile Road 1.5 miles to the entrance.

Further Information:
Stony Creek Metropark
4100 Inwood Rd.
Romeo MI 48065

18 DINOSAUR HILL NATURE CENTER

Though diminutive at 16 acres, Dinosaur Hill Nature Center, located near Rochester, is super-charged with natural programs and activities. Guided nature walks for groups of all ages, school programs, slide shows, a speakers bureau and regularly scheduled classes on nature study for preschoolers through senior citizens make this center the area's headquarters for nature education.

The center, named after a hill that local children believed looked like a sleeping dinosaur, is also a quiet, beautiful place to walk or bicycle. Three self-guided nature trails, totaling two miles, wind through the grounds: seven acres of woodland, open fields, a small swamp and wetlands, all bordered by Paint Creek.

The trails are open for cross-country skiing in winter.

County: Oakland

City: Rochester

Fees: None.

Schedule: Open year round, sunrise to sunset.

Directions: From the intersection of University Drive and Main Street in downtown Rochester, drive north on Main Street (M-150) approximately a half mile to Woodward; turn west (left) onto Woodward and go two blocks to Oak Street; turn north (right) onto Oak Street and go approximately six blocks to North Hill Circle; turn west onto North Hill Circle and drive to the entrance.

Further Information:
Dinosaur Hill Nature Preserve
333 North Hill Circle
Rochester MI 48063

---

19 JONATHON WOODS

The last glacial age in Michigan left much evidence of its passage at Jonathon Woods. The sharply rising, heavily forested hills, steep valleys, potholes, lowland swamps, ponds and bogs in this 144 acres owned by the Nature Conservancy make up a classic morainal landscape. This great diversity in habitat accounts for the 330 species of plants and equally impressive variety of other wildlife found at Jonathon Woods.

Approximately three miles of trails pass by ponds and bogs and through stands of maple, oak, aspen, ash, white pine, box elder, elm, ironwood, basswood, beech, willow and black cherry. Many of the hardwoods have reached im-

(Continued on page 23.)

JONATHAN WOODS
(Continued from page 22.)

posing size, and the trails that pass beneath them offer peace, solitude and beauty.

There is some evidence of old fence lines and attempts to clear some areas of glacial rock, but for the most part Jonathon Woods shows little disturbance from the hands of man.

County: Lapeer

City: Metamora

Fees: None.

Schedule: Open year round.

Directions: From M-24 south of Lapeer, take Dryden Road east through Metamora, then one mile past Thornville to Hosner Rd; turn south (right) onto Hosner Road and proceed 3.5 miles to Jonathon Road; turn west (right) onto Jonathon Road and go .8 miles. The Sanctuary sign is approximately 40 feet from the road opposite mailbox 3130. There is just enough room to pull a car off the road and park in front of the sign.

Further Information:
The Nature Conservancy
531 N. Clippert St.
Lansing MI 48912

20 SEVEN PONDS NATURE CENTER

You can't help but learn about nature in this 245-acre outdoor classroom owned and managed by the Michigan Audubon Society. Close-up study or just plain enjoyment of the widely divergent landscape and habitat—including glacial lakes, cedar swamps, cattail marshes, open fields and woodland—come from boardwalks, bridges, observation platforms and 7.5 miles of trails. Maps and self-guiding pamphlets, available at the interpretive building, help explain the natural setting and important features of the area. What questions the booklets don't answer, the naturalist on duty will.

Areas of special interest include an orchard managed for wildlife food and shelter, a waterfowl feeding area, an herb garden and a prairie restoration project featuring many rare and unusual grasses and flowers.

(Continued on page 25.)

SEVEN PONDS NATURE CENTER
(Continued from page 24.)

The variety of displays and educational exhibits at the interpretive building includes a Michigan bird display (with more than 100 mounted specimens), a "touch table" for children, a natural history collection and a working beehive. Printed matter at both the bookstore and the extensive library in the building focuses on environmental education and history.

Seven Ponds also offers an impressive number of formal educational opportunities. For example, the Young Naturalists Program, presented every spring, introduces the study of plants and animals to young people ages 11 to 14. The Natural History Field School, held every summer, is a two-week in-depth study of living things and their habitats. In the fall, high school students take part in Field Biology classes. Leader-training workshops are available to those who supervise nature programs, at camps, for example. Adults can also enroll in a wide variety of classes ranging from nature study to creative crafts.

Other facilities here include a small picnic area. The center is open in the winter for snowshoeing and cross-country skiing.

County: Lapeer

City: Dryden

Fees: Members of the Nature Center and Michigan Audubon Society— Free.
  Non-members—$.50 per adult and $.25 per child or $1.00 per family.

Schedule: Grounds—Open year round except Mondays.
  Building—Open Tuesday through Sunday, 9:00 a.m.-5:00 p.m.

Directions: Twelve miles south of Lapeer on M-24 turn east onto Dryden Road; go through both Metamora and Thornville, then turn south (right) onto Calkins Road, which bends to the left after approximately a mile and becomes Crawford Road; the entrance to the center is just around that bend.

Further Information:
Seven Ponds Nature Center
3854 Crawford Rd.
Dryden MI 48428

21

FOR-MAR NATURE PRESERVE
AND ARBORETUM

Nearly 400 acres of woodland, open fields, restored prairie, marshes, five ponds and Kearsley Creek make up the For-Mar Nature Preserve and Arboretum, located just a few blocks outside the limits of Michigan's "Vehicle City."

Like most Michigan nature preserves, For-Mar is dedicated to the study and enjoyment of nature, and an enjoyable learning experience here is almost guaranteed by eight nature trails. Some of the nearly seven miles of well-trodden paths follow the creek; others circle small ponds, cross open meadows or meander through woods; three are self-guided with brochures available at the DeWaters Education Center (Potter Road entrance). All provide excellent opportunities for birdwatching, searching for wildflowers, or full exploration of the variety of habitats where nearly 475 species of flora and fauna flourish.

Two trails, both of which begin at the DeWaters Education Center, are specially designed for the handicapped. A wire-guided trail designed for the visually handicapped, for example, circles through a small woods. And the Woodlot Trail, a .2-mile paved self-guided trail through the same woods, is accessible by wheelchair.

The DeWaters Education Center, which houses a variety of nature displays and exhibits, is the focal point of educational programs for all ages. Guided field trips—including wildflower walks and a spring birdwatching class—and other programs are offered throughout the year.

Other attractions at For-Mar include a 113-acre arboretum which, though still under development in the southwest corner of the grounds, already features many interesting specimens.

And the Foote Bird Museum, located at the Genesee Road entrance, displays 600 mounted birds.

County: Genesee

City: Flint

Fees: None.

Schedule: April 1-September 7— Thursday-Sunday, 8 a.m. to sunset. September 8-March 31—Open seven days a week, 8 a.m. to sunset.

Directions: From I-69 east of Flint, exit on Belsay Road; go north on Bel say Road two miles to Potter Road; turn west (left) onto Potter Road and go approximately four blocks to the park entrance. To reach the Genesee Road entrance, take Belsay Road north from I-69 approximately one mile to Davison Road; turn west (left) onto Davison Road and drive one mile to Genesee Road; turn north (right) onto Genesee Road and go approximately two blocks to the entrance.

Further Information:
For-Mar Nature Preserve and Arboretum
G-5360 E. Potter Rd.
Flint MI 48506

---

22 SHANNON NATURE SANCTUARY

Quiet and peaceful, easy to get to but off the beaten track, and small but packed with varied habitats and scenic beauty, the Shannon Nature Sanctuary is both a treat and retreat for nature lovers. Here, you can spend an hour roaming one of several short trails or spend half a day in seclusion amidst the beautiful surroundings.

A surprising number of habitats—including a hardwood forest, a cattail marsh, a flood plain, a pond, a pine plantation, two streams, an old field giving way to young trees, and the shore of Lake Shannon—make up the relatively small 19.2-acre sanctuary. The forest floor is lush with ferns, vines, shrubs and other low-growing plants. Wildflowers abound throughout the sanctuary, especially along the cattail marsh and flood plain. In fact, the whole preserve by late spring seems to be a riot of plant life.

A leaflet, available at a mailbox just inside the sanctuary gate, lists plants, birds, mammals and other wildlife to both watch and listen for. Twenty-five identified species of birds, for example, nest within the sanctuary.

Several short trails wind through the preserve. One, which begins at the sanctuary entrance, borders the northern boundary, passes through dense woods, then turns south and intercepts a small creek. A second trail, which also begins at the sanctuary entrance, borders Lake Shannon and the cattail marsh before it, too, reaches the creek. This creek is also a focal point for several other trails. One, along the west side, heads upstream. A second, on the east side, borders the stream bed, then heads further east to an old field and a pine plantation. Bridging the creek near the sanctuary's northern boundary is a fallen tree equipped with handrails and a planked trunk.

County: Livingston

City: Parshallville

Fees: None.

Schedule: Open year round.

Directions: South of Fenton on US-23, exit on Center Road and go a few hundred feet to the service road that borders the west side of the expressway; turn south (left) onto this service road and go two miles to Faussett Road; turn west (right) onto Faussett Road and drive one mile. The entrance road to the sanctuary is a chain-gated track on the south side of Faussett Road just before Faussett Road crosses the southern end of Lake Shannon. Unhook the chain and drive south .5 miles to the sanctuary parking area.

Further Information:
Michigan Nature Association
P.O. Box 102
Avoca MI 48006

23 HOLLY RECREATION AREA

The Holly Recreation Area's best-kept secret is that, in spite of the heavy use made of the park, it is a very good birdwatching area. Teenagers and young adults from northern Oakland and southern Genesee counties pack the beaches during the summer months, but the rich diversity of habitat—woods, wetland, open fields and numerous lakes—also attracts a great many birds. One enthusiastic and dedicated birder, for example, in 10 years of study identified 107 breeding species plus 88 non-nesting visitants. His impressive list includes such rare and threatened species as the Northern Harrier, Osprey, Caspian Tern and American Avocet. The best chances for seeing the greatest number of birds comes from the shorelines of McGinnis and Valley lakes during midweek, when the park is least crowded.

Three hiking trails of varying lengths wind through the park's 7,470 acres. The Wilderness Foot Trail and Saginaw Trail, each several miles in length, extend to the farthest corners of the park. The Valley-Wildwood Trail circles two lakes and stays close to the more heavily used section of the park as evidenced by the cans and other litter strewn along the path and water's edge.

Inquire at park headquarters, near the entrance, for information on the hiking trails as not all of them are marked on park maps.

County: Oakland

City: Holly

Fees: $2.00 daily vehicle permit or $10.00 annual vehicle permit valid in all state parks.

Schedule: Open year round.

Directions: About halfway between Flint and Pontiac in northwestern Oakland County, exit from I-75 at Grange Hall Road (101); go east on Grange Hall Road, cross Dixie Highway and go about a quarter mile to the park entrance.

Further Information:
Holly Recreation Area
Grange Hall Rd.
Holly MI 48442

24 INDIAN SPRINGS METROPARK

Michigan maps of the early 1800s usually had two words printed across most of the Lower Peninsula: *interminable swamp*. In the southeastern part of the state, one of the dominant natural features which contributed to that label was the great Huron Swamp. Today, one of the last vestiges of that unique physical landmark remains at Indian Springs Metropark.

But there's much more to this, one of the newest (opened June 1982) Huron-Clinton Metroparks than just a look at the "interminable swamp." Open fields, hardwood forests, a pond and the headwaters of the Huron River also make up its 2,000 acres, and the area is rich in plant and animal life. The park's bird checklist, for example, numbers more than 140 species. And a pamphlet, "Wildflowers of Indian Springs Metropark," available at the nature center, lists over 200 wildflowers native to the area. Especially beautiful in the spring are abundant marsh marigolds in the wetland area.

The best way to explore and enjoy the area is on nearly six miles of nature trails. The Woodland Trail—three loops of .75, 1.25 and 2.0 miles respectively—heads through marshy lowlands and deep woods. The paths also cross and recross the Huron River where here, at its headwaters, it is almost small enough to jump. The Woodland Trail is especially enjoyable for spring wildflowers and fall color.

Best for summer wildflowers is the Farmland Trail, a 1.75-mile round trip along forest edges and open fields. As its name suggests, the short, paved Pondside Trail circles the park's pond. And as in most Huron-Clinton metroparks, a five-mile biking, hiking and jogging trail roams through the far reaches of the park. This paved path begins at the large Meadow Lake Picnic Area.

At the end of the entrance road in the solar-heated nature center, displays and exhibits explain the history and natural significance of the area, plus nature walks and workshops are conducted year round.

All trails are open for cross-country skiing in the winter.

County: Oakland

City: Clarkston

Fees: One-day vehicle permit, $2.00; Annual vehicle permit valid in all Huron Clinton Metroparks, $7.00; Senior-citizen annual permit, $2.00.

Schedule: Open year round—May through September, 8:00 a.m.-10:00 p.m.; October through April, 8:00 a.m.-8:00 p.m.
Trails—Open daily, Dawn-Dusk.

Directions: Eight miles northwest of Pontiac on US-10 (Dixie Highway) turn southwest onto White Lake Road; at approximately 1.7 miles, jog right briefly onto Andersonville Road, then left again onto White Lake Road and continue about three miles to the park entrance.

Further Information:
Indian Springs Metropark
5200 Indian Trail
Clarkston MI 48016

25 TIMBERLAND SWAMP

Scattered across the lower part of the state, sometimes surprisingly close to major metropolitan areas, are remnants of the great wilderness that formed in Michigan as the last glaciers retreated. No matter how large or small, these last precious outposts of prehistoric Michigan inspire a feeling of awe and a unique appreciation of nature within all who see them. The Timberland Swamp Nature Sanctuary is one such area.

Just minutes from Pontiac and Detroit, yet virtually untouched by man except for a brief stint of hardwood logging, Timberland Swamp is not only a quiet, secluded retreat from the modern world but also a showcase of nature. This 245-acre preserve and Indian Springs Metropark which almost surrounds it, together form an 800-acre swamp that gives birth to three magnificent rivers: the Huron, the Shiawassee and a branch of the Clinton.

A path, which penetrates the swamp and woodlands from the end of Ware Road, is a good place to enjoy a natural theatre, beginning with a spectacular wildflower show every spring. Trillium literally carpets the forest floor in early May, and hundreds of other wildflowers add diversity and color throughout spring. The swamp also nurtures a wide variety of trees, including maples, beech and a few virgin oaks. Fox, deer, opossum, mink, woodchuck, snakes, turtles, salamanders and frogs find shelter in the swamp.

Waterthrushes, flycatchers, owls and grouse are among the many birds that inhabit the area. Thirteen species of warblers—including the beautiful blue, black and white-painted Cerulian Warbler—nest in the sanctuary. Birdwatchers also have a fair chance of seeing such relatively rare species as Cooper's Hawk and Pileated Woodpecker.

The preservation of this magnificent remnant of what was Michigan before settlers drained and tilled the soil, is an outstanding example of the work of the Michigan Nature Association. The organization, dedicated to preserving natural areas in Michigan, persevered for 11 years to acquire the land in this sanctuary.

Though the sanctuary is open to the public, please remember that this is private land and that you are the guest of the M.N.A.

County: Oakland

City: Clarkston

Fees: None

Schedule: No posted hours.

Directions: From I-75 west of Clarkston take exit 92 and drive south on Dixie Highway approximately 1.6 miles to White Lake Road; turn south (right) onto White Lake Road and drive about two miles to Andersonville Road; turn west (right) onto Andersonville Road and follow it northwest three miles to Big Lake Road; turn west (left) onto Big Lake Road and go for a short distance to Ware Road; turn south (left) onto Ware Road and proceed to the sanctuary entrance.

Further Information:
Michigan Nature Association
P.O. Box 102
Avoca MI 48006

Southeastern Lower Peninsula

26
INDEPENDENCE OAKS COUNTY PARK

Scenic views, a wide variety of plant and animal life, and good birdwatching come from nine miles of hiking and nature trails that wind through valleys, over forested hills, across creeks and marshes, and around Crooked Lake at this 830-acre Oakland County park.

Crooked Lake, which runs north and south, divides the park into nearly equal halves.

Beaches, boat ramps, playgrounds, picnic areas and ball fields line the east shoreline. The headwaters of the Clinton River also pass through this section of the park in a low marsh area.

Across the lake, which acts as a barrier to the noisier day-use activities, an interpretive center

(Continued on page 33.)

Southeastern Lower Peninsula

27 DRAYTON PLAINS NATURE CENTER

Wildflower walks, bird and tree identification, maple sugaring and general tours are among the variety of programs the 137-acre Drayton Plains Nature Center conducts year round to introduce nature to the general public.

Eight nature trails, including two that are self-guiding, wind for 7.25 miles through the private, non-profit organization's grounds, which include woodlands, open fields, 10 acres of marsh, and ponds, all located on the banks of the Clinton River. A waterfowl wildlife refuge and nesting area is also within the sanctuary's boundaries.

One trail is open in the winter for cross-country skiing.

County: Oakland

City: Drayton Plains

Fees: None.

Schedule: Open year round, 9:00 a.m.-Sunset; Closed Mondays.

Directions: Two miles north of the Pontiac city limits on US-10, turn west onto Hatchery Road; go a half mile to Edmore Road; turn southeast (left) onto Edmore Road and go to Denby Drive; bear right on Denby Drive and follow it to the entrance.

Further Information:
Drayton Plains Nature Center
2125 Denby Rd.
Drayton Plains MI 48020

INDEPENDENCE OAKS COUNTY PARK

(Continued from page 32.)

is the starting point for the quiet and peace of the hiking trails, which vary in length from .5 to 3.0 miles. Trail maps are available at this newly opened building, which overlooks a picturesque creek, and a variety of educational nature programs are also conducted there.

All facilities at the park are barrier-free. In addition, the All Visitors Trail, a short paved trail beginning on the east side of the lake near the boathouse, is specifically designed for the handicapped.

All of the trails are not only open, but also groomed in the winter for cross-country skiers. Other winter facilities for skiers include a warming house, a concession stand and restrooms. For snow conditions call (313) 625-0877.

County: Oakland

City: Clarkston

Fees: County Residents—$2.50 per day per vehicle.
Non-country Residents—$4.00 per day per vehicle

Schedule: Open year round, 8:00 a.m.-Dusk; Closed Christmas day.

Directions: From I-75 north of Pontiac, take the Sashabaw Road exit (89); go north on Sashabaw Road two miles to the entrance.

Further Information:
Independence Oaks County Park
9501 Sashabaw Rd.
Clarkston MI 48016

28 PONTIAC LAKE RECREATION AREA

Birdwatching is so consistent here that classes from a local university make regular field trips to the park for birdwatching and study. Mushroom hunters, herbalists, berry pickers and wildflower enthusiasts, too, all pay return visits.

Oak-, maple- and aspen-covered glacial hills run through the middle of the 3,700-acre park, and old farm sites, orchards and fields reverting to the wild are silent reminders of the area's early history. Marshes, springs, Pontiac Lake and the Huron River add to the variety of habitat and scenic interest.

The park's lone hiking trail connects the day-use area, tucked into the southeast corner, to a 174-site modern campground off Maceday Road. About halfway along this 1.8-mile route, the path rises to a scenic overlook of Pontiac Lake and the surrounding countryside. Hikers can also use the 17 miles of soft, sandy bridle trails that network the area.

Facilities at the park's large day-use area include a picnic area, a swimming beach, a beachhouse, a playground, and rifle, skeet and archery ranges. Other facilities scattered throughout the park include a boat-launching site, riding stables and a snowmobile area. Many stump-infested areas in Pontiac Lake, created in the 1930s by damming the Huron River, provide excellent fish habitat. Trail and road maps for the huge park are available at park headquarters.

The hiking and bridle trails are open in the winter for cross-country skiing.

County: Oakland

City: Pontiac

Fees: **$2.00 daily vehicle permit or $10.00 annual vehicle permit valid in all state parks.**

Schedule: **Open year round.**

Directions: **From the intersection of US-10 and M-59 in Pontiac, go west on M-59 approximately seven miles to Williams Lake Road; turn north (right) onto Williams Lake Road and go approximately .9 miles to Gale Road; turn west (left) onto Gale Road and go a quarter mile to the headquarters road (on the right) and the day-use area (on the left).**

Further Information:
**Pontiac Lake Recreation Area
7800 Gale Rd.
Pontiac MI 48054**

29 HIGHLAND RECREATION AREA

In northeast corner of the 5,500-acre Highland Recreation Area, nature has prepared a unique display for man. There, growing in the Haven Hill Natural Area, is every forest type found in southern Michigan.

Nearly 20 miles of beautiful hiking (including an extensive system of bridle paths) and nature trails web this diverse habitat, which supports 17 species of mammals and over 100 species of birds. Several begin at Goose Meadows (near the park entrance), then skirt Haven Hill Lake as they take their various routes through this quiet national natural landmark. Goose Meadows, itself, presents excellent opportunities for observing the variety of waterfowl attracted to Haven Hill Lake. Other trails begin at the winter-sports area, a quarter mile south of Goose Meadows on the park entrance road, and at a small parking area south of the park's maintenance building. Trail and road maps are available at the park entrance.

For a memorable view of Haven Hill Lake and the Natural Area, especially during the fall-color season, drive up a steep hill to the nature center, closed and shuttered because of state budget cuts, and walk to a scenic overlook on a high hill.

Other facilities at Highland Recreation Area include a pleasant swimming beach and a picnic area at Teeple Lake, plus other small picnic grounds scattered along the roads throughout the western edge of the park.

Cross-country skiers may use the trails in the winter.

County: Oakland

City: Milford

Fees: $2.00 daily vehicle permit or $10.00 annual vehicle permit valid in all state parks.

Schedule: Open year round.

Directions: Go west from Pontiac on M-59 approximately 15 miles to the entrance.

Further Information:
Highland Recreation Area
5200 E. Highland Rd.
Milford MI 48042

30 PROUD LAKE RECREATION AREA

Try your luck and skill at landing a trout from the quick-flowing Huron River or walk through pine plantations, over high hills, by numerous lakes, or across a quaking bog, meadows and marsh thick with wildflowers and birdlife.

You can see and do all from more than five miles of quiet, beautiful and lightly used trails that penetrate the wide variety of scenery and habitat of the 3,600-acre Proud Lake Recreation Area. The Marsh Trail, River Trail and Chief Pontiac Trail, for example, probe the area south of the Huron River, which cuts the park into north and south halves. At the end of the Chief Pontiac Trail, a new foot bridge and dam crosses the Huron River just north of Moss Lake and leads to the Ecology Trail, which makes a long loop north of the river. All trails begin at parking lots in back of and to the north of park headquarters. The trails are open for cross-country skiing in the winter.

Two picnic areas, a swimming beach, a canoe livery, an extensive bridle trail and a modern 110-site year-round campground add to the appeal of the Proud Lake Recreation Area.

> **County: Oakland**
>
> **City: Milford**
>
> **Fees: $2.00 daily vehicle permit or $10.00 annual vehicle permit valid in all state parks.**
>
> **Schedule: Open year round.**
>
> **Directions: From I-96 approximately 12 miles east of the I-96/US-23 interchange, take exit 159 (Wixom Road); go north on Wixom Road six miles to the headquarters entrance.**
>
> **Further Information:**
> **Proud Lake Recreation Area**
> **3500 Wixom Rd.**
> **Milford MI 48042**

31 KENSINGTON METROPARK

Mention Kensington Metropark, and most people will probably think of the bustling crowds of swimmers, sunbathers, picnickers, golfers, cross-country skiers, and sailboaters who flock by the thousands to this popular getaway. Not as well known is a secluded, quiet, much-less-traveled area on the 4,300-acre park's west side where visitors can experience nature and enjoy the out-of-doors on a more initimate basis.

The focal point, there, is a nature center which hugs the shore of Kingfisher Lagoon. Six beautiful hiking and nature trails, four of which are marked with helpful interpretive signs, begin near the center building. If you're looking for seclusion, take either the Chickadee or Fox Trail, both of which lead to the northern edge of

(Continued on page 37.)

(Continued on page 37.)

KENSINGTON METROPARK

(Continued from page 36.)

the nature-study area. The best place to enjoy spring wildflowers is on the Deer Run Trail's two loops, and excellent birdwatching possibilities come from the variety of cover and habitat along the 1.25-mile Aspen Trail. Completing the trail system in the nature area are Wildwing Trail, which circles for 2.25 miles around Wildwing Lake, and the half-mile Tamarack Trail, which crosses a tamarack bog.

The center building houses nature exhibits, including a working beehive, and the center's staff conducts guided hikes, nature workshops and special programs throughout the year.

At Kent Lake, the focal point of most of the park's activities, a paved hiking/bike/jogging trail passes two swimming beaches and 12 scattered picnic areas on its several-mile circuit around the lake. For a different view of the park or to explore Kent Lake's many islands, (including Labadie Island and its semi-private picnic area) use one of the park's rental rowboats or sailboats.

Miles of cross-country ski trails, ice fishing, an ice rink and toboggan runs are winter attractions.

> **County: Oakland**
>
> **City: Milford**
>
> **Fees: $2.00 daily vehicle permit or $7.00 annual vehicle permit good at all metroparks.**
>
> **Schedule: Open year round except Christmas and Thanksgiving.**
> **Trail hours—6:00 a.m.-dusk.**
> **Park hours—6:00 a.m.-10:00 p.m.**
>
> **Directions: Four miles east of US-23 on I-96, exit on either Kensington Road or Kent Lake Road and go north a few hundred feet to the entrances and the numerous parking lots which ring Kent Lake.**
>
> **Further Information:**
> **Kensington Metropark**
> **2240 W. Buno Rd.**
> **Milford MI 48042**

32 ISLAND LAKE RECREATION AREA

Without a doubt, the best way to appreciate the quiet beauty of Island Lake State Recreation Area is to canoe the Huron River, which neatly bisects the park along an east-west line. Often canopied by gently leaning trees, the river passes through a thick second-growth forest, sharply twists around steep hills and lazily loops through open meadows on its seven-mile journey within the park's boundaries. Canoe rentals are available at a livery on the eastern end of the park at

Kent Lake; those who have their own canoes can put in at either of two access points on Island Lake. Other facilities for canoeists include two beautiful riverside picnic areas and a campground, reached only by river.

Hikers, too, can get some good views throughout the park's picturesque 3,466 acres. A several-mile-long trail circles through the area

(Continued on page 38.)

ISLAND LAKE RECREATION AREA

(Continued from page 37.)

along both banks of the Huron River and also climbs to the higher ground that frames the river valley. The land here generally rises from the river to rolling hills whose terrain alternates between undulating meadows and second-growth woods. Small swamps and marshes dot other sections of the park. The trail crosses several small creeks and passes a small rustic (no electricity or flush toilets) campground that is also accesssible by car. Trails begin at the picnic grounds at either Kent or Island lakes (at opposite ends of the park) or behind the park headquarters, located at the intersection of Grand River and Kensington roads.

Other facilities at the park include swimming beaches at Kent and Island lakes plus several adjacent picnic areas.

County: Livingston

City: Brighton

Fees: $2.00 daily vehicle permit or $10.00 annual vehicle permit valid in all state parks.

Schedule: Open year round.

Directions: From the west, drive east on I-96 approximately 2.5 miles from the US-23/I-96 junction to the Kensington Road exit; turn south onto Kensington Road, cross Grand River Road and go less than half a mile to the park entrance. From the east (Detroit area) exit from I-96 at Kent Lake Road; go south several hundred feet to Grand River Road; turn west (right) onto Grand River Road and go approximately 1.7 miles to Kensington Road; turn south (left) onto Kensington Road and go less than half a mile to the park entrance.

Further Information:
Island Lake Recreation Area
12950 E. Grand River
Brighton MI 48116

33 BRIGHTON RECREATION AREA

The best views of the high, rolling hills, glacial depressions and 10 lakes that make up 4,913-acre Brighton Recreation Area come from two hiking trails that wind through the eastern section of the park. The Penosha Trail loops for five miles over rolling terrain, across foot bridges and corduroyed wetlands, and along the shore of a small lake. A short turnoff about three-quarters of the way around the circuit climbs steeply to a high scenic overlook from which you can see the countryside for miles around. If you pack a bedroll, you can unroll it at a small campground—with fire pits, pit toilet and garbage disposal—that mark's the trail's halfway point.

The less-strenuous two-mile-long Kahchin Trail loops through the same type of terrain as the longer trail but also passes old stone fences, abandoned fields reverting to their natural state, second-growth oak/hickory woodland and other evidence of the area's former use as farmland. Both trails begin adjacent to the parking area at the intersection of Bishop Lake Road and Rolison Trail.

A beautiful display of wildflowers and good morel mushrooming are spring calling cards to the area.

Facilities in the Brighton Recreation Area include three picnic areas, two swimming beaches—one at Bishop Lake, the other at Chilson Pond—and camping. Seventy-three rustic sites make up the Appleton Campground, on the north side of Bishop Lake Road; facilities at the 149-site Bishop Lake Campground, to the south of Bishop Lake Road, are modern.

Fishing—especially for panfish, bass and pike—is good on the park's 10 lakes. Appleton Lake, on the northern edge of the park, is stocked annually with rainbow trout.

County: Livingston

City: Brighton

Fees: **$2.00 daily vehicle permit or $10.00 permit valid at all state parks.**

Schedule: **Open year round, 8:00 a.m.-10:00 p.m.**

Directions: **From I-96 approximately 2.5 miles west of the US-23/I-96 interchange, take exit 145 (Grand River Road); go south on Grand River Road approximately 1.2 miles to Brighton Road; turn west (right) onto Brighton Road and go 1.5 miles to Baur Road; turn south (left) onto Baur Road and go two miles to Bishop Lake Road, turn west (right) onto Bishop Lake Road and go one mile to the campgrounds, hiking trails and day-use area.**

**Further Information:
Brighton Recreation Area
6360 Chilson Rd.
Howell MI 48843**

34 PINCKNEY RECREATION AREA

A hike on one of southeast Michigan's longest and most rustic trails, the Potawatomi, is the main attraction for nature lovers to this sprawling 9,994-acre area. The trail, named after Indians who once used the area as their traditional summer hunting grounds, stays as far as possible from area roads as it circles for 17 miles through the wild, undeveloped heart of the recreation area. Constructed by Boy Scouts and marked by cedar posts with orange discs, the trail is easy to follow as it passes many of the dozen major lakes within the park, climbs over rolling forest-covered hills and crosses numerous small streams. Hikers can pick up the trail at several different places, but the easiest to find with good parking is at Silver Lake off Dexter Townhall Road near the park headquarters.

The Crooked Lake Trail and Silver Lake Trail, both two to three miles long, also begin at the Silver Lake parking lot. A several-mile-long trail connects the Pinckney Recreation Area trails to the Waterloo Recreation area trail system and creates the opportunity for week-long hikes of 50 to 60 miles.

Other facilities and activities in the area include a total of 255 campsites at three different campgrounds, picnic areas, swimming, fishing, concession stands and cross-country skiing. Rustic campgrounds at Halfmoon Lake and Crooked Lake are only a short distance from the Potawatomi Trail. A boat-launching area, a swimming beach and the park's only modern campsites line the shore of Bruin Lake. Day-use areas include a beach at Silver Lake and a beach, changehouse, large picnic area and concession stand at Halfmoon Lake. Anglers can use boat access sites at more than a dozen good-sized lakes within the park's boundaries. In the winter, two cross-country ski trails, two and four miles long, begin and end at the parking area at Silver Lake.

These facilities are scattered across two counties and are connected by a of web of roads, so unless you're extremely familiar with the area, stop at the headquarters and get a map.

Counties: Washtenaw and Livingston

City: Pinckney

Fees: **$2.00 daily vehicle permit or $10.00 annual vehicle permit valid in all state parks.**

Schedule: **Open year round.**

Directions: **To the reach headquarters, take exit 49 (North Territorial Road) from US-23 north of Ann Arbor; drive west on North Territorial Road 12 miles to Dexter Townhall Road; turn north (right) onto Dexter Townhall Road and drive one mile to Silver Hill Road; turn left and drive a half mile to the park entrance and headquarters.**

Further Information
Pinckney Recreation Area
8555 Silver Hill, Route 1
Pinckney MI 48169

35 HUDSON MILLS METROPARK

chair.

Four of southeast Michigan's most beautiful picnic areas—three near the banks of the river—are spread throughout the 1,545-acre park. The northernmost overlooks one of the few rapids of the Huron River. Another connects, via a small foot bridge, to a small island in the middle of the river. Groves of stately trees and open meadows are the settings for the remaining two.

Several access sites and two overnight campgrounds cater to canoeists, who consider this one of the finest sections of the Huron River to paddle.

Other facilities include several ball diamonds and children's playgrounds (usually near the picnic areas), plus bike and ski rentals and a food concession at an Activity Center on the east side of the park.

The park maintains groomed cross-country ski trails in the winter.

Some of the most picturesque picnic areas in southeast Michigan, scenic trails and the beauty of the Huron River are good reasons to visit Hudson Mills Metropark.

Two trails, one barrier free, wind through the former site of a sawmill, a gristmill, a cidermill and a plastermill, the earliest dating back to 1827. Helpful interpretive signs mark the .75-mile Acorn Nature Trail, which begins near the Oak Meadows Picnic Area, borders the river then loops past areas of swamp, marsh and woods. A paved hiking/jogging/bike path, which circles the perimeter of the park, passes through woods, crosses open meadows, traverses a small island via two foot bridges, and for over a third of its approximately two-mile length, borders the river. This trail is easily accessible by wheel-

County: Washtenaw

City: Ann Arbor

Fees: **$2.00 daily vehicle permit or $7.00 annual vehicle permit valid in all Metroparks.**

Schedule: Open year round.

Directions: Six miles north of Ann Arbor on US-23 take exit 49 (North Territorial Road); drive west on North Territorial Road approximately seven miles to the park entrance.

Further Information:
Hudson Mills Metropark
8800 N. Territorial Rd.
Dexter MI 48130

ANNE AND LEONARD WING
NATURE PRESERVE

A wide variety and large number of plants; the almost constant calls of Red-winged Blackbirds, warblers and herons; the rare opportunity to experience and study a wetlands habitat at very close range; and great natural beauty are reasons why, per square foot, this very small (2.5 acres) area is as much, if not more, of a treat for the senses than some larger, better-known preserves.

Framed on three sides by gently rolling, wooded hills, the entire preserve is set in a small wetlands consisting of a marsh, a pond and a tamarack bog. The marsh supports a profusion of water-loving plants and wildflowers, and food and shelter at both the marsh and the pond draw a great number of birds. The only trail, an 80-yard-long boardwalk, cuts through the heart of the marsh past a small stand of tamarack to the edge of the pond.

The Washtenaw Audubon Society owns the preserve, which is named after a husband and wife who were known respectively as a nationally prominent ornithologist and a nature writer.

County: Washtenaw

City: Ann Arbor

Fees: None.

Schedule: No posted hours.

Directions: On the east side of Ann Arbor take Dixboro Road (which runs parallel to and east of US-23) north to Warren Road (which runs parallel to and north of M-14); go east on Warren Road about a half mile to the preserve entrance, on the north side of road.

Sanilac Petroglyphs State Park (page 16)

37 EXHIBIT MUSEUM

Call it what you will—the University of Michigan Museum of Natural History, the Alexander G. Ruthven Museum or the Exhibit Museum—the imposing four-story brick building by any name, is a fascinating and educational place to spend an afternoon. Here, various University of Michigan departments or disciplines—such as paleontology, zoology and anthropology—have filled three of the building's floors with extensive collections, exhibits and displays.

The complete skeletons of a giant Michigan mastodon and an allosaurus, for example, dominate the second-floor exhibits on prehistoric life. Complementing this awesome display are the fossilized bones of some of prehistory's most impressive dinosaurs, which line the back of the large hall. Along the remaining walls and rounding out this display are fossils of prehistoric mammals, early reptiles, amphibians, plants and invertebrates, plus explanations of their place in the evolution of the planet.

Extensive collections of Michigan fish, plants, reptiles and amphibians, plus a large exhibit of mounted native birds and mammals—many realistically posed in their natural habitats—are housed on the third floor.

A North American Indian display—including numerous artifacts—plus exhibits on primitive technologies, geology, mineralogy, biology, astronomy and a wide variety of other interesting subjects are spread throughout the top (fourth) floor. A museum gift shop and planetarium theatre are also located on this floor. Researchers work on the first floor, which is not open to the public.

County: Washtenaw

City: Ann Arbor

Fees: None.

Schedule: Monday through Saturday, 9:00 a.m.-5:00 p.m.; Sundays, 1:00 p.m.-5:00 p.m.

Directions: From I-94 south of Ann Arbor take exit 177 and go north on State Street approximately 2.6 miles to North University; turn right, onto North University, and go 2 1/2 blocks.

Further Information:
Alexander G. Ruthven Museums
1109 Geddes Avenue
Ann Arbor MI 48109

38 MATTHAEI BOTANICAL GARDENS

The University of Michigan's Matthaei Botanical Gardens offers one of the most unusual classes conducted at any nature center—or educational facility of any type for that matter—in Michigan. Students enrolled in the class titled Aerial Ecology study botany and wildlife habitats from the basket of a hot-air balloon as it drifts across the countryside. This center for research, education and the study of nature hosts a *(Continued on page 45.)*

MATTHAEI BOTANICAL GARDENS

(Continued from page 44.)

wide range of "normal" adult education classes as well. Birdwatching, Edible Wild Plants, Herb Garden Design, Japanese Flower Arranging, and Mushrooms of Michigan are among the many classes available to both the educational community and the general public.

But you don't have to ride in a hot-air balloon or sit in a classroom to learn from or simply enjoy the 250-acre Gardens. Three separate habitat rooms in the Conservatory building, for example, display tropical, desert and temperate plants. And a detailed, beautifully illustrated 54-page guide to the garden's three nature trails is a thorough, interesting and enjoyable introduction to the natural world. The excellent booklet not only identifies many of the plants found throughout the trails' diverse habitats, but also fully explains each species' place in the plant society.

The hikes vary greatly in length, terrain and habitat. The .6-mile Red Trail, for example, follows Fleming Creek through its flood plain, past thick shrubs, a small stand of tamaracks and a grove of very old burr oaks, then passes a wildflower garden and a juniper garden. The Yellow Trail winds for 1.2 miles through a recently established prairie area, then follows the east side of Fleming Creek past a large, marshy pond. The garden's longest path, 1.6-mile Blue Trail, meanders through a pine plantation and an upland forest, then passes two small ponds. Perennial, herb, rose, rhododendron and other special gardens color the grounds along all trails.

To really appreciate the full dimensions of the Matthaei Botanical Gardens, plan to pay return visits at various times of the year. In the dead of winter, for example, the trails are so quiet, white and peaceful that owls and hawks often perch, especially along the Blue Trail, unconcerned in trees. And the Conservatory, with its profusion of plants, is just about a sure antidote to February's gloom. Spring brings abundant wildflowers, flowering shrubs and migrating songbirds followed by blooming prairie plants in summer. Beautiful fall-color walks are best September through October.

County: **Washtenaw**

City: **Ann Arbor**

Fees: **Trails and grounds free; $1.00 admission to the Conservatory.**

Schedule: **Open year round, except Christmas and New Years Day. Grounds—Open 8:00 a.m.-Sunset. Conservatory—Open 10:00 a.m.-4:30 p.m.**

Directions: **From US-23 on the east side of Ann Arbor, exit on Geddes Road (39) and drive east approximately a quarter mile to Dixboro Road; turn north (left) onto Dixboro Road and go approximately 1.5 miles to the entrance.**

Further Information:
**Matthaei Botanical Gardens
1800 N. Dixboro Rd.
Ann Arbor MI 48105**

39 SEARLES NATURAL AREA

What might a day-dreaming nature-lover in a crowded urban area wish for as a quick and nearby escape from the roads, cars and people? He or she might imagine a small haven where, except for the chatter of birds, quiet would reign in a woods lush with plant life. Trees would shade and cool the forest floor, even on the hottest of days. And a trail, though well worn, would be crowded with shrubs and trees as it wound through an oak/hickory hardwood forest and along a gently flowing creek.

Such a place exists and it's called the Searles Natural Area. Only a few miles from downtown Ann Arbor and barely a mile from the busy US-23 expressway, the 50-acre haven, owned by the Washtenaw Audubon Society, offers peace, seclusion and the opportunity to get away from the urban sprawl. It's the answer to an urban nature-lover's wish.

County: Washtenaw

City: Ann Arbor

Fees: None.

Schedule: No posted hours.

Directions: South of Ann Arbor, from US-23 take exit 31 and drive east on Willis Road; at approximately 1.3 miles, where Willis Road bends to the south, continue east (straight) on a dirt road .3 miles to the preserve, on the north side of the road.

40

NANKIN MILLS NATURE CENTER

and

WILLIAM P. HOLLIDAY FOREST

"If only the walls could talk," as the saying goes, the knotted planks of the Nankin Mills Nature Center would whisper several chapters of Michigan history to its 20th-century visitors. Constructed before the Civil War as a gristmill, the building first absorbed the concerns, politics and gossip of farmers who brought in their wheat to be ground. Later within the same walls, escaping slaves huddled as they made their way to Canada via this and other depots along the Underground Railroad. Even Henry Ford—who sometimes seems to have touched everything in Michigan during his lifetime—did in fact remodel this mill in the 1920s to produce electricity.

Today the walls and hand-hewn beams of the restored mill reflect natural history, and visitors now pass by the placid millrace pond to learn from natural displays—including live animal exhibits—and an interpretive program.

The picturesque nature center is also an excellent starting point for a short walk or extensive hike into the adjacent William P. Holliday Forest and Wildlife Preserve. This 500-acre uniquely shaped sanctuary (several miles long and only several hundred yards wide at its broadest point) serpentines its way along Tonquish Creek.

Six nature trails—varying in length from half-mile loops to the 12-mile round-trip Tonquish Trail—follow the stream's course while also making short exploratory circuits away from it. The tree-canopied paths continually cross and recross the creek as they enter then leave a variety of other habitats, including a five-acre marsh, 15 acres of open meadows, the mill pond and several smaller creeks. Comfort stations and shelters are spaced at regular intervals along the trails, which are also accessible from Cowan Road.

The nature center and wildlife preserve also abut the Middle Rouge Parkway, a 2,250-acre park stretched along the Middle Rouge River from Northville to Dearborn. Facilities there—most scattered along Hines Drive, which runs the length of the park—include ball fields, play areas, picnic areas and several lakes.

County: Wayne

City: Westland

Fees: None.

Schedule: Trails hours vary but generally open one-half hour before sunrise and close one-half hour after sunset. Contact Nankin Mills Nature Center for exact hours.

Directions: From I-96 east of Plymouth, take exit 174 and drive south two miles on Farmington Road to Ann Arbor Trail; turn east (left) onto Ann Arbor Trail and go 100 feet to the entrance.

Further Information:
Nankin Mills Nature Center
33175 Ann Arbor Trail
Westland MI 48185

41

DEARBORN
ENVIRONMENTAL STUDY AREA

Just about anyone who has visited Greenfield Village (along with many who haven't) recognizes that Henry Ford expended a great deal of time, money and energy to preserve the past. What most people don't know, however, is that the great industrialist was almost equally devoted to the conservation and the enjoyment of nature.

When Ford built his Fair Lane Estate along the

County: Wayne

City: Dearborn

Fees: None.

Schedule: Open year round, Dawn-Dusk.

Directions: From US-39 (Southfield Freeway) in Dearborn, exit on M-153 (Ford Road) and go west approximately one mile to Evergreen Road; turn south (left) onto Evergreen Road and go approximately three quarters of a mile to the University of Michigan-Dearborn campus. The sanctuary is located on the west side of the campus on Fair Lane Road. Park across from the Henry Ford Estate or farther east on Fair Lane Road.

Further Information:
  University of Michigan-Dearborn
  Department of Natural Sciences
  Dearborn MI 48128

Rouge River, he set out to create a place where he could retreat from the world in a setting of natural beauty. To do so, he hired the then-world-famous landscape architect, Jens Jensen. Ford chose the right person. Jensen's work at Fair Lane—including Fair Lane Lake and a meadow (later renamed in the great architect's honor) linking the lake to Ford's mansion—has been recognized as one of the finest examples of American landscape architecture.

Much of Jensen's work and the Ford estate remains today as a large portion of the Dearborn Environmental Study Area. Set aside by the University of Michigan-Dearborn and located on their campus, this 72-acre sanctuary not only serves as an outdoor classroom, training facility and site for several wildlife-study projects but also as a place where the general public can go to enjoy nature as Henry Ford did more than 50 years ago.

Three trails totaling three miles pass by an incredibly diverse array of sights including an abandoned orchard (there long before Ford bought the property), marshes, Fair Lane Lake, the Rouge River, a sycamore/willow flood-plain forest, a stand of virgin timber featuring some of the largest beech and maple trees in the estate, old farm fields, an arboretum and a rose garden. These and other special points of interest, plus a map are included in a helpful and educational brochure available at the entrance. For a very different perspective of the natural environment

(Continued on page 49.)

42   OAKWOODS NATURE STUDY AREA

One of the most unusual trails in Michigan can make a visit to this park a cut above the ordinary. The unique and appropriately named Walk-in-the-Water Trail is a formal, designated canoe "path" that circles for a mile through the many channels and islands of the Huron River. Floating markers along the route explain and interpret river ecology.

Those who like to keep their feet on the ground can use more than 3.75 miles of earthen trails to explore the variety of scenery and habitats of the 400-acre nature-study area area nestled along the southern shore of the Huron River about 10 miles upstream from its mouth on Lake Erie. The Big Tree Trail, for example, circles for .75 miles through a hardwood forest.

The one-mile Sky-Come-Down Trail skirts a large pond, but the main attraction along it is a classic display of "edge effect," that is, the meeting, overlapping and blending of two different plant communities—meadows and woods in this case. Formally called *ecotones*, these edge areas support a variety of plant species from both habitats and, as a result, are usually excellent places to observe wildlife, especially birds.

Other trails include the park's longest, the Long Bark Trail, which follows the edge of the Huron River for nearly a mile before winding its way back through deep woods for another mile to the Nature Center.

County: Wayne

City: Flat Rock

Fees: **$2.00 daily vehicle permit or $7.00 annual vehicle permit valid for all Huron-Clinton Metroparks.**

Schedule: **Trails—Open year round, Dawn-Dusk.**
Building—Summer, 10:00 a.m.-5:00 p.m.; School Year, 1:00 p.m.-5:00 p.m.

Directions: **From I-275 on the Wayne-Monroe County Line take exit 8 (Will Carleton Road); go east on Will Carleton Road for .75 miles to Romine Road; turn north (left) onto Romine Road and go approximately 1.5 miles to Willow Road; turn east (right) onto Willow Road and go a quarter mile to the park entrance.**

Further Information:
Oakwoods Metropark Nature Center
P.O. Box 332
Flat Rock MI 48134

Numbered posts—which correspond to numbered paragraphs in a pamphlet available at the

(Continued on page 50.)

DEARBORN ENVIRONMENTAL AREA
(Continued from page 48.)

here, pick up a self-guided audio tape and cassette player (both available at either the Fair Lane Estate or the circulation desk of the university library) and, along the Sensory Nature Trail, explore nature with senses other than sight.

The diverse habitat here attracts a wide variety of birds: 192, according to a checklist available at the sanctuary entrance. Local birders know the area as an excellent one for spotting migrating wood warblers in May, and more than 30 species of these brightly colored, energetic little birds have been sighted at the property.

Picnicking is not allowed in the Environmental Study Area, but picnic tables are available in the campus courtyard across the road.

43   LAKE ERIE METROPARK

Lake Erie Metropark completes a string of nine Huron-Clinton Metroparks that are scattered along the banks of the Huron River from its beginnings at Indian Springs in northern Oakland County to its end, 100 miles later, at Lake Erie. Here, scenic views of flowing waterways, quiet lagoons, and Lake Erie inlets and islands mark the point where not only the Huron, but also the Detroit River empties into Lake Erie.

No formal designated hiking or nature trails mark the landscape, but casual walkers will have no trouble exploring the expansive open meadows and extensive shoreline. On the edges of one large grassy meadow, the waters of the Detroit River and a long lagoon frame a large picnic area.

The park's real estate also includes the northern end of the Lake Erie marshes, so birdwatching opportunities for waterfowl and shorebirds are good, especially during spring migration. The park is also a prime area for observing hawks, particularly during the fall migration season.

Other facilities at the park, located in the extreme southeastern tip of Wayne County, include a wave pool and a marina.

County: Wayne

City: Rockwood

Fees: $2.00 daily vehicle permit or $7.00 annual vehicle permit valid in all Huron-Clinton Metroparks.

Schedule: Open year round.

Directions: From I-75 south of Detroit take exit 27 (North Huron River Drive); drive east on North Huron River Drive two miles to West Jefferson; turn north (left) onto West Jefferson and go less than a block to the park entrance.

Further Information:
Lower Huron Metropark
17845 Savage Rd.
Belleville MI 48111

OAKWOODS NATURE STUDY AREA
(Continued from page 49.)

Nature Center Building—identify and interpret flowers, trees and other natural points of special interest along all trails. In addition, a tape cassette, also available at the Nature Center, guides handicapped or elderly visitors down the 700-foot paved Split Log Trail.

A variety of exhibits inside the Nature Center Building includes a live animal display. The park's staff conducts nature walks and classes throughout the year. Oakwoods does not allow picnicking, but Willow Metropark, just to the north, has numerous picnic areas.

44

POINTE MOUILLEE STATE GAME AREA

trails and the dike system is available at the headquarters

Excellent birding plus good hiking are the draws to the Pointe Mouillee State Game Area, which stretches from the Huron River mouth south along nearly four miles of western Lake Erie shoreline.

The vast marsh, open waters, diked ponds and inlets of the game area and its adjoining wildlife refuge attract large numbers of birds year round, but early spring and before the opening of waterfowl hunting season in the fall are the best times to see large concentrations. Ducks, geese, shorebirds, gulls and terns plus many rare and unusual species make stopovers here during spring and fall migrations. The area, which encompasses a significant portion of the Lake Erie marsh system, also provides nesting habitat for many waterfowl and shorebirds during the summer breeding season.

A good place to spot shorebirds, songbirds and waterfowl is in a small section of the game area that lies along Pointe Mouillee Road north of the Huron River in Wayne County. Located on a point within this area, the park headquarters marks the mouth of the Huron River.

Hikers and birders can take trails from any of several parking areas along Dixie Highway and Roberts Road, both of which border the western edge of the state game area. These trails lead into the woods and marshes and alongside both Mouillee Creek and the Lautenschlager Drain. Trails from a parking area at the end of Sigler Road (which crosses Dixie Highway just south of the Huron River) lead to an extensive dike system, which in turn leads to the wildlife refuges within the game area. There, you can walk for several miles next to marshes, diked pools and open water. A map that marks the parking areas,

County: Monroe

City: Rockwood

Fees: None.

Schedule: Open year round, but admittance to many sections is restricted during waterfowl season, plus the many hunters make birdwatching during this time at best, difficult, and at worse, dangerous.

Directions: From I-75 south of Detroit exit, onto North Huron Road (27) and go east two miles to West Jefferson; turn south (right) onto West Jefferson and drive about 1.5 miles to Campau Road; turn east (left) and go a half mile to Pointe Mouillee Road; turn south (right) onto Pointe Mouillee Road and drive to the headquarters.

Further Information:
Pointe Mouillee State Game Area
37205 Mouillee Rd., Rt. 2
Rockwood MI 48173

45 STERLING STATE PARK

Sterling State Park, Michigan's only state park on Lake Erie, nearly marks the halfway point of one of the prime birdwatching areas in the state, a stretch along the eastern end of Lake Erie from the mouth of the Detroit River to the Ohio state line. The Lake Erie shoreline, the park's four lagoons and small marsh area, and the Sandy Creek Outlet all attract numerous shorebirds and waterfowl from spring migration through summer and into fall.

An added plus for birdwatchers, especially during inclement spring weather, is the fact that they can observe most of the bird activity in this 1,000-acre area from the comfort of their car. Several roads closely border the park's four lagoons, which attract egrets, Great Blue Heron, smaller shorebirds, Coots, Mergansers, Blue-winged Teal and many other species. If you want to explore the less-traveled area of the park in search of the more elusive birds, take a nearly mile-long foot trail that circles the largest lagoon.

Other facilities here include a swimming beach, a large open picnic area (on a low rise back from the beach) with a panoramic view of Lake Erie, and a 288-site campground (near the entrance) with modern facilities but little shade and no privacy. A boat basin, with four well-sheltered boat-launching ramps and plenty of parking, connects through the Sandy Creek Outlet to Lake Erie. Those without boats can fish from several docks built out into two of the lagoons.

County: Monroe

City: Monroe

Fees: $2.00 daily vehicle permit or $10.00 annual vehicle permit valid in all state parks.

Schedule: Open year round.

Directions: From I-75 near Monroe exit on Dixie Highway and drive northeast approximately one mile to the park entrance.

Further Information:
Sterling State Park
2800 State Park Rd., Rt. 5
Monroe MI 48161

---

46 ERIE MARSH PRESERVE

The 2,618-acre Erie Marsh Preserve and the shoreline of Lake Erie from the Ohio border north to Point Mouillee is one of the finest birdwatching regions in the state. The area—one of the last large remnants of a great prehistoric marsh and wetlands that once stretched along the south and west shores of Lake Erie—attracts impressive numbers of waterfowl, shorebirds and

(Continued on page 53.)

Southeastern Lower Peninsula

ERIE MARSH PRESERVE

(Continued from page 52.)

other species. Most birds—including hawks and rare terns and gulls, such as Forester's Tern, Great Black-backed Gull and Icelandic Gull—pass through the wet meadows, marshes, diked pools and open waters of North Maumee Bay during spring and fall migration. But a significant number—including Great Blue Herons, Coots, Gallinules, terns, several species of ducks, gulls (including some species rare in the state) and egrets—also nest here in the summer.

The preserve—11 percent of state wetlands found between Port Huron and the Ohio line—is also home to many rare and interesting plants. The rare swamp rose mallow and the American lotus, for example, grow in the wetlands and bloom in profusion during late summer.

A system of dikes circles the preserve, and miles of trails atop them give access to the area. The Nature Conservancy, owner of the preserve, requests, however, that all visitors use only the inner dikes. Birdwatchers are very visible when walking on the raised dikes and, as a result, should carry binoculars and spotter scopes because waterfowl are difficult to approach. In some areas, the dikes are tree-lined or bordered by brush and shrubs, and birders there have a better chance for close observation.

The entire area surrounding the Erie Marsh Preserve also affords great birdwatching. Mud flats, lagoons, drains and floodings border many local secondary roads such as Dean, Summit and Bay Creek, and you can spot numerous waterfowl, shorebirds, gulls, and terns without leaving your car.

County: Monroe

City: Monroe

Fees: None.

Schedule: Open year round except for the months of October and November.

Directions: Two miles north of the Ohio Line on I-75, exit on Summit Road (2), which passes over the expressway. Make a *U*-turn at the bait shop just south of the overpass and head back north on Summit Road a half mile to Bay Creek Road; turn right, onto Bay Creek Road, and drive a half mile to Dean Road; turn right, onto Dean Road, and go .5 miles to the parking area at the Erie Shooting Club.

Further Information:
The Nature Conservancy
531 N. Clippert St.
Lansing MI 48912

---

47   HIDDEN LAKE GARDENS

With the retreat of glaciers from northwest Lenawee County, nature slowly unveiled the rounded hills, steep valleys, conical depressions and sweeping vistas she had painstakingly created over millenniums. Centuries later, man applied strokes of his own: thousands of trees, shrubs and other plantings. Together they created a living work of art framed by the untouched woodlands and open meadows of the Irish Hills and titled, "Hidden Lake Gardens."

Harry A. Fee, a prominent Adrian businessman who was interested in scenic beauty and landscaping, began man's involvement in 1926 when he personally planned and implemented plantings on 226 acres of land he had purchased.

County: Lenawee

City: Tipton

Fees: $1.00 per person per visit or $15.00 family season pass.

Schedule: April through October weekdays, 8:00 a.m. to One-half hour before sunset; November through March weekdays, 8:00 a.m.-4:30 p.m.; Weekends and holidays, 9:00 a.m. to same closing hours as weekdays.

Directions: From Cambridge Junction go east on M-50 seven miles to the entrance. Or from the intersection of M-52 and M-50 north of Adrian, go five miles west on M-50 to the entrance

Further Information:
Hidden Lake Gardens
Tipton MI 49287

Nineteen years later, he donated his gardens to Michigan State University and also established a trust to ensure their further development. Since then, the gardens have tripled in size, plantings have multiplied (more than 2,500 species planted since 1960), and Mr. Fee's desire "to create landscape pictures...(and) attract anyone interested in the out-of-doors" has been carried out brilliantly by Michigan State University.

You don't even have to leave your car to appreciate the beauty of the 760-acre area. Six miles of one-way drives wind through the gardens past thousands of labeled plants and trees—massed plantings of azaleas, crabapples, cherries, lilacs, magnolias, rhododendrons, roses, spruces, a wide variety of hardwoods, and the outstanding Harper Collection of dwarf and rare conifers, to name just a few. If you would like to temporarily lose site of the asphalt, park in any of 10 different areas spaced along the drives and wander among a variety of collections—spruces, willows, a demonstration vegetable garden and All American Trials of bedding annuals, again to name just a few.

Those who would like to explore the farther reaches of Hidden Lake Gardens can do so on any of four nature trails. The trails, totaling five miles in length, pass through oak upland forests, border old fence rows and cross rolling countryside. An extensive, in-depth 28-page trail guide points out plants and natural features along the routes and makes the walks and nature study, including some excellent birdwatching and wildflower identification, even more enjoyable.

Three separate rooms in the Conservatory, located near the center of the gardens, feature a fascinating array of plants—bamboo, cactus, ba-

(Continued on page 55.)

HIDDEN LAKE GARDENS

(Continued from page 54.)

nana, cocoa, coffee, fig, palm tapioca and others—in their respective tropical, desert or temperate environments. A short walk from the Conservatory, more indoor plant displays, plus gardening and landscaping information—including programs on gardening and nature study—is available at the Gardens Center Building. A small but beautiful picnic area is located just west of the Conservatory.

HIDDEN LAKE GARDENS COLOR SCHEDULE

April—Autumn: Ornamental shrubs and wildflowers

Mid-April—Early May: Narcissus, Forsythias, Primroses

Early May—Mid-June: Tulips, cherries, redbuds, crab apples, dogwoods, azaleas, rhododendrons, lilacs

Mid-September—Early November: Autumn colors

48 W. J. HAYES STATE PARK

A setting of natural beauty that reminded early Irish settlers of their native countryside has drawn visitors to northwest Lenawee County for decades. Located in the midst of this southern Michigan tourist mecca is W.J. Hayes State Park, 654 acres of rolling terrain, sparkling lakes and picturesque scenery. Though there are no designated hiking or nature trails within the park, there is plenty of room to wander.

Campers can choose between open meadows and heavily wooded areas at a 210-site campground which wraps around the southern shore of Round Lake. Facilities at a day-use area at Wamplers Lake—only a few hundred yards west of Round Lake but across M-124, which passes through the park—include a large picnic area, playgrounds, a 1,000-foot-long swimming beach, change rooms and a concession stand. Boat-launching sites are available at both lakes, but the one at Round Lake is limited to use by campers only.

For those who enjoy man-made attractions, a variety of activities—including giant waterslides, a dinosaur park, a wildwest town and an international speedway—are within an easy drive from the park.

County: Lenawee

City: Cambridge Junction

Fees: $2.00 daily vehicle permit or $10.00 annual vehicle permit valid in all state parks.

Schedule: Open year round.
Day use area—Open daily, 8:00 a.m.-10:00 p.m.

Directions: The park is located approximately four miles east of Cambridge Junction at the junction of US-12 and M-124.

Further Information:
Hayes State Park
1220 Wamplers Lake Rd.
Onsted MI 49265

49 GOOSE CREEK GRASSLANDS

Goose Creek Grasslands is a 69-acre echo of the vast, open prairie that once covered large areas of lower Michigan and extended from the Midwest to the state of New York. This original, untouched Michigan tract, located on the western edge of the Irish Hills, encompasses prairie meadows, marshes and the "largest untouched calcareous fen (low land partially covered by wa-ter) known in Michigan."

Amateur and professional naturalists alike will want to pay return visits to Goose Creek. More than 220 plant species—including sedges, rushes, bog plants, native orchids and several rare and endangered species—have been identi-

(Continued on page 57.)

GOOSE CREEK GRASSLANDS
(Continued from page 56.)

fied in the preserve. Aquatic plants thrive here, as do 20 different types of grasses, including some spectacular varieties that grow to over five feet tall. Wildflowers cover the area, especially in the spring, and prairie plants reach maturity and flower in mid to late summer. But whether in April, July or August, Goose Creek always has something different and beautiful to show off.

Birds peculiar to open meadows and marshes—such as Bobolinks, wrens, swallows and meadowlarks—inhabit the preserve. Records show that 38 species of birds, including waterfowl and gamebirds, have nested at Goose Creek.

The best way to see and appreciate the area is by boat or canoe, but you can also walk the shoulder of the road and wander through the area north of the bridge on the east side of Cement City Highway. The Michigan Nature Association conducts guided tours of the preserve on several dates throughout the year. Contact them at the address below for a schedule.

Goose Creek recently joined the 18 other original prairie remnants included in the more than 200 nature preserves owned by the Michigan Nature Association. As part of its ongoing efforts to acquire and preserve important natural areas in the state, the 26-year-old non-profit organization is currently attempting to raise funds to purchase land in a 700-acre tract adjacent to Goose Creek that private companies are offering for development.

County: Lenawee

City: Cement City

Fees: None.

Schedule: None.

Directions: Located in the extreme northwest corner of Lenawee County, the preserve is .7 miles north of US-12 or .5 miles south of Cement City on Cement City Highway. The parking area is on the east side of the road just south of the bridge which crosses Goose Creek.

Further Information:
Michigan Nature Association
P.O. Box 102
Avoca MI 48006

50

DAHLEM

ENVIRONMENTAL EDUCATION CENTER

The Dahlem Environmental Education Center—established in 1973 by Jackson Community College for the improvement, understanding and appreciation of our natural environment—has received national recognition for excellence in science education and for good reason. A wide variety of public programs, workshops, guided hikes, summer camps, classroom visits (elementary through college) and special projects such as the annual Bluebird Festival make this 300-acre preserve an outstanding outdoor classroom for teachers, students, naturalists and the general public.

Five miles of trails and boardwalks wind through gently rolling terrain that features a varied habitat of marshes, wetlands, spring ponds,

open fields, evergreen plantings, hardwood forest and a creek. The trails are open in the winter for cross-country skiing. Also located on the grounds is the 16-acre Fannie Beach Arboretum.

The center is supported by fund raising, local grants, donations and memberships.

County: Jackson

City: Jackson

Fees: $.75 per student for class visits.

Schedule: Nature trail—8:00 a.m.-8:00 p.m., during Easter Standard Time; 8:00 a.m.-9:30 p.m. during Eastern Daylight Time.

Directions: From I-94 in Jackson, take exit 138 (West Avenue); go south on West Avenue to High Street; turn east (left) onto High Street and go to 4th Street; turn south (right) onto 4th Street and go to Horton Avenue which branches off to the west; from Horton Road turn south (left) onto Jackson Road and proceed to 7117 S. Jackson and the entrance to center.

Further Information:
Dahlem Environmental Education Center
c/o Jackson Community College
2111 Emmons Rd.
Jackson MI 49201

51 LEFGLEN NATURE SANCTUARY

Nearly 700 native Michigan plant species, more than a third found in the state, have been identified in this unique Michigan Nature Association area, where northern and southern fauna co-exist. Bring plant and wildflower field guides to fully enjoy and identify the rare wildflowers, including nine species of native orchids.

Birds as well as plants are abundant at Lefglen. More than 50 species, including a pair of Sandhill Cranes at Lake Nirvana, nest in the wide variety of habitats such as swamp, marsh, bogs, true prairie and woods

Two unconnected mile-long trails, separated by extensive wetlands, provide access to the 210-acre sanctuary. The south trail—which follows the property's boundary, generally on high ground—skirts marshland, passes through woods, then ends at one of the few areas of native prairie left in the state. The north trail briefly follows the northern boundary, then turns south and follows an esker (a serpentine ridge of gravel and sand left by a glacier) into a large swamp.

County: Jackson

City: Grass Lake

Fees: None.

Schedule: No posted hours.

Directions: From I-94 east of Jackson, take the Grass Lake exit (150) and go south to the town of Grass Lake; turn west (right) onto Michigan Avenue, go through town approximately one mile, then turn south (left) onto Wolf Lake Road; go 4.5 miles to a small parking area opposite 5344 Wolf Lake Road; the south trail begins at the back of the parking area. To reach the northern trail, park at County Park, directly opposite Little Wolf Lake about a half mile north of the south trail parking lot, and walk north to a Michigan Nature Association cottage at 4583 Wolf Lake Road. The trail begins there.

Further Information:
Michigan Nature Association
P.O. Box 102
Avoca MI 48006

52
PHYLLIS HAEHNLE
MEMORIAL SANCTUARY

The main calling card to the Haehnle Memorial Sanctuary is the large number of Sandhill Cranes—some standing four feet tall with wing spans of over six feet—that crowd into the marsh every spring and fall. It is not unusual to see 200 to 400 of these magnificent birds during peak migration periods in the fall, and on one November 1980 day, a record 1,325 were counted. Though some cranes nest here annually, most use the sanctuary as a stopover during their long fall migration flights.

The last two weeks in October and the first two weeks in November, between midafternoon and sunset, have proven to be the best viewing periods. The best observation spot, a high crest overlooking the marsh in the southwest corner of the sanctuary (the only area open to the public) is just a short walk northwest from the parking area. Be sure to bring binoculars, or you may have difficulty spotting the birds in the nearly mile-wide expanse of open water and thick stands of cattails.

Cranes are not the only attraction here. The sanctuary has long been recognized as a spectacular birding site, and its varied habitats—marsh, river, floodplain, climax forest and old farmland—attract a great many other birds. One avid birdwatcher, over a 20-year span from 1935 to 1955, sighted 135 different species, including Yellow Rails, Prairie Chickens and Great Blue Herons. The sanctuary also has a thriving colony of Black Terns.

Casper Haehnle donated the area to the Michigan Audubon Society in 1955 as a memorial to his daughter.

County: Jackson

City: Jackson

Fees: None.

Schedule: Open year round.

Directions: Approximately seven miles east of Jackson on I-94, take exit 147 and go north on Race Road 2.5 miles to Seymour Road; turn west (left) onto Seymour Road and go 1.5 miles to a parking area on the southwest corner of the sanctuary.

Further Information:
Michigan Audubon Society
409 West E. Avenue
Kalamazoo MI 49007

Stony Creek Metropark (page 21)

Southeastern Lower Peninsula

53 WATERLOO NATURE CENTER

The Waterloo Nature Center is the focal point for nature study in the Waterloo Recreation Area, which contains 17 lakes, miles of hiking trails, four campgrounds, several picnic areas and a bridle path spread over 18,000 acres in two counties. The interpretive building is closed due to state budget cuts, but eight open nature trails totaling five miles cut through the center's 1,700 acres. The Geology, Spring, Pond, Lowland, and Oak Woods nature trails wind through deep woods, swamps, open fields and over rolling hills rich in a diversity of plant and animal life. Interpretive signs along several of the trails identify plant life or point out and explain other natural features.

A walled, gated bridge over a swampy stream bars access to two trails, the Beech Woods Trail and the Floating Bog Trail. Why? Because the ecosystems along both are so unique and fragile that man's carelessness and vandalism can do and has done irreparable damage. As a result, a park naturalist must accompany anyone—with an occasional exception for naturalists, teachers and professors—entering those areas.

While walking along the Beech Woods Trail through a magnificent stand of mature beech trees, it quickly and sickeningly becomes evident why such measures are necessary. Thoughtless vandals have carved names and graffiti into the soft paper-smooth bark of almost every tree. Each blade mark not only disfigures each beautiful specimen but also drastically shortens its life by opening the tree to disease and insect infestation.

(Continued on page 63.)

Counties: Jackson and Washtenaw

City: Chelsea

Fees: $2.00 daily vehicle permit or $10.00 annual vehicle permit valid in all state parks.

Schedule: Open year round.

Directions: Nature Center—From I-94 west of Chelsea, take exit 157; go north two miles on Pierce Road to Bush Road; turn west (left) onto Bush Road and go approximately .75 miles to the entrance.

Recreation Area—From I-94 west of Chelsea take any of exits 147, 150, 153, 156 or 157. However, because the Waterloo Recreation Area consists of a vast checkerboard of state land interspersed with private parcels, all of which is crisscrossed by numerous roads, first-time visitors should write in advance for a map of the area. Roadside signs throughout the area also point the way to the nature center, headquarters, campgrounds and public access sites on the many lakes.

Further Information:
Waterloo Recreation Area
16345 McClure Rd.
Chelsea MI 48118

54 RIVERBEND NATURAL AREA

If you could create a natural area, you would probably first find an out-of-the-way area. Then you might take a flood plain, a creek and a pond and place them among 285 acres of mature forests and open fields. To complete your creation, you could nestle it all in a sweeping bend of a large river, then lace the parcel with five miles of nature trails.

You could, but you don't have to. It's already there, on the east bank of the Grand River on the western edge of Ingham County, and it's called Riverbend Natural Area.

At Riverbend, there are plenty of opportunities for solitary walks, nature study, photography or the search for wildflowers and birds along seven trails, which vary in length from the quarter-mile Timber Doodle Trail to the 1.3-mile Deer Run Trail. Two are self-guided; small wooden plaques along the trail point out and explain many of the natural features. The trails are open for cross-country skiing in the winter.

Preschoolers through adults can also take part in guided nature walks, canoe trips and night walks as well as attend programs presented on a variety of subjects throughout the year.

There are no picnic facilities in this quiet, picturesque area, but a drive a quarter mile east on Nichols Road, then a mile north on Grovenburg Road leads to a large picnic area at Grand River Park.

County: Ingham

City: Lansing

Fees: None.

Schedule: Open year round, 8:00 a.m.-Sunset

Directions: From US-127 south of Lansing, take the Holt Road exit; go west on Holt Road slightly more than two miles to Aurelius Road; turn south (left) onto Aurelius Road and go three miles to Nichols Road; turn west (right) onto Nichols Road and proceed 3.5 miles to the park entrance.

Further Information:
Riverbend Natural Area
c/o Ingham County Parks
301 Rush St.
Mason MI 48854

WATERLOO NATURE CENTER
(Continued from page 62.)

The Beech Woods Trail leads to the Floating Bog Trail and its boardwalk built into the middle of another fascinating and fragile ecosystem. Anyone careless or thoughtless enough to leave the boardwalk here will, with every step, not only crush delicate plants but leave a depression that will last for years. The Waterloo Natural History Association regularly schedules public Bog Walk programs through this area year round. Contact the park office at (313) 475-8307 for information and schedules.

Short nature trails also probe the areas around Portage Lake Campground, on the extreme west end of the recreation area, and Sugarloaf Lake Campground, northwest of the nature center.

If you really feel like stretching your legs past countless lakes and several campgrounds, take all or part of a trail that travels through the entire Waterloo Recreation Area, then east to the Pinckney Recreation Area. Access to the potential 25 miles of great hiking on this trail comes from the nature center area, Green Lake Campground or Portage Lake Campground.

55 FENNER ARBORETUM

The opportunity for solitude along an extensive system of nature trails, the chance to see buffalo and a Bald Eagle, and a wide variety of fascinating exhibits and programs are reasons to visit Fenner Arboretum, a 120-acre city park located on the eastern edge of Lansing.

Five miles of trails—lined with many labeled trees, lush plant life and wildflowers—wind through diverse habitat to a variety of attractions. The Pioneer Trail, for example, skirts the northwestern edge of the park and passes through meadows as it leads to a centennial cabin and pioneer garden. Constructed in 1959, the cabin is a replica of homes found in the area 100 years earlier. The garden, too, is typical of one planted in the pioneering days.

The Prairie Trail crosses grassland to a pond with a photoblind, then meanders to a prairie scene, complete with two live bison, located at the southern edge of the park. The mile-long Tamarack Trail passes through a swamp and borders a secluded pond on its way to Sam, a Bald Eagle confined to a cage because of injury. The Sugar Bush Trail, as the name implies, passes a

maple grove in its .75-mile circuit from the Natural Science Building, where all trails originate.

Exhibits and facilities inside the interpretive center, located up a long driveway from the arboretum entrance, include small-animal displays, a wildlife feeding station, a touch table for hands-on experience with nature, trail maps, a gift shop and a nature library. Bird talks and nature walks are among the regular programs conducted at Fenner throughout the year. Special programs include the Apple Butter Festival, held in October, and the Sugar Bush Festival, held in March.

A pleasant grass-covered picnic area shaded by large, stately trees is located at the park entrance. All trails are open for cross-country skiing.

County: Ingham

City: Lansing

Fees: None.

Schedule: Park—Open year round, 8:00 a.m.-Dark
Building—Open Tuesday through Sunday, 9:00 a.m.-4:00 p.m.

Directions: From US-127/I-496 in Lansing, take the Trowbridge Road exit; go east on Trowbridge Road to Harrison Road; turn south (right) onto Harrison Road and drive .5 miles to Mt. Hope Road; turn west (right) onto Mt. Hope Road and drive 1.5 miles to the entrance (just before Aurelius Road).

Further Information:
Fenner Arboretum
2020 E. Mt. Hope
Lansing MI 48910

Fenner Arboretum

Southwestern Lower Peninsula

Southwestern Lower Peninsula

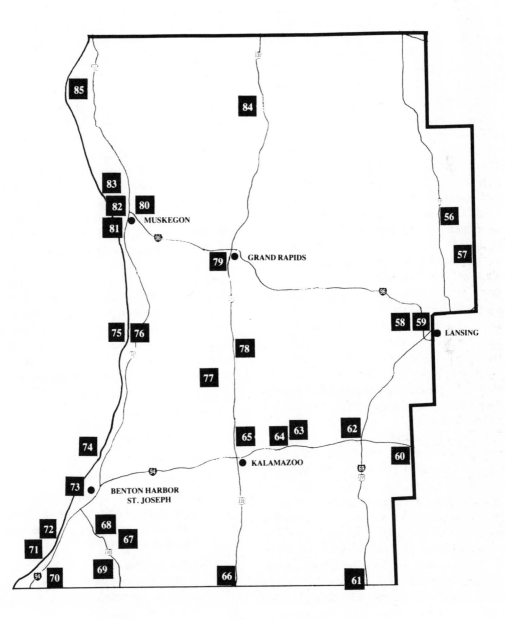

56 MAPLE RIVER STATE GAME AREA

The 1,170 acres of the Wetland Wildlife Management Units of the Maple River State Game Area make up the largest wetland complex in central Michigan. That alone just about guarantees good birdwatching, and there's even an added plus: This parcel isn't hidden away in some hard to find geographic nook or cranny. The major north-south highway in central Michigan, US-27, cuts right through the middle of the game area, so during peak migration periods, even speeding motorists get some outstanding views of hundreds of waterfowl and shorebirds.

The wetlands habitat—composed of meadows, forest, river, marshes, pools, canals and adjoining farmland—attracts huge numbers of birds throughout the year. Egrets, Great Blue Herons, Whistling Swans, Canada Geese and numerous duck species, for example, nest here or stop briefly on their migrations. Songbirds, too, make migratory stopovers as do shorebirds, including members of the maddeningly difficult to identify Sandpiper family. Wild turkeys, if planned releases are carried out, will soon roam the area. Best birding is from March to May and September to November, when thousands of migrating birds pass through the area. But because of the many nesting birds, even midsummer holds good possibilities.

The Maple River State Game Area is an excellent example of what can be accomplished when groups and agencies combine forces toward a common goal. In this case, the groups and agencies included the Michigan Duck Hunters Association, the Audubon Society, the Michigan Wildlife Habitat Foundation, and the Department of Natural Resources, to name just a few. Their goal: to help restore an area of Michigan's original, vitally important wetlands habitat, only a third of which is left in the state. Some donated money. Others contributed equipment and supplies. Most donated time and sweat to improve this ecosystem. Many, for example, built or improved dikes, channels and spillways; erected Osprey nesting platforms; or placed numerous Wood Duck nesting boxes throughout the area.

Wildlife photographers, birdwatchers, nature lovers or hikers looking for an out-of-the-ordinary walk can best enjoy the results of the groups' and individuals' extraordinary efforts from the tops of several miles of dikes. The level, easy-to-walk dikes penetrate the heart of the area and offer spectacular close-up views of the countless birds that pervade the flooded pools, marshes, meadows and woods.

To reach the dikes, park at any of three different areas, all reached via US-27 north of the Maple River. The easiest to get to is a half mile north of the river on the east side of US-27. The dikes from this lot lead to a panoramic view of the area from atop a 15-foot observation tower. To reach the other two parking areas, drive about a mile north of the river on US-27 to Ranger Road. Turn either east or west onto Ranger Road, drive to the first crossroad in either direction, then turn south and go approximately one-half mile to the parking area.

County: Gratiot

City: St. Johns

Fees: None.

Schedule: No posted hours.

Directions: Drive approximately eight miles north of St. Johns on US-27 and park in one of the areas as mentioned in the text.

Further Information:
Gratiot-Saginaw State Game Area
13350 S. Meridian Rd.
Brandt MI 48614

---

57 SLEEPING HOLLOW STATE PARK

Extensive hiking and cross-country ski trails, which appear to be lightly used, and a large man-made lake are the main attractions to the relatively new 2,678-acre Sleepy Hollow State Park.

Hikers can wander along the extensive shoreline of Lake Ovid, created by the damming of the Little Maple River. Hiking and cross-country ski trails, which begin at either of the two east-side parking areas, also wind around the north and east sides of the park. Though these paths don't offer much variety or seclusion, hiking is pleasant and easy over open rolling fields and meadows interrupted only occasionally by isolated stands of mature trees. Cross-country skiers, especially, will like the easy traveling to scenic winter vistas.

Good canoeing and angling is reported on the lake which is dotted with several islands. Facilities, widely spaced around the lake's edges, include a swimming beach, three picnic areas and a boat-launching and rental dock. A small 20-site campground, on an open hilltop adjacent to one of the large swimming beach parking lots, is neither shaded nor private.

County: Clinton

City: Laingsburg

Fees: $2.00 daily vehicle permit or $10.00 annual vehicle permit valid in all state parks.

Schedule: Open year round..

Directions: From US-27 approximately five miles south of St. Johns, take Price Road east six miles to the park entrance.

Further Information:
Sleepy Hollow State Park
7835 Price Road
Laingsburg MI 48848

---

58 FITZGERALD COUNTY PARK

Erosion doesn't have to be ugly, as evidenced by the quiet, patient work of the Grand River, which over the past several thousand years, has slowly carved one of the most unique spots in southern Michigan. A place so compelling that Indians and early settlers went miles out of their way to view nature's handiwork; a place so mystic that an 18th-century religious group constructed a building there to conduct seances; and a place so beautiful that turn-of-the-20th-century tourists flocked to resorts here by the thousands.

What is the magnet that has attracted such a diverse group of visitors? The answer can be summed up by the name of the nearby city: Grand Ledge. Eons ago, what is now Michigan was covered by a great sea. Time and pressure slowly changed its beaches and bottom to sedimentary bedrock. Then recently, geologically speaking, the Grand River cut through the rock and left a mile-long series of magnificent 270-million-year-old sandstone outcroppings.

In addition to the sheer beauty and distinctive geological character of these ledges, another attraction to nature lovers is an ecosystem that is unique to Lower Michigan. Eastern hemlocks and other evergreens seem to grow right out of the rock. And mosses, lichens and liverworts—some of which are found nowhere else in the Lower Peninsula—cover the edges.

The best views of the Fitzgerald County Park's 80-acres come from the half-mile self-guiding Ledges Trail. A large red barn—built and used in the late 1800s by the Grand Ledge Spiritualists Association for meetings and seances—marks the trail's beginning. The trail then follows the 270-million-year-old sandstone ledges that border the river before ending at the park's boundary, marked by a railroad trestle. The trail continues across private property for another .6 miles to Island Park in downtown Grand Ledge. Three other nature trails, totaling about two miles, wind through steep ravines, into woods, around ponds and past a dam.

Other facilities here include a newly opened nature center, athletic fields, a picnic area, a winter sledding hill and cross-country ski trails. Canoe and cross-country ski rentals plus cross-country ski lessons are all available at the park.

County: Eaton

City: Grand Ledge

Fees: $1.00 per car daily pass; $7.00 per vehicle annual pass; or $4.00 per vehicle senior-citizen annual pass.

Schedule: Open year round, 8:00 a.m.-Sunset.

Directions: From the junction of M-43 and M-100 just south of Grand Ledge, drive two miles west on M-43 to Grand Ledge Highway; turn north (right) onto Grand Ledge Highway and go a half mile to the park entrance.

Further Information: Fitzgerald County Park 3808 Grand Ledge Hwy. Grand Ledge MI 48837

Fitzgerald County Park

59 WOLDUMAR NATURE CENTER

Located on an old farm amid expressways, residential areas and urban sprawl, the 188-acre Woldumar Nature Center is an oasis to both wildlife and people. Open fields, 100 acres of woodland, marshes, ponds, two streams and the Grand River attract a wide variety of animal life including 125 species of birds. Deer, for example, feed in an old apple orchard; raccoons and opossum, on the other hand, find food and shelter in the woods. And migrating waterfowl make regular spring and fall stopovers at the ponds and lagoon.

A mature oak/beech climax forest is an excellent example of the Eastern woodland forest that covered great portions of the eastern United States before the arrival of European settlers. This hardwood stands in sharp contrast to the white pine and spruce also planted at the center.

Five nature trails totaling five miles make full exploration of the Center's different environments a pleasure.

The farm's barn now houses the center's administrative offices, meeting room, library, nature exhibits and gift shop. A wide variety of programs, including guided field trips and day camps, for pre-schoolers through adults are available.

> **County: Eaton**
> **City: Lansing**
> **Fees: Members—Free.**
>   **Non-members—50 cents.**
> **Schedule: Trails—Open year round.**
>   **Building—Open September through May, Tuesday through Friday, 8:00 a.m.-5:00 p.m.; June through August, Monday through Friday, 8:00 a.m.-5:00 p.m.**
> **Directions: From the junction of US-27 and I-96 in southwest Lansing, drive northeast one mile on US-27 to Lansing Road; exit and drive northeast on Lansing Road one-half mile to the entrance.**
> **Further Information:**
>   **Woldumar Nature Center**
>   **5539 Lansing Rd.**
>   **Lansing MI 48917**

60 WHITEHOUSE NATURE CENTER

Though less than 15 years old, this relatively young nature center has, especially through its energetic and growing reclamation and restoration projects, earned a respected position on the roster of outstanding Michigan nature areas.

The center's transformation of an unsightly garbage dump and gravel pit, for example, into an eight-acre wildlife habitat is an excellent ex-

(Continued on page 73.)

WHITEHOUSE NATURE CENTER

(Continued from page 72.)

ample of performing reconstructive surgery on land scarred by man, then returning it to nature. Food, shelter and water—the three essential ingredients for wildlife maintenance and sustenance—were provided by the creation of shallow ponds and the planting of selected grasses, legumes, shrubs and trees.

Also typical of the center's ongoing work is the restoration of a tall-grass prairie area and the creation of a native wildflower garden. Tall-grass prairie once covered extensive portions of Michigan and the Midwest until farmers plowed it under to the point of near extinction. Whitehouse is re-establishing this threatened ecosystem by taking seeds from native plants along railroad tracks in Michigan and from areas in Indiana and Illinois, then planting them in a special three-acre site. Adjacent to the prairie are wildflower specimens that have been transplanted from natural habitats that are being destroyed. Both projects are tucked between a marsh at the edge of the Kalamazoo River and another of the center's developments, an arboretum that will eventually include nearly 100 different native Michigan trees and shrubs.

Located on the campus of Albion College, the 125-acre center's other varied habitats—including open fields, farmland, marshy areas along the edges of the east branch of the Kalamazoo River, and 25 acres of woodland—support nearly 400 kinds of plants and more than 160 species of birds.

Printed guides (available at the interpretive building) to four of the center's five trails, do an excellent job of explaining the various ecological communities and special features found along each trail. Hiking opportunities here total more than six miles and vary in length from the half-mile Marsh Trail, a boardwalk path along the Kalamazoo River, to the 2.4-mile Ecology Trail, which follows the center's boundaries.

The center also serves as an outdoor classroom for college biology courses, individual field studies and public school visitors.

County: Calhoun

City: Albion

Fees: None.

Schedule: Open year round, Dawn-Dusk.
Interpretive Building—Open Monday through Saturday, 8:00 a.m.-4:00 p.m.; Sunday, 2:00 p.m.-4:00 p.m.

Directions: From I-94, exit on Business Route I-94 (#121) and follow the route (which becomes Michigan Avenue) into Albion to Albion College; at the college campus, turn south onto Hannah and go approximately three blocks, then turn left immediately after crossing the railroad tracks and follow the gravel road to the nature center parking lot.

Further Information:
Whitehouse Nature Center
Albion College
Albion MI 49224

61

KOPE KON NATURE SANCTUARY

and

ADALINE KERSHAW WOODS

The last untouched shoreline on a lake shared with Ohio and an adjacent parcel representing one of Michigan's last virgin wilderness areas combine for a total of 56 acres of unique natural beauty. Second-growth forest and open fields add to the variety of habitat, and more than 50 birds, including five species of woodpeckers, nest within the area.

Named after a Potawatomi Indian chief whose people lived in this Michigan/Ohio border area, Kope Kon Nature Sanctuary hugs a small inlet on Lake George's northern shore. There, cattail marshes, water lilies and shallow coves attract many shorebirds and waterfowl, including Green Herons, Great Blue Herons and Canadian Geese. Wood Ducks nest in hollow trees in a red-maple swamp back from the shoreline.

The unusual Kentucky coffee tree—with its double compound leaves and seeds that early pioneers used to make a substitute coffee—grows in Kope Kon as does the rare king-nut (a member of the hickory family). More common of the 30 different species found here are pawpaw, red maple, tulip, sassafras, beech, basswood and three species of elm.

(Continued on page 75.)

County: Branch

City: Coldwater

Fees: None.

Schedule: No posted hours.

Directions: Approximately nine miles south of Coldwater on I-69/US-27, take exit 2 (the last exit before the state line) and go west on Copeland Road about a quarter of a mile to Old US-27; turn south (left) onto Old US-27 and go approximately two miles to Kope Kon Road; turn right and follow the road to its end.

Further Information:
Michigan Nature Association
P.O. Box 102
Avoca MI 48006

62 BERNARD W. BAKER SANCTUARY

This 871 acres of swamp and wetlands near Battle Creek probably is the nation's first Sandhill Crane sanctuary and definitely is the first and largest of the Michigan Audubon Society's 10 sanctuaries.

During the first three decades of this century in Michigan, the number of Sandhill Cranes diminished at an alarming rate, mainly due to the draining of marshland throughout the state. Many voiced concern; Bernard W. Baker, a Muskegon businessman, artist and conservationist, took action. In 1941 he purchased 491 acres that made up part of the swampland known as the Big Marsh and donated it to the Michigan Audubon Society as a refuge for the cranes. The establishment of this and subsequent sanctuaries throughout the state helped the Sandhill Crane population to slowly recover to normal levels.

Today, though virtually within sight and sound of I-69, the sanctuary is quiet, beautiful and little used by the general public. For panoramic views

of the lowlands, close-up looks at native Michigan wildflowers, and good birding for a variety of species in addition to cranes, walk along the Iva E. Doty Native Flower Trail. This nature path begins to the left of a small interpretive building near the entrance, then cuts through open fields, crosses a marsh boardwalk, and enters deep woods along 1.5 miles of the sanctuary's eastern edge.

County: Calhoun

City: Battle Creek

Fees: None.

Schedule: Open year round.

Directions: From I-69 take exit 42 (first exit north of the junction of I-94 and I-69); go west on N Drive North 100 yards to 16 Mile Road; turn north (right) onto 16 Mile Road and drive 3.3 miles (just past Garfield Road) to the sanctuary sign.

Further Information:
   Michigan Audubon Society
   409 West E. Avenue
   Kalamazoo MI 49007

KOPE KON/ADALINE KERSHAW WOODS
(Continued from page 74.)

Just back from Lake George and adjoining Kope Kon Nature Sanctuary is Kershaw Woods, named after the woman who deeded this land to the Michigan Nature Association in 1979. In sharp contrast to the modern homes built just across the road, much of Kershaw Woods—with its towering oaks, flowering dogwood, rare plants, wildflowers and ferns—remains as it was before settlers came to the state.

From the end of Kope Kon Road, two trails circle into Kope Kon Sanctuary and two others lead several hundred feet into Kershaw Woods.

63

KINGMAN MUSEUM OF NATURAL HISTORY
and
LEILA ARBORETUM

Have you ever wondered what it might have been like to stand and watch the prehistoric glaciers create the Michigan we know? Immediately after entering the Kingman Museum, you have a chance to not only watch, but also actively recreate the movements of the last great walls of ice that gradually retreated from our state. There, in a Michigan Ice Age exhibit, you can crank a working glacier up and down and watch it gouge out the modern Michigan landscape. Nearby are skeletal remains of several mammals, including a saber-toothed tiger, a dire wolf and an American bison. A mastodon, discovered in the area, may be touched and studied. Eskimo soapstone carvings and American Indian artifacts primitively but poignantly illustrate the effect of the glacial environment on man.

From the Ice Age exhibit, a timber-lined passageway leads to "A Journey Through the Crust of the Earth." There, hands-on and glass-enclosed samples of rocks, minerals and fossils line the walls of the simulated cave. If you'd like to play amateur geologist you can—by using a microscope and a key to minerals' five basic physical properties—identify one or more "mystery" specimens. On the outside wall of the cave, a large cross-sectional and topgraphical painting of the earth explains the motions and forces constantly at work within our planet's crust.

A space-science exhibit, also located on the main floor of the three-story building, includes a planetarium, a "window to the universe" photographic display and a space suit from the Apollo 14 moon mission.

Of special interest to birders, nearly 100 mounted specimens of Michigan birds, plus examples of all of North America's extinct species—including the Ivory-billed Woodpecker, Carolina Parakeet and Passenger Pigeon—are displayed on the upper (mezzanine) level.

County: Calhoun

City: Battle Creek

Fees: Adults, 50 cents; Children, 25 cents.

Schedule: Tuesday through Saturday, 9:00 a.m.-5:00 p.m.; Sunday, 1:00 p.m.-5:00 p.m.; Open Mondays, July and August only.

Directions: From downtown Battle Creek, drive west on M-89 (Michigan Avenue) about two miles to the entrance, on the north side of street.

Further Information:
Kingman Museum of Natural History
West Michigan Ave.
Battle Creek MI 49017

(Continued on page 77.)

64   KELLOGG BIRD SANCTUARY

County: Kalamazoo

City: Augusta

Fees: Adults, $1.00; Children under 17, 50 cents; Children under four, free.

Schedule: Open year round, 8:00 a.m.-Dusk.

Directions: Follow M-89 (Michigan Avenue) northwest out of Battle Creek to 40th Street; turn north (right) onto 40th Street and go approximately one mile to C Avenue; turn west (left) and drive a quarter mile to the entrance.

Further Information:
W.K. Kellogg Bird Sanctuary
Michigan State University
12685 East C Avenue
Augusta MI 49012

For the closest and clearest look you may ever get at a virtual Audubon's *Who's Who* of birds of prey, visit the Kellogg Bird Sanctuary, northwest of Battle Creek. The sanctuary has become one of the Midwest's largest havens for magnificent avian predators, many which because of injury or because they were raised as pets, can no longer survive in the wild. Outdoor flight cages here, for example, house hawks such as Cooper's, Rough-legged, Red-shouldered, Red-tailed, Broad-winged and Goshawk. Representatives from the owl family include Great Gray, Barred, Great Horned and Screech. And a Bald Eagle is on loan from the U.S. Fish and Wildlife Service.

In spite of that awesome display of power and predatory efficiency, the overall atmosphere at Kellogg is one of peace and serenity. Even "hiking" seems to be too strong a term to use here. "Leisurely stroll" seems more appropriate to the beautifully landscaped, paved paths that curve gently through the sanctuary, where Wild Tur-

(Continued on page 78.)

KINGMAN MUSEUM
LEILA ARBORETUM
(Continued from page 76.)

The lower level houses "A Walk in the Footsteps of the Dinosaurs" exhibit (which includes the 10-foot leg bone of a diplodocus dinosaur), plus an area for changing exhibits.

Special school programs are conducted at the museum's auditorium. Natural-history and telescope-making workshops, plus travel and nature films are other reasons why the museum's educational program is rated strong.

Other facilities at Kingman, which is totally accessible to the handicapped, include a gift shop and a library.

Surrounding the museum are the 72 rolling, hilly acres of the Leila Arboretum. Groupings of native trees and shrubs plus unsual specimens such as mugo pine (native to the mountains of Switzerland), Japanese pine, red pine, black pine and Siberian elm cover the former golf course. Future plans call for specialty, aquatic, research and demonstration gardens.

Casual strollers will enjoy the several fine scenic overlooks and vistas, plus fine views of the tree groupings along the open expanses. A paved roadway also winds through the grounds.

KELLOGG BIRD SANCTUARY

(Continued from page 77.)

keys and peafowl freely roam the grounds along with flocks of geese, ducks, swans, and even white-tailed deer. Ducks dabble and dive practically within arm's reach in display ponds around the edge of Wintergreen Lake. In fact, more than 20 species of ducks and geese plus 30 swans of five different species—Whistling, Trumpeter, Mute, Whooper and Austrailian Black—are residents.

This large number of different birds, their closeness to the visitor and the hand feeding of the Canadian Geese make the Kellogg Sanctuary an ideal place for a first exposure to nature study and birding, especially for children.

Kellogg Sanctuary, begun by cereal magnate W.K.Kellogg in 1927 as a private refuge, is also an excellent place for a continuing education in nature study. For casual learners, the Overlook Museum at Wintergreen lake features self-guiding displays and exhibits. For more serious students, Michigan State University—which received the sanctuary from Kellogg in 1928 and has maintained and operated it ever since—offers college classes, adult education programs and summer day camps, all available to the general public. The sanctuary also serves as a wildlife-management research center and field laboratory for MSU.

65 KALAMAZOO NATURE CENTER

A wide variety of demonstration projects—from a 128-year-old functioning pioneer farm to a modern Solar Homestead and Solar Garden—are the main attractions to one of Michigan's premier nature centers.

Eleven trails totaling 7.5 miles lead to a natural spectrum of special projects and demonstrations. Nine hundred native Michigan-area trees and shrubs, for example, fill a 25-acre arboretum. A formal garden and a prairie restoration project have their own reserved sites within the 640-acre center, too. Early American crafts and early rural Michigan life are played out at the DeLano Homestead, a completely restored functioning pioneer farm, originally built in 1858. Modern gardening and farming techniques, on the other hand, are demonstrated at the Youth Solar Garden and the Tillers Small Farm Program. And at yet another demonstration project, easy-to-install, low-cost energy conservation equipment has turned a drafty old house into an energy efficient Solar Homestead.

A variety of exhibits that interpret Michigan's natural history plus a live-animal display, an extensive nature library and a book shop compete for space inside the busy interpretive center. The building is also the focal point for an ambitious number of programs—ranging from summer camps and family picnics to conservation and natural history workshops—geared to students, educators and the general public. The Kalamazoo Nature Center is also the state headquarters for the Michigan Audubon Society

Not lost among the dazzle of the exhibits and outdoor projects and displays is the quiet beauty of nature. Most of the outstanding natural features—including the Kalamazoo River and more than 200 acres of mature beech/maple forest—that drew James Fenimore Cooper as a regular visitor to the area more than 100 years ago are even more impressive today. Walkers can also stroll along forest paths, explore the banks of a small stream or investigate marshes and ponds. And both birdwatchers and wildflower enthusiasts will pay return visits here.

County: Kalamazoo

City: Kalamazoo

Fees: Members—Free.
   Non-members—Nominal fee.

Schedule: Monday through Saturday, 9:00 a.m.-5:00 p.m.; Sunday, Memorial Day, July 4 and Labor Day, 1:00 p.m. - 5:00 p.m.; Closed Thanksgiving, Christmas, New Years Day and the first 14 days following Labor Day.

Directions: From US-131 about six miles north of Kalamazoo, exit on Avenue D and drive three miles east to Westnedge Avenue; turn south (right) onto Westnedge Avenue and drive one mile to the entrance.

Further Information:
Kalamazoo Nature Center
7000 N. Westnedge Ave.
Kalamazoo MI 49007

66

WHITE PIGEON RIVER
NATURE SANCTUARY

Fifty-eight acres of steep hillsides, old river channels, flooded bottomlands, lagoons and riverbanks, plus a riot of plant and animal life are good reasons to visit and explore this premier example of the work of the Michigan Nature Association.

The sanctuary is quickly and justifiably earning a reputation as a great birding spot, especially at the height of activity in May and June. According to a 24-hour bird count by the

M.N.A. in 1975, 55 species—including warblers, vireos, kingfishers and two species of flycatchers—nest in the sanctuary's varied habitats. Prothonotary Warblers, which winter in South America, also make their summer home in wooded swamps at White Pigeon River. A glimpse of this rare Michigan nester, whose deep, brilliant yellow head and breast are set off by contrasting blue-gray wings, would, alone, make a visit here worthwhile. Great Blue Herons from a rookery just to the north of the sanctuary, plus gloriously colored Cerulean Warblers, Scarlet Tanagers, Indigo Buntings, Rose-breasted Grosbeaks and Wood Ducks are prominent spring and summer visitors to the sanctuary.

A tremendous diversity of plant life also covers the sanctuary. Shrubs, vines, trees, aquatic plants and wildflowers compete for space along the riverbanks. Back from the river, wild roses, violets, May-apple, Solomon's seal, Jack-in-the-pulpit and other wildflowers blanket the hillsides in spring and are scattered throughout the property, spring through fall. Six species of oak, four of ash, three kinds of maple, plus honey locust, hackberry, basswood, black willow, sycamore, redbud, black willow and mulberry are among the many trees that thrive here.

White-tailed deer, rabbits, fox, squirrels, woodchucks, raccoons, numerous toads and frogs, Massasauga rattlesnakes and prodigious snapping turtles are among the wildlife that call the White Pigeon River area home. Twenty-seven species—including giant swallowtail, tiger

County: St. Joseph

City: White Pigeon

Fees: None.

Schedule: No posted hours.

Directions: From the junction of US-12 and US-131 just west of White Pigeon, drive two miles west on US-12 to Burke Road; turn south (left) and drive one mile to the corner of Burke and Silver Creek roads; Burke Road, which marks the sanctuary's western boundary, is closed south of this intersection. Park off the road at the intersection but do not block the gate because, though closed to traffic, local farm tractors occasionally use the road.

Further Information:
Michigan Nature Association
P.O. Box 102
Avoca MI 48006

(Continued on page 81.)

67 DOWAGIAC WOODS

Barely touched by man, this 220-acre tract is so fertile that you can often find over a dozen plants growing in a single square foot. The land here has never been farmed, grazed or, except for sporadic lumbering operations, otherwise disturbed. Its owner, the Michigan Nature Association, in fact, believes that Dowagiac Woods may be the largest moist virgin-soil woodland left in Michigan.

You might expect such an area to support a

profusion of plants and animals, and it does. Four hundred identified plants—hepatica, bloodroot, anemones, trilliums, five species of orchids, and more than 20 kinds of ferns, to name just a few—thrive in Dowagiac Woods. The area also shelters nine plants and animals—including swallowtail butterflies, spotted turtles and marsh blue grass—that are endangered in Michigan. The sanctuary is, in fact, a giant living outdoor natural history museum.

Spring is without a doubt the best time to visit. Fifty different blooming species of wildflowers literally carpet the forest floor then in a spectacular display. The star of the show?—the blue-eyed Mary, a delicate blue-and-white flower which blooms from April to June in the damp, open woods of only four southern Michigan counties.

Although Dowagiac Woods puts on its greatest show in spring, visits in summer and fall pay dividends, too. Prairie grasses and wildflowers, for example, bloom in July and August. And 45 different kinds of trees—including blue beech, chinkapin oak, cork elm, hackberry, and Ohio buckeye, which is endangered in Michigan—just about guarantee beautiful autumn color.

Birdwatchers, too, will not be disappointed.

(Continued on page 82.)

County: Cass

City: Dowagiac

Fees: None.

Schedule: No posted hours.

Directions: From Dowagiac, go west on M-62 for about four miles to Sink Road; turn south (left) onto Sink Road and go one mile to Frost Road; Turn east (left) onto Frost Road and go about one mile to the parking area on the north side of road.

Further Information:
Michigan Nature Association
P.O. Box 102
Avoca MI 48006

WHITE PIGEON RIVER SANCTUARY
(Continued from page 80.)

swallowtail, viceroy, bronze-copper and hackberry—make up a partial list of butterflies found at the sanctuary.

The easiest way to negotiate the area's extremes in terrain and habitat is on a nature trail that begins at the intersection of Burke and Silver Creek roads, follows closed and gated Burke Road south, then turns east into the sanctuary.

This easy-to-walk trail generally travels through high, dry hillsides except near the river, where the sanctuary is overgrown and somewhat difficult to get through

The White Pigeon River Nature Sanctuary, acquired by the Michigan Nature Association, is just one of many outstanding reasons why the people of Michigan owe a debt of gratitude to this important non-profit organization dedicated to preserving our state's natural heritage.

68   LOVE CREEK NATURE CENTER

Be sure to bring your camera when you visit this plant and wildlife sanctuary. Then step up to a one-way wildlife observation window in the center's interpretive building and photograph a variety of animals and birds from a closeness you may never approach again.

Your camera will also come in handy during walks down any of the 100-acre center's 13 nature trails. In spring and summer, an abundance of wildflowers—from Cutchman's britches and trillium to marsh marigolds—line nearly six miles of trails interrupted now and then by wooden bridges and trailside benches. At any time of year, the beech/maple climax forest, open fields, pond, small two-acre marsh, Love Creek and observation tower overlooking a marsh provide not only a variety of photo opportunities but also an ideal setting to simply contemplate the quiet beauty of nature.

Love Creek personnel conduct guided field trips, programs for school children, and classes on wildlife and ecology plus year-round nature walks and slide shows. Other natural displays and exhibits complement the interpretive center's main window attraction. Birdwatching here is rated good, especially during the spring migration season.

Hiking and showshoeing, plus more than five miles of groomed cross-country ski trails of varying difficulty are winter attractions.

County: Berrien

City: Berrien Springs

Fees: None.

Schedule: Trails—Open daily, Dawn-Dusk.
    Building—Open Wednesday through Friday, 9:00 a.m.-5:00 p.m.; Saturday and Sunday, 10:00 a.m.-5:00 p.m.

Directions: In Berrien Springs on US-31/33 approximately a half mile east of the St. Joseph River, turn east (left) onto Pokagon Road and go two miles to Huckleberry Road; turn north (left) onto Huckleberry road and drive one mile to the entrance.

Further Information:
Love Creek Nature Center
223 L Huckleberry Rd.
Berrien Center MI 49102

DOWAGIAC WOODS
(Continued from page 81.)

Forty-nine species nest in the sanctuary, and many more pass through, especially during spring migration. Northern Yellowthroats, Acadian Flycatchers, woodpeckers, Wood Ducks, Scarlet Tanagers, grosbeaks, and Indigo Buntings are just a few of the many species birders might spot here.

Hikers can use three trails to explore the sanctuary. The main trail begins at the north edge of the parking lot, then circles for 1.5 miles through the sanctuary. An extension of this loop reaches to the northern limits of the sanctuary. Both trails occasionally cross wet ground, especially in the spring. A short, easy trail—especially beautiful in the spring when the woods are blanketed with wildflowers—begins on Frost Road west of the parking area in the extreme southwest corner of the sanctuary.

The Michigan Nature Association purchased this area in 1983 with funds from 550 individual contributors plus a grant from the Kresge Foundation.

69 FERNWOOD INC.

Nature provided the raw materials: ravine-cut hills that sharply rise 125 feet from the St. Joseph River to a gently rolling terrain of woodland, open fields and a tall-grass prairie. Later, man added some finishing touches of his own: numerous gardens, plantings and an arboretum. Together, they created Fernwood, a 100-acre privately owned preserve and botanical garden on the east bank of the St. Joseph River where you can enjoy the peace and beauty of nature from a poolside gazebo, a river bank, the midst of a garden or a hillside full of azaleas.

Twelve nature trails, though totaling only three miles, pass by a startling array of mini-ecosystems that results from the great difference in elevation and soil types here. The River Trail, for example, switchbacks down the steep fern-covered banks of the St. Joseph River. The Wilderness Trail, on the other hand, wanders through 18 acres of untouched forest. Other trails—including one guided by a helpful brochure, available at the entrance—probe a cattail marsh, a trout pond, a creek, a lily pond and steep ravines.

Trails also lead to a 45-acre arboretum and a five-acre tall-grass prairie. The Arboretum Trail (the longest in the park) wanders through carefully arranged plantings of ornamental and native shrubs and trees. To reach the tall-grass prairie, north of the arboretum in the extreme northeast corner of the preserve, take a cutoff from either the Arboretum or Wilderness trails. The best views of this small sample of the great prairie system that once spanned large areas of the Midwest come from an observation platform located at the midpoint of a trail that skirts the prairie's southern edge.

Flowering trees, shrubs, annuals and perennials fill a large main garden, located near the entrance. Throughout the preserve, smaller specialized gardens include the Rock and Bog gardens—which display unusual and rare ferns, dwarf conifers and plants from around the world—and a colonial Williamsburg Garden, currently under development. Hanging and potted tropical plants fill a greenhouse, and wildflowers, herbs, perennials, lilac, boxwood, iris and daylily cover other special planting areas scattered throughout the grounds.

County: Berrien

City: Niles

Fees: Members, Free; Non-members, $1.00.

Schedule: Open March through November—Weekdays, 9:00 a.m.-5:00 p.m; Saturdays, 10:00 a.m.-5:00 p.m.; Sundays, Noon-5:00 p.m.

Directions: From US-12 about four miles west of Niles, take Buchanan Road north into Buchanan to Walton Road; go northwest on Walton Road across the St. Joseph River to Range Line Road; drive north on Range Line Road about 1.5 miles to the entrance.

Further Information: Fernwood, Inc. 1720 Range Line Rd. Niles MI 49120

70 WARREN WOODS NATURAL AREA

In 1879, Mr. E.K. Warren of Three Oaks came up with a rather radical idea. He took a look at a 200-acre parcel in the extreme southwest corner of Michigan and decided he'd buy the virgin timberland for only one reason: to keep it that way. Radical idea? Yes, because wilderness then was still thought of as something to be cleared, settled, cut, drained, tamed or somehow put to use. Only a few years before had some of the first land in the *nation*, Yellowstone Park, been set aside for public use. So, at the time, Warren's real-estate deal brought him only ridicule.

Today, E.K. Warren's vision and foresight brings us the rare gift of being able to experience natural Michigan as it was before European settlers claimed the land. Most of his 200-acre tract, now aptly named Warren Woods, has never been touched by man. Even deadfalls, as far as anyone knows, have never been cleared. The result is southern Michigan's final stand of primeval beech/maple forest, with such outstanding individual specimens that it has been designated a Natural National Landmark.

An added plus: This natural area has long been considered one of the best birding spots in the state, especially for warblers—including Hooded, Cerulean and Kentucky warblers—and songbirds such Acadian Flycatchers and Louisiana Waterthrushes. The impressive crow-sized Pileated Woodpecker—with its black back, brilliant red crest, and voice that the creator of Woody Woodpecker copied for his cartoon character—also frequents the woods as do Redheaded Woodpeckers and Barred Owls. Other birds spotted here include many that are usually only found farther south.

There are two entry points to Warren Woods. A foot trail begins on the south side of Warren Woods Road just before the road cuts across the northern edge of the preserve a few hundred feet west of the Galien River. Soon after leaving the road, the trail forks. The east fork travels a short distance to the Galien River, which bisects the park. The longer west branch follows the Galien River for much of its route as it loops though the central portion of the natural area. The second access point is a picnic area parking lot at the south entrance off Elm Valley Road. A short trail from the area makes its way north to the Galien River.

County: Berrien

City: Three Oaks

Fees: None.

Schedule: Open year round.

Directions: From I-94 just south of Warren Dunes State Park near Sawyer, take exit 12 (Sawyer Road); go west a half mile to Three Oaks Road (the first intersection reached); turn south (right) onto Three Oaks Road and go approximately three miles to Warren Woods Road and the northern entrance or one mile farther south to Elm Valley Road and the southern entrance; the natural area is less than a mile west of Three Oaks Road on either of the two roads.

Further Information:
Warren Dunes State Park
Route 1 Red Arrow Hwy
Sawyer MI 49125

---

71 WARREN DUNES STATE PARK

Most first-time visitors are attracted to Warren Dunes State Park by the rugged beauty of its well-known massive dunes and the two-mile stretch of magnificent sandy beach lying in front of them. Most leave (and often pay return visits) with the realization that far more contributes to the park's beauty.

Behind the dunes, for example, picturesque Painterville Creek winds past several picnic areas and one of the park's two campgrounds before it empties into Lake Michigan. Other diverse habitats —including ponds, swampy areas, and oak/hickory and beech/maple woods— make up the rest of the park's 1,507 acres.

But for most visitors, there's no denying that the beach and dunes are the main attraction here. The swimming beach is as beautiful as any in the state. And the mountains of sand, some towering 240 feet above the shore (high enough that hang gliders launch themselves from the tops), not only offer breathtaking vistas but also a close-up chance to watch nature wage an ongoing battle with itself to both destroy and preserve what it's created. As a first defense against the ongoing assaults from destructive winds, nature sends in grasses to stabilize the sand. Shrubs gradually replace the colonies of grasses and are themselves later supplanted by heavy artillery: quick-growing but short-lived trees such as aspen and willow. Finally occupational forces—oak/hickory followed by beech/maple forests—cover the dunes. But even these impressive defense forces are sometimes not enough, and offshore winds blow away or bury centuries of painstaking work.

For excellent and varied views of or from the dunes, take one or more of the several lengthy trails, which also probe other areas of the park.

Other facilities include several picnic areas and 197 modern campsites divided between two

campgrounds. Tobaggoning and cross-country skiing are winter attractions.

County: Berrien

City: Bridgman

Fees: $2.00 daily vehicle permit or $10.00 annual vehicle permit valid in all state parks.

Schedule: April 1 through September 30, 8:00 a.m.-10:00 p.m. October 1 through March 31, 8:00 a.m.-Dusk.

Directions: From I-94 12 miles south of St. Joseph, take exit 16 and follow the signs to the park, which is just off the expressway.

Further Information:
Warren Dunes State Park
Route #1 Red Arrow Highway
Sawyer MI 49125

72 GRAND MERE STATE PARK

Over 10,000 years ago, as the last of the great prehistoric glaciers receded from Michigan, they left huge gouged-out basins that filled with water and became the Great Lakes. The great sheets of ice also scooped many small depressions strung along the Lake Michigan shoreline that evolved into interdunal lakes and wetlands.

Today, these interdunal lakes are the dominant feature at Grand Mere State Park. Because a buffer zone of surrounding sand dunes protects this fragile ecological area, it has remained as almost a textbook example of the evolution and plant succession from aquatic to terrestrial and from bare sand to forested hills. In addition to a profusion of common wildflowers, grasses and woody plants, many rare and endangered plant species survive in this designated National Natural Landmark area.

Grand Mere is also a great birdwatching spot, not too surprising when you consider that it's located in the county that not only holds the state record for most species seen in one day but also has recorded sightings of such rare visitors to Michigan as Yellow-throated Warblers, Dickcis-

sels, Mockingbirds, Bell's Vireo and White-eyed Vireo, to name just a few. Common Loons, Red-throated Loons, Coromorants, herons, ducks and gulls all frequent the Grand Mere area. Spring migration attracts large numbers of warblers and other song birds; hawks are plentiful during both spring and fall migration.

Recent land acquisitions have doubled the park's shoreline and have also greatly reduced what was formerly a patchwork of private and public lands. Several trails web the wooded dunes, interdunal lakes and Lake Michigan shoreline.

Grand Mere is a day-use only park with a picnic grounds but no camping facilities. Just six miles south, however, is Warren Dunes State Park with nearly 200 camping sites.

County: Berrien

City: Stevensville

Fees: $2.00 daily vehicle permit or $10.00 annual vehicle permit valid at all state parks.

Schedule: Open year round.

Directions: At Stevensville take exit 22 from I-94, then drive south on Thorton Road (which parallels the west side of expressway) approximately two miles to Willow Road; turn west (right) onto Willow Road and drive less than half a mile to the entrance.

Further Information:
Grand Mere State Park
c/o Warren Dunes State Park
Route #1 Red Arrow Highway
Sawyer MI 49125

Southwestern Lower Peninsula

73 SARETT NATURE CENTER

Those who like to view the natural world from as many angles as possible will enjoy the Sarett Nature Center. There, in a gallery of man-made structures—towers, elevated platforms, benches, boardwalks and an extensive system of woodchip-covered paths—you can view 350 acres of swamp and flood-plain forest, cattail marshes, tamarack bogs, meadows, streams, man-made ponds and upland forest from a wide range of perspectives. Plus, a beautifully illustrated guide advises what to look for at each stop along five trails totaling more than six miles.

And there is much to see. Located on the banks of the Paw Paw River, this fine sanctuary is composed of many different habitats which support a wide variety of plant and animal life. Tamarack, willow, alder, spice bush, hardwoods, wild swamp rose, multiflora rose, ferns, sedges and a multitude of wildlfowers, for example, are among the flora found here.

Shorebirds and waterfowl are attracted to Sarett's extensive wetlands, and rails, marsh wrens and ducks nest in its cattail marshes. Hawks and owls, too, are common visitors to the sanctuary, owned by the Michigan Audubon Society, and spring migration is an excellent time to spot songbirds here. Sarett Nature Center encourages those visits through an extensive program of wildlife plantings to provide food and shelter for birds and animals.

To attract human visitors and to meet its stated goal to "provide quality environmental education to the community," Sarett offers a wide range of facilities—meeting rooms, exhibits, a bookshop, a library and an observation room—plus quality public programs, including natural history classes and guided field trips and expeditions. And attract people it does. In 1985, alone, more than 19,000 school children from southwestern Michigan took part in the center's programs.

Trails are open for cross-country skiing in the winter.

County: Berrien

City: Benton Harbor

Fees: None.

Schedule: Tuesday through Friday, 9:00 a.m.-5:00 p.m.; Saturday, 10:00 a.m.-5:00 p.m.; Sunday, 1:00 p.m.-5:00 p.m.

Directions: East of Benton Harbor from the junction of I-94 and I-196/US-31, drive north on I-196 approximately one mile to the first exit (Red Arrow Highway); go southwest on Red Arrow Highway approximately a half mile to Benton Center Road; turn north (right) onto Benton Center Road and go one mile to the entrance.

Further Information:
Sarett Nature Center
2300 Benton Center Rd.
Benton Harbor MI 49022

74   VAN BUREN STATE PARK

Sand dunes covered with maple, oak and beech forests plus 2,800 feet of beautiful Lake Michigan shoreline are reasons why more than a quarter-million visitors come to Van Buren park each year.

Swimming is excellent, but 205 lightly shaded sites at a campground a short walk from the beach and picnic area provide only a minimum of privacy.

Other facilities at the 346-acre park include a bathhouse and a concession stand, both on the beach.

County: Van Buren

City: South Haven

Fees: $2.00 daily vehicle permit or $10.00 annual vehicle permit valid in all state parks.

Schedule: Open year round, 8:00 a.m.-10:00 p.m.

Directions: Take the Blue Star Highway south out of South Haven for two miles to Ruggles Road; turn west (right) and follow Ruggles Road to the park entrance.

Further Information:
Van Buren State Park
23960 Ruggles Rd.
South Haven MI 49090

75   SAUGATUCK DUNES STATE PARK

If you'd like to stroll in relative seclusion for more than two miles along one of the most beautiful shorelines in the country, pay a visit to Saugatuck Dunes State Park.

Twenty-to 180-foot-high windswept dunes appear to stand guard over the beautiful Lake Michigan beach here, but that's not what keeps most visitors off the two-mile stretch of sand. The one-mile hike from the parking lot to the beach plus the lack of facilities (no campground, vault toilets and only one picnic area) evidently does, since this is one of the least-visited state parks along the southern Lake Michigan coastline.

For those who don't mind (or even perhaps enjoy) the relative lack of amenities, Saugatuck State Park is a great place to hike, cross-country ski, beachcomb and picnic. Back from the shore and towering dunes are interdunal wetlands and terrain, ranging from rolling hills to steep slopes, blanketed by a pine/hardwood forest. Pitcher's thistle, spotted wintergreen, genseng, and the not-so-common, Common Tern—all on the state's threatened species list—are among the

(Continued on page 89.)

76 DE GRAAF NATURE CENTER

The DeGraaf Nature Center is a perfect example of the old adage, "good things come in small packages." Though only 13.4-acres big, the area is packed with a wide variety of habitats and plant and animal life.

As a result, visitors receive great rewards for little effort. Trillium, lady's-slippers, wild roses and other wildflowers, plus a variety of shrubs and trees line the six short trails that lead variously to a stream, a pond, woodland, a meadow and a marsh. A wide range of animals and birds—including Great Blue Herons, Green Herons and Belted Kingfishers—find food and shelter in these diverse habitats.

Self-guiding brochures for all trails are available at the trailhead, and groups can arrange for guided tours of the center, which is operated by the city of Holland.

County: Ottawa

City: Holland

Fees: None.

Schedule: Open year round, Monday through Saturday.

Directions: From downtown Holland, drive south on River Avenue, then bear right onto Michigan Avenue, which angles to the west, and drive to West 22nd Street; turn left onto West 22nd Street and go 1.25 miles to Graafschap Road; turn south (left) onto Graafschap Road and go a half block to the entrance, on the right side of the road.

Further Information:
DeGraaf Nature Center
600 Graafschap Rd.
Holland MI 49423

SAUGATUCK DUNES STATE PARK

(Continued from page 88.)

wide variety of flora and fauna found here.

Fourteen miles of cross-country skiing and hiking trails lace the 1,100-acre parcel. Many range through hilly and steep terrain and in winter are marked in degree of difficulty from novice to expert.

Facilities at the park's single picnic area, adjacent to the parking area, include tables, grills and vault toilets.

County: Allegan

City: Saugatuck

Fees: $2.00 daily vehicle permit or $10.00 annual vehicle permit valid in all state parks.

Schedule: Open daily, 8:00 a.m.-10:00 p.m.

Directions: From I-196/US-31 just north of Saugatuck exit on Blue Star Highway and go west to 64th Street; turn north (right) onto 64th Street and go one mile to 138th Avenue; turn left onto 138th and drive less than a mile to the park entrance.

Further Information:
Saugatuck Dunes State Park
c/o Van Buren State Park
23960 Ruggles Rd.
South Haven MI 49090

---

77 ALLEGAN STATE GAME AREA

Scenic beauty, easy hiking, four campgrounds and some of the state's best birdwatching are good reasons to pay a visit to the Allegan State Game Area.

In this large area of marshlands, the Kalamazoo River branches into many bayous, and during fall migration, waterfowl by the thousands stop along the river, marshes, streams and ponds. Some—including Canada Geese and even a few Snow, Ross', Barnacle, and White-fronted geese—winter over in the area.

In May during spring migration, large numbers of warblers—including Golden-winged War-

blers and Hooded Warblers—move north through the area. The Allegan State Game Area also is one of the few places in the state that hosts large numbers of Prothonotary Warblers. Best locations to spot the warblers plus other songbirds are along creeks near the river and at Swan Creek Pond. Among the many other birds to look for here are Pileated Woodpeckers, several different thrushes, Scarlet Tanager and Wild Turkeys.

An 18-mile web of well-marked, level, easily walked hiking trails laces through a beautiful setting of streams, marshes, lakes, forests and open fields. Most of the trails, plus half of the park's campgrounds are included in the Swan Creek Foot Trails System. This trail network is composed of several one- to two-mile loops that variously follow the course of Swan Creek, circle Swan Creek Pond, skirt wetlands and thrust into other areas of the park. Forty-one sites at Pine Point Campground, located on Swan Creek Pond, plus 10 sites at Swan Creek Campground, north of the pond, accommodate campers.

To the west of the Swan Creek System, one 10-mile circuit loops past the park's other two campgrounds. Hikers who enter this trail from the north end of Swan Creek Pond will reach the 50-site Horsemen's Campground after a four-mile walk. Two and a half miles farther (or 3.5 miles from the south end of Swan Creek Pond) is the park's largest overnight facility, 80-site Ely Lake Campground, and its small system of trails. Another trail connects the two campgrounds via a three-mile generally north-south route.

All hiking trails and campgrounds are clearly marked on a map available at the park headquarters on 118th Avenue.

County: Allegan

City: Allegan

Fees: None.

Schedule: Open year round.

Directions: From M-89 in Allegan, go west on 115th Avenue about six miles to 44th Street. Just north of this intersection are parking areas that give access to the southern end of the trails. Two miles north on 44th Street, at the intersection of 118th Avenue, is another parking lot. The headquarters and its parking area is west on 118th Avenue approximately one mile.

Further Information:
Allegan State Game Area
4590 118th Ave.
Allegan MI 49010

78

YANKEE SPRINGS RECREATION AREA

Algonquin hunters boldly roamed this land while European colonists still timidly hugged America's eastern seacoast, and it was not until 1835 that the first white settlers came to settle the area. Today, the rugged, rolling terrain and streams, marshes and bogs of the 5,004-acre Yankee Springs Recreation Area attracts campers, hikers, fishermen, cross-country skiers and other outdoor enthusiasts.

The park's five trails, totaling 15.5 miles, are as varied as their names. The Long Lake Trail— at five miles, the park's longest—passes north of Long Lake, traverses a bog area, follows an old wagon road to a scenic overlook on Graves Hill, then continues to the junction of several trails at the Devils Soup Bowl. To reach Long Lake Trail, start at Gun Lake Campground and take the park's shortest path, the Sassafras Trail (also the park's only interpretive trail), a half mile to the main route. Or take the Long Lake trail directly from Gun Lake Road just north of the recreation area headquarters. The two-mile-long Hall Lake Trail also climbs Graves Hill, after bordering Hall Lake, then returns to its starting point across from the Long Lake Outdoor Center on Gun Lake Road.

The Devils Soup Bowl is the destination for both the Chief Noonday and Deep Lake trails. The Chief Noonday Trail, named after an Ottawa Chief who once lived in the area, is a four-mile round trip from the Williams Lake Fishing Site access road past MacDonald Lake and a scenic overlook to the Devils Soup Bowl, then back. From the Deep Lake Campground, the Deep Lake Trail, also four miles total, circles south around a bog, heads to the Devils Soup Bowl, then returns to the campground along the north side of the lake. A map, available at the entrance, details the park's trails.

Three hundred forty-five sites at two campgrounds—Gun Lake, with modern facilities, and Deep Lake, with primitive facilities—accommodate campers. A peninsula jutting into Gun Lake is the setting for a beautiful picnic grounds. And boaters or fishermen can launch from sites on eight of the park's nine lakes.

County: Barry

City: Middleville

Fees: $2.00 daily vehicle permit or $10.00 annual vehicle permit valid in all state parks.

Schedule: Open year round.

Directions: Two miles west of Hastings on M-37 where it jogs northwest, leave M-37 and continue west on Gun Lake Road for about 14 miles to the park.

Further Information:
Yankee Springs Recreation Area
2104 Gun Lake Rd.
Middleville MI 49333

---

79 BLANDFORD NATURE CENTER

When you enter the interpretive building at the Blandford Nature Center, don't be shocked if you come almost eyeball to eyeball with a live owl, hawk, crow or other form of wildlife that may be perched on bookshelves, desks, pieces of driftwood or light fixtures. One of the Center's rooms, you see, serves as a wild-animal hospital and the patients are sometimes given the run of the building. On a recent visit they included more than half a dozen Screech, Barred, Great Horned and Long-eared owls which were loose and within hand-shaking distance. Also recuperating out of their cages that day were a Red-tailed Hawk and a crow. Several songbirds completed the patient list.

A visit with sick animals probably isn't why most people come to Blandford, however. Most visitors would rather spend an afternoon or a day exploring the Center's variety of natural attractions and displays. And the best way to do that is on seven trails totaling five miles that wind through the Center's 143 acres of woodland, open fields, marsh and farmland plus by several ponds and Brandywine Creek. The trails include

two short self-guided paths that circle a heavily wooded ravine.

Still other trails lead to a variety of outdoor exhibits such as the Pioneer Heritage Complex. Fully restored and furnished buildings there include a homesteader's log cabin built in 1866, a school house and various outbuildings. Planted around the structures are an herb garden, a dye-plant garden and a family garden typical of the era. Or along another path, sample rural life at a small family farm, complete with barn, farm animals and gardens.

Facilities at the interpretive building include a meeting room, a book shop and large viewing windows that overlook a wildlife feeding station and wooded ravine. A 1.5-mile cross-country ski trail is open in the winter.

County: Kent

City: Grand Rapids

**Fees: City residents—Free.
Non-residents—50 cents.**

**Schedule: Open year round.
Pioneer Heritage buildings—Open Sundays, 2:00 p.m.-5:00 p.m.
Interpretive Building—Open Monday through Friday, 9:00 a.m.-5:00 p.m.; Sunday, 2:00 p.m.-5:00 p.m.; closed Saturdays and holidays.**

Directions: From I-196 in downtown Grand Rapids, exit on Leonard Street and go west three miles to Hillburn Avenue; turn north (right) onto Hillburn Avenue and go one-half mile to the entrance.

**Further Information:
Blandford Nature Center
1715 Hillburn Ave., N.W.
Grand Rapids MI 49504**

80

FIVE LAKES

MUSKEGON NATURE SANCTUARY

To the untrained eye, the Five Lakes Muskegon Nature Sanctuary appears to be not much more than a pleasant, attractive and peaceful place to walk. Naturalists and conservationists, on the other hand, shake their heads in wonder and amazement at the tremendous number of unusual and rare grasses, sedges and rushes that thrive here. Outside of this area, many of the species grow only along the Atlantic Coast.

Why here? The gradual drying of a large lake that once covered the entire area in the early

County: Muskegon

City: Muskegon

Fees: None.

Schedule: No posted hours.

Directions: From I-96 southeast of Muskegon, take exit 10, then go north on Maple Island Road 10 miles to Evanston Road; drive two miles just past Wolf Lake Road and continue on Evanston Road, which angles southwest; just past the point where Evanston bends due west again, park on the north side of the road on a short turnoff just east of the Eagle Alloy Company.

Further Information:
Michigan Nature Association
P.O. Box 102
Avoca MI 48006

1800s created near-perfect growing conditions—an open sunny area of wetlands ringed by trees—for an incredible variety of grasses, sedges, rushes and prairie plants.

So be sure to bring plant and wildflower identification guides to fully enjoy your visit. And though you can spend as little as an hour on an enjoyable walk, you may end up taking an entire day—spring, summer or fall—identifying and marveling at the rich diversity of plant life virtually always underfoot. Birders will find hawks as well as a wide variety of waterfowl and songbirds, including herons and bluebirds, that visit or nest in the sanctuary.

Access into the sanctuary is through a 200-yard-long panhandle-shaped easement from Evanston Road. At the end of the easement, two mile-long trails—one leading east, the other heading northeast—branch into the 53-acre sanctuary.

81 KITCHELL DUNE PRESERVE

Tucked away on the north shore of the Grand River a few hundred yards from where it empties into Lake Michigan at Grand Haven, the Kitchell Dune Preserve is a living showcase for a typical Michigan dunal ecosystem, where nature patiently and efficiently changes a sandy, barren dune into a hardwood forest.

For a walking textbook tour of the progressive stages of this dunal plant succession, take the .75-mile Connie Lindquist Trail through the 52-acre sanctuary. Dune grass, which stops erosion and stabilizes the sand, dominates at the trails beginning. Farther inland along the trail, cottonwoods and shrubs have displaced the dune grass,

and near the end of the hike, oak and maple mark the climax of the natural succession process. This easy-to-walk trail also skirts several interdunal ponds, briefly cuts through an area of pine plantings and passes many plants typical of this ecosystem, including sassafras, bearberry, horsetails, sand cherries and the rare pitchers thistle, found only along Great Lakes shores.

A self-guiding brochure, an excellent aid to the enjoyment and understanding of the fragile and fascinating environment, is available by mail from the Nature Conservancy, which owns and maintains this preserve.

(Continued on page 95.)

82 P. J. HOFFMASTER STATE PARK

The *world's* largest accumulation of sand dunes bordering a body of fresh water stretches from the Michigan/Indiana border along Lake Michigan all the way to the Straits of Mackinac. These beautiful, majestic dunes, then, are not just a state, and not just a national, but a global treasure.

And one of the most outstanding examples of this unique, precious and precarious environment is the 2.5 miles of heavily forested dunes and sandy beaches at P.J. Hoffmaster State Park. Most of the park's 1,043 acres is a textbook example of a dune ecosystem. The gently sloping beach here builds to low foredunes then dips into a shallow trough before sharply rising to the stunning, precipitous barrier dunes which mark the sand's farthest encroachment inland.

Ten miles of hiking trails fully network the area, very little of which is level. The majority wind over the dunes; many end up at the beach. Birdwatching, good throughout the park, is best—with chances of spotting Hooded Warblers and Acadian Flycatchers—along a path that follows Little Black Creek. Photographers, in particular, will want to take a short walk from the Gillette Nature Center to a long flight of stairs

(Continued on page 96.)

KITCHELL DUNE PRESERVE   *(Continued from page 94.)*

County: Ottawa

City: Grand Haven

Fees: None.

Schedule: No posted hours.

Directions: From US-31 just north of Grand Haven, take the Ferrysburg exit. Go west on the exit road, which becomes Pine Street; follow Pine Street as it curves to the north, then turn west (left) onto Beach Road; drive 1.5 miles on Beach Road (which becomes North Shore Drive) to Berwyck Street, just before the Grand River; turn east (left) onto Berwyck Street and park at the marina just a few hundred yards east. The trail begins on the north side of Berwyck Road where it curves sharply in front of a "Captain Cove" sign.

Further Information:
Nature Conservancy
531 N. Clippert St.
Lansing MI 48912

P.J. HOFFMASTER STATE PARK
(Continued from page 97.)

which climb to the summit of a 190-foot-high barrier and some magnificent views of Lake Michigan and the rest of the park. Guided hikes also leave from the Center.

Inside the Center, a six-projector multi-image slide program, presented daily at regular intervals, not only beautifully illustrates the dune's splendor, but also dramatically explains their origins and clearly interprets their ecology. In the Center's Exhibit Hall, dioramas and other displays on the natural history of the dunes plus many special programs complement the slide show. The Center—named after one of this state's most tireless conservationists, Genevieve Gillette—is barrier free and easily accessible by the handicapped.

Other facilities at the park include several secluded picnic areas, a fine swimming beach, 333 wooded campsites and in the winter, a 2.5-mile cross-country ski trail.

County: Muskegon

City: Muskegon

Fees: $2.00 daily vehicle permit or $10.00 annual vehicle permit valid in all state parks.

Schedule: Open year round, 8:00 a.m.-10:00 p.m.; Gillete Nature Center is closed Mondays.

Directions: From US-31, approximately halfway between Grand Haven and Muskegon, exit on Pontaluna Road and go west approximately three miles to the park entrance.

Further Information:
P.J. Hoffmaster State Park
6585 Lake Harbor Rd.
Muskegon MI 48441

83 MUSKEGON STATE PARK

The five miles of sandy Lake Michigan beach at Muskegon State Park almost guarantee hours of relatively private beachcombing. Good birdwatching, hiking, a scenic drive and some outstanding angling on the waters of lakes Michigan and Muskegon are other calling cards to this 1,300-acre park.

The park—with its varied habitat of wooded dunes, extensive shoreline, open water and dense woodland—attracts more than 200 species of birds including scoters, cormorants, egrets, herons and rails. Both waterfowl and shorebirds regularly visit and nest here, and May is a particularly good time to observe the spring migration of warblers. Migrating hawks sometimes pass through the area as they move south in the fall. The best chance for spotting them is at the southern end of the park on the peninsula separating Lake Muskegon from Lake Michigan.

Other facilities and attractions include fishing piers, a picnic area and 348 camping sites divided among three campgrounds. An extensive network of hiking and cross-country ski trails cover the north end of the park, and the beautiful Scenic Drive winds through the length of the park past sand dunes and along the Lake Michigan shoreline.

County: Muskegon

City: Muskegon

Fees: $2.00 daily vehicle permit or $10.00 annual vehicle permit valid in all state parks.

Schedule: Open year round.

Directions: From US-31 north of Muskegon exit on M-120 and go southwest approximately 2.1 miles to Lake Avenue (called Water Street on some maps), where M-120 turns south; continue southwest on Lake Avenue about a half mile to Ruddiman; go southwest on Ruddiman approximately 2.6 miles to Memorial Drive; go west on Memorial Drive approximately 2.5 miles to the park entrance.

Further Information:
Muskegon State Park
3560 Memorial Dr.
North Muskegon MI 49445

84 NEWAYGO STATE PARK

If you're looking for peace, seclusion and rustic beauty far from any sizable city or major highway—in other words, if you want to "rough it" for awhile—Newaygo State Park is the place to go.

You can camp in relative privacy at one of this out-of-the-way park's 99 primitive (no electricity, flush toilets or picnic facilities) sites spread thinly through heavy woods. Unmarked trails wind west from the campground into the park's 257 acres of oak, aspen and white pine. Along these trails, look for wildflowers and songbirds.

Located on the south side of Hardy Dam Pond—a six-mile-long by one-mile-wide (at its broadest point) body of water created by the damming of the Muskegon River—even the park's mile of shoreline is undeveloped. As a result, swimming is rated only fair, birdwatching for waterfowl is fair, but canoeing and fishing—especially for walleye, pike and smallmouth bass—is good.

County: Newaygo

City: Newaygo

Fees: **$2.00 daily vehicle permit or $10.00 annual vehicle permit valid in all state parks.**

Schedule: **Open year round.**

Directions: **Approximately 43 miles north of Grand Rapids on US-131, take the Morley exit and go west seven miles on USF-5104 (Jefferson Road) to Beech Road; turn north (right) onto Beech Road and go a half mile to the park entrance.**

Further Information:
Newaygo State Park
Box 309-A
Newaygo MI 49337

85 SILVER LAKE STATE PARK

Vast sandy beaches, Sahara-like sand dunes and water dominate the 2,685-acre Silver Lake State Park.

Here, you can experience sun, sand and water in two very different ways. You can leisurely roam for nearly three miles beside the rolling, roaring surf of Lake Michigan. Or from the quiet, sandy beaches of inland Silver Lake,

you—or particularly small children—can wade or enjoy a safe swim in shallow water.

A one-mile-wide expanses of towering sand dunes fills the expanse between these two beaches, and all but about one square mile of this dune area is open to hiking and exploring.

(Continued on page 99.)

Southwestern Lower Peninsula

SILVER LAKE STATE PARK

(Continued from page 98.)

That tiny parcel, on the northern end of the park, is an extremely busy area reserved for off-road vehicles. Dune buggy enthusiasts from around the state converge here, and one of the few commercial dune-buggy rides left in Michigan operates out of the park.

Other facilities here include a 250-site campground, a picnic area and a boat-launching ramp, all clustered on the eastern shore of Silver Lake.

County: Oceana

City: Mears

Fees: $2.00 daily vehicle permit or $10.00 annual vehicle permit valid in all state parks.

Schedule: Open daily, 8:00 a.m.-10:00 p.m.

Directions: From US-31 five miles south of Hart turn west on Shelby Road and drive six miles to Scenic Drive (16th Avenue); turn north onto Scenic Drive and go 4.5 miles to the park entrance.

Further Information:
Silver Lake State Park
Route 1, Box 187
Mears MI 49346

Northern Lower Peninsula

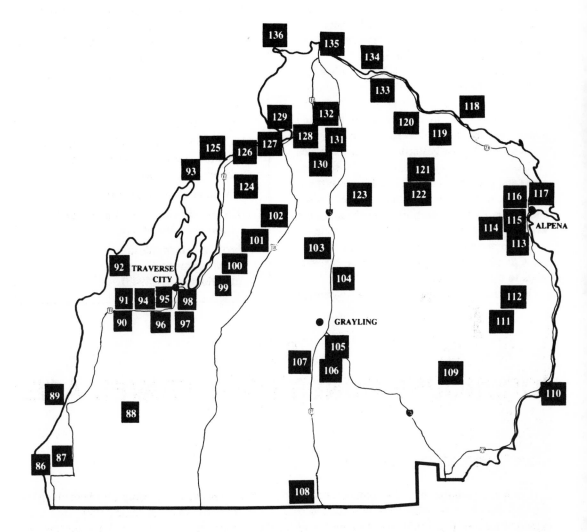

86 LUDINGTON STATE PARK

Three quarters of a million photographers, hikers, campers, beachcombers, fishermen and other outdoor lovers visit Ludington State Park each year. Most pay repeat visits because they discover that the blend of scenery and outdoor opportunities here are hard to match.

Ten varied hiking trails, totaling 20 miles, extend into every corner of the park, and there are a lot of corners to probe. Forty-five hundred acres of woodland, miles of beaches and sand dunes, and the Big Sable River are all sandwiched between the beautiful sweeping beaches of Lake Michigan and the intricately sculpted coves and inlets of Hamlin Lake. It's not surprising, then, that there's something different to see and do on each of the trails, which take anywhere from an hour to more than four hours to walk. Some border lakes; others climb dunes, cross foot bridges and pass through forests; one leads to the Point Sable Lighthouse.

Other facilities at the park include swimming beaches on both Lake Michigan and Hamlin Lake, several picnic areas and 398 campsites divided among three campgrounds. Regularly scheduled slide shows are presented in an auditorium at the park's nature center, which also houses a small exhibit hall.

County: Mason

City: Ludington

Fees: $2.00 daily vehicle permit or $10.00 annual vehicle permit valid in all state parks.

Schedule: Open year round.

Directions: Go seven miles north of Ludington on M-116.

Further Information:
Ludington State Park
Ludington MI 49431

87
NORDHOUSE DUNES FOOT TRAVEL AREA

If your main requirement of an outdoor area is the opportunity to get away from the hustle and hassle of modern life, you'll like the Nordhouse Dunes Foot Travel Area. Rugged trails, extensive beach and other facilities in this 4,300-acre area of the Manistee National Forest all appear to be lightly used.

You can backcountry camp anywhere along the more than 10 miles of hiking trails that wind through an area rich in animal and birdlife and abundant with wildflowers. Not all trails in this out-of-the way area are clearly marked, so carry

(Continued on page 103.)

NORDHOUSE DUNES

(Continued from page 102.)

(Continued from page 102.)

a compass.

You can get to the trails from several points. You can begin at the trailhead at the end of Forest Trail Road, but you might get sidetracked swimming, beachcombing or strolling in solitude along the miles of beautiful Lake Michigan shoreline. The south side of the foot-travel area can be reached from a parking area at the end of Nurnberg Road. Perhaps the best access is from a state-forest campground at the Lake Michigan Recreation Area on the north end of Nordhouse Dunes. This campground not only makes a good base camp for hikers, but also is the only spot in the area that has potable water. Adjacent to the campground is a beautiful, secluded picnic area.

County: Mason

City: Ludington

Fees: None.

Schedule: No posted hours.

Directions: From Ludington go north on US-31 approximately 12 miles to Forest Trail Road; turn west (left) onto the paved road and follow it to Lake Michigan and the trailhead.

Further Information:
Huron-Manistee National Forest
421 S. Mitchell
Cadillac MI 49601

88 ARBORETUM TRAIL

Many immigrants have taken root at this "Ellis Island" of Michigan arboretums. In 1940 the United States Forest Service planted this out-of-the-way arboretum in the Manistee National Forest to determine the adaptability and growth potential of trees from Europe, Asia and various non-Michigan climate areas of the United States. After more than 40 years, the impressive survivors of that experiment stand tall here.

A nearly mile-long self-guided trail leads to all the major stands of specimen trees, which include Scotch, pinon, pitch, white, red, table top, jack, Balkan and Austrian pine; white, blue and Norway spruce; and Darvain larch, hemlock, Douglas fir, and black cherry. Interpretive signs identify the trees and explain the natural setting, and several benches scattered throughout the grounds allow for long, relaxed looks.

County: Manistee

City: Wellston

Fees: None.

Schedule: No posted hours.

Directions: From M-55 one mile west of Wellston, turn south onto Bosschem Road; go one mile on Bosschem Road to Pine Lake Road; turn east (left) onto Pine Lake Road and go just a few yards to the parking lot, on the south side of road.

Further Information:
Manistee National Forest
Forest Supervisor
421 S. Mitchell St.
Cadillac MI 49601

89 ORCHARD BEACH STATE PARK

Located on a high bluff overlooking Lake Michigan, Orchard Beach State Park is one of Lower Michigan's most picturesque and scenic camping and picnicking spots.

An old orchard on the landward side of the bluff's crest shelters 175 grassy, semi-shady but not very private camping sites. A long stairway near the southern edge of the campground drops to a narrow half-mile-long beach at the base of the bluffs.

A beautiful, scenic view of Lake Michigan comes from the large, grassy picnic grounds sitting atop the bluff at the northern edge of the campground. A half-mile self-guiding nature trail begins and returns to the eastern side of the picnic parking area. A brochure available at the 221-acre park's headquarters lists the plants, trees and shrubs found along the trail.

County: Manistee

City: Manistee

Fees: $2.00 daily vehicle permit or $10.00 annual permit valid in all state parks.

Schedule: Open daily, 8:00 a.m.-10:00 p.m.

Directions: Go two miles north of Manistee on M-110.

Further Information:
Orchard Beach State Park
2064 Lakeshore Rd.
Manistee MI 49660

90 PLATTE SPRINGS PATHWAY

Hikers will find that the Platte Springs Pathway is a great place to "get their feet wet." No, this is not necessarily the best place in Michigan for someone to take their first hike. Hikers here really do have to get their feet wet because, to both reach and leave the trail, they have to take off shoes and socks, roll up pant legs and cross the Platte River. The ford is usually less than a foot and a half deep, but the sandy riverbed and the fairly strong current make it an exhilarating way to begin and end this hike.

Even without its unusual beginning/end this short but strenuous, rugged and scenic trail would be a magnet to hikers. The 1.25-mile main trail plus several shorter loops border the picturesque Platte River and climb steep ridges—with abrupt elevation gains of up to 150 feet—to the hills overlooking its valley. Free-flowing springs and several small streams occasionally interrupt the trail on their way down the hillside

(Continued on page 105.)

PLATTE SPRINGS PATHWAY

(Continued from page 104.)

(Continued from page 104.)

to join the Platte. Hikers must often climb under or over fallen trees that block the way. The trail also crosses old logging roads, follows game trails and passes through small stands of virgin hardwood where the terrain is so rugged, lumbermen couldn't fell and drag the trees out. One grand old sugar maple, that took root when Michigan became a state, measures two and a half feet in diameter.

Blue paint blazes and 26 numbered posts mark the trail. Corresponding numbers in a pamphlet available from any DNR office identify and interpret special points of interest. Many trees and shrubs are also marked and identified.

Attractions to anglers include excellent trout fishing and heavy fall salmon runs. A secluded, quiet state-forest campground completes this near-perfect outdoor spot.

County: Benzie

City: Honor

Fees: None.

Schedule: Open year round.

Directions: One mile east of Honor on US-31, turn south onto Pioneer Road, then follow the signs to the Platte River State Forest Campground, which is on Goose Road. The trail begins at the south end of campground.

Further Information:
Michigan Department of Natural Resources
P.O. Box 30034
Lansing MI 48909

91 GRAVEL RIDGE PATHWAY

The Gravel Ridge Pathway, though short, passes through an area rich in both natural and human history. In fact, 21 points of special interest—an average of one about every 85 yards—are marked by numbered posts along the one-mile trail. Corresponding to the numbered posts are descriptions in a pamphlet, which also includes a trail map, available by mail from the DNR in Lansing.

The trail begins at the Veterans Memorial State Forest Campground, follows the Platte River for about a quarter of a mile, then climbs to a ridge and passes a gravel pit used in early road construction in the area. In 1915, wagons hauled gravel to surface a nearby road. And in 1926-27, gravel from the same site ended up in concrete used to pave the same highway, now US-31. Deep scars in the landscape inflicted by the mining operations remain after more than 50 years. The trail crosses the old wagon road and an abandoned railroad grade before returning to the campground.

Just a few hundred yards east on US-31 is the Platte River State Anadramous Fish Hatchery, whose rearing ponds for trout and salmon are the largest of their type in the world. The hatchery is open to the public.

County: Benzie

City: Honor

Fees: None.

Schedule: No posted hours.

Directions: On US-31, drive 3.5 miles east of Honor and park at the Veterans Memorial State Forest Campground. The trail begins across the highway.

Further Information:
Michigan Department of Natural Resources
Box 30034
Lansing MI 48909

Glen Lake, Sleeping Bear Dunes (page 107)

92

SLEEPING BEAR DUNES
NATIONAL LAKESHORE

As the glaciers of the last ice age receded from Michigan some 12,000 years ago, they shaped and sculptured a remarkable landscape of rolling hills, countless small lakes and magnificent Great Lakes. But the masses of ice, in cooperation with wind and water, seem to have taken special care in creating Michigan's endlesssly beautiful coastlines.

Nowhere is this fascinating glacial legacy more visible than along the 40-mile stretch of northwestern Lower Peninsula coast included in the Sleeping Bear Dunes National Lakeshore. Massive bluffs jutting into Lake Michigan, some of the world's most beautiful inland lakes, awesome sand dunes and two offshore islands are major features of the park, which takes up 68,000 acres of coastal area between Frankfort and Leland.

Indians, lumbermen, Great Lakes sailors and early farmers, like the glaciers, left reminders of their passing. Old Indian trails, abandoned farms, ghost towns and other remnants of the logging era, are scattered throughout the park. Three lighthouses and an equal number of former U.S. Life Saving Stations remain as evidence of the area's rich nautical heritage. Today, lake freighters on the Great Lakes shipping route from the Straits to Chicago still pass between the mainland and South Manitou Island, just seven miles offshore.

A former state park, other state land and considerable private property was combined to make up Sleeping Bear Dunes, which was officially established as a national lakeshore in 1970. The

County: Leelanau

Fees: None.

Schedule: Open year round.

Further Information:
  Sleeping Bear Dunes National Lakeshore
  400 Main St.
  Frankfort MI 49635

towns of Empire and Glen Arbor and the private property surrounding them divide the park into almost three equal sections. Highway M-22 runs the park's entire length and along with M-109 provides easy access to almost all points of interest and activities.

The list of things to do here is impressive: hiking, beachcombing, scenic drives, dune climbing, fishing, canoeing, backpacking, mushrooming, berry picking, camping, cross-country skiing, hang-gliding and swimming, to name just a few. The area is also an excellent place to hunt for Petoskey Stones, the official state stone. Forty-nine species of mammals—including deer, racoons, white-footed mice, porcupines, mink, red fox, and two species of flying squirrels—plus 326 species of birds and 87 species of fish thrive in the park.

(Continued on page 108.)

**SLEEPING BEAR DUNES
NATIONAL LAKESHORE**
(Continued from page 107.)

FRANKFORT TO EMPIRE

Hiking is the name of the game in this section of the park.

Two 2.2-mile loops of the Old Indian Hiking Trail both lead to a scenic overlook of Lake Michigan and the Platte Plains Dunes. As the name implies, this trail follows parts of an old Indian path as it parallels the coast along forest-covered dunal ridges that once marked the shorelines of prehistoric Lake Michigan. The trail begins off M-22 on the southern edge of the park just west of the M-22/Sutter Road junction.

A network of old logging roads and the abandoned grade of a narrow-gauge railroad make up most of the 15 miles of hiking and backpacking paths of the Platte Plains Hiking Trail. The routes wind to several scenic overlooks of Lake Michigan, past the ghost town of Aral, along old dunal ridges, through pine plantations, around several lakes and beside a stream with an active beaver community. Backcountry camping is permitted at White Pine Campground, near Platte Bay. Trails can be reached from the south at the Platte River Campgrounds. Access to the middle of the system is at the end of Trails End Road. At the north end of the trail complex, Esch Road deadends at Lake Michigan giving easy access not only to the trails but also to miles of beach. A historical plaque here marks the site of Aral, a once-prosperous lumbering town now reduced to a few crumbling foundations.

For a breathtaking overlook of Lake Michigan, take the 1.5-mile round trip Empire Bluff Self-guiding Hiking Trail to the park's perched dunes, some of which tower 400 feet or more above the lake. Nature created these perched dunes by depositing wind-driven sand on top of bluffs—large deposits of gravel, boulders and other debris—left by the receding glaciers. Beach dunes, on the other hand, are formed by wave and wind action on sandy shoreline. Beach dunes, such as those found at the Platte Plains area, sometimes reach heights of over a 100 feet. Perched dunes—like those at Empire, Sleeping Bear and Pyramid Point bluffs—can be imposing behemoths camped several hundred feet above the lake or may be little more than small sand piles resting atop the highlands.

To reach Empire Bluff, take the self-guiding path from the trailhead, which is just south of Empire on Wilco Road. Numbered descriptions in a brochure available at the trailhead correspond to numbered points of interest along the route, such as glacial boulders, a beech/maple forest and an old farm. At Empire Bluff, for a short distance along the shoulder of the dune, the trail is surfaced by a cord matt, which protects the fragile area from foot traffic. This bluff and Pyramid Point are popular hang-gliding spots.

(Continued on page 109.)

SLEEPING BEAR DUNES NATIONAL LAKESHORE

(Continued from page 108.)

EMPIRE TO GLEN ARBOR

The world's most famous sand dune, one of the state's most unusual picnic areas, Michigan's shortest highway, a scenic drive and the park's most strenuous (and rewarding) hikes are packed into this section.

The focal point for all this activity is the Visitors Center, located on M-109 three miles north of Empire. Natural and human history exhibits, displays and programs there include a regularly scheduled slide show on the history of the park, plus interpretive programs conducted by park rangers. Other services and facilities at the Center—open daily from mid-May to mid-October and weekends the rest of the year—include trail maps for the entire park, a book shop and schedules for interpretive programs.

North of the Visitors Center, one of the most unusual and scenic seven miles of paved road in the country, Pierce Stocking Drive, leaves M-109. Good views come from three observation platforms constructed along this one-way route on top of the dunes. An especially stunning look at Lake Michigan comes from one which juts out from the shoulder of the 450-foot-high crest of the largest dune. From the edge of this platform, you feel as though you are looking almost straight down at the narrow strip of beach that separates dune from water, and the beachcombers below look no larger that ants. You may be tempted to make the journey down the face of the dune to the beach—and it does look inviting—but be warned, it is a long, difficult climb back to the top. Easier foot exploration of several dunes along the drive comes at numbered stops which correspond to numbered text in an interpretive pamphlet available at the drive's entrance.

Also on the 7.6-mile route, you can picnic at an area unlike any other in the state and possibly the nation. At the unusual location, over 400 feet above Lake Michigan atop a gigantic dune, picnic tables are tucked into a shaded, grass-covered, sheltered area.

Pierce Stocking Drive, open daily from 10:00 a.m. to sunset, is an especially good way for the handicapped to enjoy and view the dunes. Steps at two of the three observation platforms, unfortunately, limit wheelchair access, but improvements are planned. Trailers, bicycles, and motor homes longer than 24 feet or higher than 11 feet are not allowed on this road.

Just north of Pierce Stocking Drive is the world's most famous sand dune—from which the park got its name—Sleeping Bear Dune, itself so named by Indians who thought the then tree-covered dune, from the lake, looked like a sleeping bear curled on top of a massive bluff.

More than nine miles of trails, the majority of which follow an old dune-buggy-ride road, cover this giant four-square-mile perched dune. Difficult access and strenuous trail conditions are reasons the park service warns prospective hikers to wear shoes and bring hats, sunglasses, suntan lotion and water. Access from M-109, for example, is an arduous (one seems to slip one step backward for every two forward) 150-foot ascent up the dune. Once on top, it is a hard four-mile loop to the lake and back. From Sleeping Bear Point Coast Guard Station in Glen Haven (the other access point) the shortest loop to the dune and back measures nearly 6.5 miles. To get to Glen Haven from M-109, take M-209, which, at

(Continued on page 110.)

SLEEPING BEAR DUNES
NATIONAL LAKESHORE
(Continued from page 109.)

.4 miles, is Michigan's shortest state highway.

Two much easier hiking trails begin just south of the Visitors Center. The shortest, the 1.5-mile Windy Moraine Trail, circles south of the Center. The 2.4-mile Schauger Hill Trail crosses M-109, enters a hardwood forest, then passes over hilly terrain which includes some moderate climbs. Wildflower and mushroom hunters will enjoy spring hikes on this trail; fall color is spectacular; and cross-country skiers can use the route in the winter.

Other hiking and cross-country trails in this section include an extensive system at Alligator Hill, located three miles north of the Visitor Center and west on Day Forest Road. Four loops at this former 1920s golf course range in length from 1.5 to 2.7 miles, and an additional .7-mile trail leads to a scenic overlook.

GLEN ARBOR TO LELAND

Solitude and a wide selection of short walks, day trips and wilderness backpacking ventures are attractions to this section of the park.

Less used and more secluded than most areas

in the park, for example, is the Pyramid Point Hiking Trail, a 2.5-mile route through meadows and forests and behind bluffs. A quarter-mile branch trail climbs steeply to the top of one of the dunes and a magnificent view of Lake Michigan, the Manitou Islands and boats negotiating the shipping lanes. You might be in the company of hang gliders who launch from here, but you can walk along the crest of the dunes in either direction with little chance of meeting the crowds found in other areas of the park. The trail begins at a parking lot reached by going 4.7 miles north and east of Glen Arbor on M-22, then 2.9 miles north on Basch Road, which—because it resembles a roller coaster more than a road—is in itself an adventure.

East of Pyramid Point, County Road 669 runs north from M-22 and ends at Good Harbor Bay, with its miles of little-used beaches. A sand road leads east from the end of CR669 a few hundred yards to the Good Harbor Bay Picnic Area and another 2.5 miles of hiking trails.

Seven miles offshore from Leland is South Manitou Island, whose eight square miles and 5,260 acres are packed with both natural and man-made attractions. The Manitou Island Transit Company in Leland makes one daily run to

(Continued on page 111.)

SLEEPING BEAR DUNES
(Continued from page 110.)

the island. But since the ferry returns only three and a half hours after its arrival, day visitors who want to see everything should take the motorized island tour.

Overnight visitors (excluding pets, which are prohibited) have their choice of three campgrounds. Travel light but carry a backpacker's cook stove. The closest camping area is more than a mile from the ferry dock, and open fires are restricted to community fire rings only. Light lunches and a limited supply of camping items are available at a restaurant located about a half mile north of the dock.

The best way to explore is along the miles of old logging trails and roads that crisscross the island. Hidden away in the southwest corner of the island is the world's largest white cedar tree. This 90-foot-tall, 17.5-foot-diameter specimen—along with the other virgin white cedars, many over 500 years old, located in the Valley of the Giants—somehow miraculously escaped being turned into cordwood or homes. On the northeast corner of the twelve miles of beaches that encircle South Manitou is a gull colony. A palisade of perched dunes lines the west coast, and an old, unused schoolhouse, a cemetery and abandoned farms occasionally interrupt the landscape. The Island Post Office serves as the South Manitou Island Visitors Center, which, with its historical pictures and displays, hints at being a museum.

On the island's southeast side, a dock, built in 1835 to load cordwood fuel onto lake steamers, marks South Manitou's first settlement. Five years later, the island's first lighthouse began pointing the way into the sheltered bay (the only natural harbor between here and Chicago) and guiding ships through the Manitou Passage. The dangers of this coast are dramatically illustrated by the still-visible hulk of the *Francisco Morazan*, which, in 1961, ran aground about three miles west of the beacon. A new lighthouse was constructed in 1858, and it in turn was replaced 13 years later by the present lighthouse, now open to the public. A U.S. Life Saving Station, established in 1901, now serves as an island reception center staffed by park rangers.

For a true wilderness camping or backpacking adventure—no stores, no designated campgrounds, no potable water and no sanitary facilities—schedule a ride on a local charter boat then stake out your own spot anywhere on the 15,000 heavily wooded acres of North Manitou Island.

93 LEELANAU STATE PARK

Spring brings both birds and birdwatchers to Leelanau State Park, located at the tip of the "little finger" of Michigan's "mitten." Most birds, but especially hawks and songbirds, dislike crossing open water and will fly over land as long as possible as they migrate north. As a result, birds moving up the state's western shoreline funnel into the Leelanau Peninsula, and at the northern tip, the park becomes a staging area where the birds rest, feed and gather the courage to cross the waters of Grand Traverse Bay. Elsewhere in the park, deep woods, marshy areas and lakeshore attract shorebirds, waterfowl and songbirds during spring, summer and fall.

(Continued on page 113.)

County: Leelanau

City: Northport

Fees: $2.00 per day vehicle permit or $10.00 annual vehicle permit valid in all state parks.

Schedule: Open year round.

Directions: Southern Section—From Northport go north on County Road 629 approximately four miles to Densmore Road (just north of Woolsey Airport); turn west (left) onto Densmore Road and follow to its end.
Northern Section—From Northport go north on County Road 629 approximately eight miles to its end.

Further Information:
Leelanau State Park
Northport Unit
Route #1 Box 49
Northport MI 49670

94 CHAIN O' LAKES PATHWAY

Before hiking here, be sure to stop at the Platte River Hatchery, on US-31 east of Honor, and pick up an excellent printed guide to the area. The pamphlet includes not only a trail map but also 20 numbered descriptions of special points of interest which correspond to numbered posts along the Pathway's two trails. Blue paint spots also mark the routes, especially where they pass through sometimes thick undergrowth and clusters of 100-year-old white-pine stumps, reminders of the area's lumbering past.

The Chain O' Lakes Pathway's two loops begin and end at the Lake Ann State Forest Campground, on the west shore of Lake Ann. Both the 1.25- and 2.0-mile loop probe a variety of habitats including the Platte River, bogs, two lakes and several clearings over rolling terrain. Stands of maple, birch, aspen, blackberry and white pine cover the higher ground while the vegetation changes to cedar, spruce, tamarack, dogwood, mosses and ferns as the land drops to the bogs and natural springs that flow near the Platte River. Many of the trees and shrubs are labeled for easy identification.

The trails are open in the winter for cross-country skiing.

Sites at the Lake Ann State Forest Campground are grass-covered, shady and fairly private.

County: Benzie

City: Lake Ann

Fees: None.

Schedule: Open year round.

Directions: Go 4.5 miles west from Interlochen on US-31 to Reynolds Road; turn north (right) onto Reynolds Road and go four miles to Lake Ann State Forest Campground.

Further Information:
Area Forester
Betsie River State Forest
Platte River Hatchery & Field Office
15200 Honor Highway
Beulah MI 49617

LEELANAU STATE PARK
(Continued from page 112.)

Spring also brings an abundance of wildflowers to the park. And white-tailed deer plus raccoons, squirrels, rabbits, fox, porcupine and other small mammals are among wildlife that roam the area year round.

Leelanau State Park is divided into two sections which are separated by private land. Attractions to the smaller northern parcel, at the very tip of the peninsula, include a rustic campground at the water's edge, a picnic area, rocky beach and a lighthouse, constructed in 1916 as the most recent in a series of beacons that have guided Great Lakes shipping from this point since 1852.

Sandy Lake Michigan beaches and low dunes edge the southern section, which makes up most of the park's 1,253 acres. Behind the dunes, pockets of low cedar and tamarack wetlands give way to an inland mixed hardwood/conifer climax forest and the marshy shore of Mud Lake. More than eight miles of trails—all beginning at a parking lot at the end of Densmore Road and all open for cross-country skiing—probe this section.

95 LOST LAKE NATURE PATHWAY

When you're walking on this trail system past Lake Dubonnet, don't think your eyes are playing tricks on you if you happen to see a chunk of land moving across the water. It probably is.

In 1956, controlled flooding from a dam created Lake Dubonnet from two smaller lakes, and in the process, large areas of lowland along the former shorelines were uprooted. Today, one of those chunks remains as a one-acre floating island, complete with 40-foot trees and brush, that gets blown back and forth across the lake at the wind's whim. Other evidence of the extent of that flooding comes from the dead trees sticking out of the water on the north end of the lake. Waterfowl nest in the habitat, and beaver, too, have built a house there.

The "bottom" (and the shortest, at 1.5 miles) loop of the Pathway's three circular trails, which are "stacked" south to north, begins at the Lake Dubonnet State Forest Campground, in the Fife Lake State Forest, then follows the Lake Dubonnet shoreline for half its length.

The 3.5-mile middle loop passes blueberry bogs, a beaver dam, red-pine plantings and white-pine stumps, evidence of the area's involvement in the lumbering era.

The 5.5-mile "top" loop crosses an aban-doned logging railroad grade, then at its northern rim, skirts the lake from which the Pathway gets its name. Lost Lake is an excellent example of the slow process of natural plant succession that eventually fills in all lakes. More than half of its original area has turned into bog, and over the next several hundred years, the bog will replace the entire lake.

Orange paint spots mark the Pathway, and 28 numbered posts along all loops correspond to descriptions in a self-guiding brochure available at any DNR office. The brochure, however, is not entirely necessary here because the same information is attached to several of the numbered stops, plus many of the trees and shrubs are also labeled.

The trail system is open for cross-country skiing and has a winter "extension" that adds one mile to the total distance of each loop.

County: Grand Traverse

City: Interlochen

Fees: None.

Schedule: Open year round.

Directions: From US-31 1.5 miles west of Interlochen Corner (M-137/US-31 junction), just past the Interlochen Golf Club, turn north (right) onto Wildwood Road and drive approximately 1.5 miles to the state-forest campground entrance. The Pathway begins just north of the day-use parking lot.

Further Information:
Michigan Department of Natural Resources
Box 30034
Lansing MI 48909

96 INTERLOCHEN STATE PARK

The opportunity to combine the pleasures of nature and the fine arts annually draws nearly 300,000 visitors to Interlochen State Park. No wonder then, that our first state park is, with 545 sites, also Michigan's largest state camping facility. The sites are divided into four campgrounds, two on Duck Lake, at the park's east boundary, and two on Green Lake, at the 186-acre park's west boundary. Right next door to the park is the world-reknowned Interlochen Center for the Arts, which includes the Interlochen Arts Academy and the National Music Camp. So during the summer, campers can attend daily public concerts, art shows, plays, and tours at the Center.

Getting away from people, then, is not the main objective, but there are a few opportunities for some brief sessions of solitude along several short trails that wind through virgin pine and hardwood forests. And the North Park Trail, a self-guiding nature trail with numbered stops that correspond to numbered paragraphs in an interpretive brochure, circles through the northern section of the park.

County: Grand Traverse

City: Interlochen

Fees: **$2.00 daily vehicle permit or $10.00 annual vehicle permit valid in all state parks.**

Schedule: **Open daily, 8:00 a.m.-10:00 p.m.**

Directions: **From the intersection of M-137 and US-31, approximately 12 miles southwest of Traverse City, drive south on M-137 about three miles to the park entrance.**

Further Information:
**Interlochen State Park
Interlochen MI 49643**

Other facilities at Interlochen State Park include beaches and boat-launching sites at both Duck and Green lakes, plus a picnic area next to the beach at Duck Lake. Anglers report good catches of perch, bluegill, northern pike and trout from the two lakes and nearby streams.

97 MUNCIE LAKES PATHWAY

If there were a printed menu for hikers to select from when they come to Muncie Lakes Pathway, it would probably say something like: "From column *A* pick a length: from a short 1.5-mile walk to a demanding nine-mile overnighter. Then from column *B*, choose a destination: se-cluded lake, beautiful forest, or crystal-clear stream."

Over nine miles of hiking and cross-country ski trails divided into a number of loops make up

(Continued on page 116.)

MUNCIE LAKES PATHWAY

(Continued from page 116.)

this hiker's smorgasbord in the Pere Marquette State Forest. Maps posted at all trail intersections orient the hiker and note mileage to various points. Blue triangular markers then guide the way over gently rolling wooded terrain.

And there are a variety of distances and destinations to choose from. For example, Muncie Lakes, a cluster of small lakes and marshy area rich in wildlife, is 2.5 miles from the parking lot on Ranch Rudolf Road. Dollar Lake, at the extreme northeastern edge of the trail system, is another two miles farther. The southern loop of the pathway is rarely more than half a mile from the shallow, crystal-clear Boardman River, one of the most scenic streams in the Lower Peninsula. In two places the trail brushes the heavily wooded banks of this twisting, turning excellent trout stream.

Backpackers can camp anywhere off the trails and back from the lakes. Also, Sheck's State Forest Campground connects to Muncie Lakes Pathway's south trail via a hiking/riding path that passes the camping area and joins the Pathway

County: Grand Traverse

City: Traverse City

Fees: None.

Schedule: Open year round.

Directions: Go south from Traverse City on Garfield Road (County Road 611) about eight miles to Hobb's Highway; turn east (left) onto Hobb's Highway and go approximately four miles to Ranch Rudolf Road; turn south (right) onto Ranch Rudolf Road and follow it to the parking area.

Further Information:
Michigan Department of Natural Resources
P.O. Box 30028
Lansing MI 48909

about .2 mile north of the campground parking lot.

In winter the trails are marked for cross-country skiers by green, blue or black markers, which indicate increasing difficulty.

98

GRAND TRAVERSE NATURAL EDUCATION PRESERVE

Strung like a ribbon along the west bank of the Boardman River, the 370-acre Grand Traverse Education Preserve wraps a peaceful natural package of hiking trails, dams, ponds and scenic picnic areas, all only two miles from the heart of Traverse City.

The preserve hugs the river for over two miles and in many places, especially when squeezed between river and railroad tracks, is only 100 yards wide. Scenic rest areas and picnic grounds

(Continued on page 117.)

GRAND TRAVERSE
NATURAL EDUCATION PRESERVE
(Continued from page 117.)

are often located in the broader areas. Two dams on the river within the park have created large ponds that attract waterfowl. A pair of Mute Swans, for example, which nest in and around the Grand Traverse region, can usually be spotted along the Boardman here.

Four trails, including one that is self-guided, wind for six miles along the river through marshes, grasslands and forest areas, and across several small streams that empty into the Boardman.

County: Grand Traverse

City: Traverse City

Fees: None.

Schedule: Open year round.

Directions: From the intersection of Cass and Airport roads in Traverse City, drive south two miles on Cass Road to the entrance.

Further Information:
Grand Traverse Natural Education Preserve
1125 W. Civic Center Dr.
Traverse City MI 49684

99 SAND LAKES QUIET AREA

Sand Lakes Quiet Area is rated "G," that is, suitable for even very young children. Easy walking over rolling sandy hills and through a mixed hardwood/conifer forest is the norm here, whether you take a day hike or a short backpacking excursion to one of the many lakes scattered throughout the area.

More than 10 miles of trails cover Sand Lakes' 2,500 acres of Pere Marquette State Forest land. Motorized traffic is barred, and hikers can backcountry camp anywhere within the trail system. Several secluded lakes, with fine swimming and fishing, are especially good places to set up camp. Sites are also available at the Guernsey Lake State Forest Campground, on the eastern end of the Quiet Area off Guernsey Lake Road.

You can reach the trail system from several roads which border the Quiet Area. A large parking lot on Broomhead Road at the northeast corner, for example, provides easy access and is the only entry point in the winter for cross-country skiers. You can also enter the area from a few pulloffs along Island Lake Road and from a parking lot at the state-forest campground.

Maps of the trail system are posted thoughout the area or are available from any local DNR office.

> **County: Grand Traverse**
>
> **City: Williamsburg**
>
> **Fees: None.**
>
> **Schedule: No posted hours.**
>
> **Directions: On M-72 go either six miles east of Acme or 11.5 miles west of Kalkaska to Broomhead Road; turn south onto Broomhead Road and go four miles.**
>
> **Further Information:**
> **Michigan Department of Natural Resources**
> **Box 30034**
> **Lansing MI 48909**

100 SKEGEMOG LAKE WILDLIFE AREA

Quicksand, Massasauga rattlesnakes, and the wet and wild terrain were enough to keep out 19th-century loggers and farmers but not 20th-century real-estate developers. So in the 1970s, private and public organizations, plus 900 individual contributors had to combine forces to save this uniquely beautiful 2,700 acres of marshes, quaking bogs, streams, cedar swamps, and ponds, all wrapped around the southeastern end of Lake Skegemog.

Through their efforts, much more than a unique and beautiful landscape was saved. The Lake Skegemog Wildlife Area, located partially within the Pere Marquette State Forest, is home to a wide variety of wildlife including many rare and endangered species. Repeated sightings of

(Continued on page 119.)

101 GRASS RIVER NATURAL AREA

SA H

There are usually two ways into a natural area: on foot or by car. At the Grass River Natural Area you have a third choice: by boat. The preserve is located on the Grass River, which connects Lake Bellaire and Clam Lake, and boaters can reach the natural area from either lake and tie up at a dock large enough to accommodate two or three craft.

No matter how you get here, it's well worth the trip. More than a mile of boardwalks plus several bridges, benches and observation platforms guarantee easy access to and added enjoyment of this 965-acre area of upland forests, meadows, riverside marshes and cedar swamp, all ribboned by a creek and a river. And the man-made structures don't detract from the beauty of the natural setting.

Most of the trails here loop through the cedar swamp and marsh area bordering the Grass River, which cuts through the park's northern section just before flowing into Clam Lake. The bark- and wood-chip covered paths are easy walking over level ground and vary in length from an eighth of a mile to a little more than a mile. Where the ground is not firm, boardwalks carry foot traffic (some are also wide enough for

(Continued on page 120.)

SKEGEMOG LAKE WILDLIFE AREA
(Continued from page 118.)

two adult and two juvenile Bald Eagles, for example, is good evidence that those great birds nest in the area, as do osprey. Bobcats, otter, black bear, ruffled grouse, mink, beaver, weasels and badgers roam the marshes and forests, and some of the state's largest muskellunge prowl the shallow stump-infested waters of the lake.

For an outstanding panoramic view of not only the entire Skegemog Lake Wildlife Area, but also Elk Lake and the Torch River, drive to a scenic turnout off M-72 about eight miles west of Kalkaska. Good views also come from a platform reached from the Torch River Road on the park's north side near the mouth of the Torch River.

For a more intimate look at the Lake Skegemog area, walk an old railroad grade which cuts through the western edge of the preserve. This 4.5-mile hiking/skiing trail, closed to all motorized use, runs from the park's southern boundary at M-72 to the northern edge at Schneider Road. Don't wander off the trail; it's too easy to become lost in the trackless swamps and bogs that conceal quicksand and Massasauga rattlesnakes.

One of the best ways to appreciate this unique piece of wilderness area is to quietly coast along the shore of Lake Skegemog in a canoe. Boggs Road on the south and the Torch River on the north both have public access points.

County: Kalkaska

City: Kalkaska

Fees: None.

Schedule: Open year round.

Directions: The trail begins off M-72 approximately 8.9 miles west of Kalkaska (.9 miles west of the scenic turnout), just west of Barker Creek Nursery.

Further Information:
 Skegemog Lake Natural Area Project
 P.O. Box 23
 Williamsburg MI 49690

GRASS RIVER NATURAL AREA
(Continued from page 119.)

wheelchairs) over the swamp and marsh. The walkways—which seem to merge and become a part of the natural setting—also border and repeatedly cross scenic little Finch Creek as it splits into several channels before emptying into Grass River.

Several foot bridges and three platforms, too, are as pleasing in this natural setting as the view from them. Many of the bridges, for example, have incorporated benches into their design so that visitors can sit and enjoy the whispering creek or contemplate the beauty of the surrounding swamp. Panoramic views of the river, Clam Lake and the grassy marsh bordering the riverbank come from two observation platforms located next to the Grass River on either side of the mouth of Finch Creek and a third set next to the creek about 100 yards back from the river.

Wildflowers proliferate in the Grass River Natural Area, and more than 300 species of plant life have been identified within its varied habitat and ecosystems. Forty species of mammals and 53 varied bird species also call the park home.

County: Antrim

City: Bellaire

Fees: None.

Schedule: Open year round, Dawn-Dusk.

Directions: From the intersection of US-131 and M-88 in Mancelona, go west 2.5 miles on M-88 to where M-88 jogs north at Alden Highway; continue west on Alden Highway and go approximately one mile to Grass River Natural Area Road; turn north (right) and go .8 miles to the parking lot.

Further Information:
Grass River Natural Area, Inc.
P.O. Box 231
Bellaire MI 49615

This Antrim County park is funded by public donations and is managed by a volunteer organization. Future plans call for the construction of an interpretive building and the publication of self-guiding brochures for the nature trails.

102   JORDAN RIVER PATHWAY

Catch even just a glimpse of the Jordan River, say from the top of Deadman's Hill or maybe from the river's edge just a few feet from Jordan River Road, and you will immediately understand why, in 1972, it was dedicated as Michigan's first Natural Scenic River. Even such quick images of this river—hurrying around small islands; twisting, turning and looping back on itself; lined by leaning pine and cedar that shelter wild iris and orchids; bed atumble with moss- and lichen-covered fallen trees; and all magnificently framed by sharply rising hills—are hard to forget.

For an indelible memory of the sublime beauty of the Jordan's setting in the Mackinaw State Forest, hike all or parts of two trails, one short, one long, and both of which begin and end at Deadman's Hill (so named because, in 1903, a Big Wheel—a huge single-axled device used to drag logs in the summer—broke loose, crashed down the hill and killed an unlucky lumberjack).

County: Antrim

City: Alba

Fees: None.

Schedule: Open year round.

Directions: On US-131, drive about 11.5 miles north of Mancelona to Deadman's Hill Road; turn west (left) onto Deadman's Hill Road and go approximately two miles to the parking lot and trailhead.

Further Information:
Michigan Department of Natural Resources
P.O. Box 30028
Lansing MI 48909

Panoramic views of the Jordan River Valley plus many intimate contacts with the river itself come from an 18-mile trail, which begins at the hill then passes over high hills, crosses countless small spring-fed streams, passes old logging railroad grades, skirts a beaver dam and cuts through deep woods. Several short sections of this trail are also accessible from county roads that cross it. For those who would like to hike the entire 18 miles (a two-day trip), an overnight stay at the Pinney Bridge Campground marks the halfway point. Facilities at this site of an old logging camp include pit toilets but no electricity.

A short three-mile loop, which only takes about two hours to hike, also begins at Deadman's Hill, descends into the valley (with brief glimpses of the river), then returns. Just before reclimbing Deadman's Hill, a quarter-mile side-trip to the quiet beauty of an old beaver dam and pond is well worth the time and effort.

Section-by-section mileage plus historical and natural points of interest along both trails are included on a detailed map and brochure published by the Department of Natural Resources and available by mail from their Lansing offices.

Several scenic views that require virtually no walking come from pulloffs along the Jordan River Road, which descends into the valley from US-131 then borders the river for about 10 miles.

103 OTSEGO LAKE STATE PARK

Some of the finest campsites in the state-park system, plus a mile and a half of outstanding beach on a beautiful lake make up this small 62-acre park.

The park's 203 campsites are divided into two large loops which are nestled in a stand of red oak, red pine and white pine on a slight rise overlooking the exceptionally pretty lake. The shaded, semi-private sites here are larger than those at most state parks.

A day-use area and an excellent 1.5-mile-long sandy beach marks the park's western edge. Facilities there include a bathhouse, a picnic area, a playground and a boat-launching site.

Between the day-use area and the campground, the park land is almost entirely developed, so there are no wide expanses of natural habitat here. Some orchids and low bush cranberries, however, grow on a small point which

County: Otsego

City: Gaylord

Fees: **$2.00 daily vehicle permit or $10.00 annual vehicle permit valid in all state parks.**

Schedule: **Open year round.**

Directions: **Go seven miles south of Gaylord on Old US-27.**

Further Information:
**Otsego Lake State Park
Route 3, Box 414
Gaylord MI 49735**

nudges out into the lake near the center of the park.

Fishing in Otsego Lake is good for pike, bass and panfish.

104 HARTWICK PINES STATE PARK

During the last 30 years of the 19th century, lumberjacks cut down more than one billion Michigan trees, and not surprisingly, the state led the nation in lumber production. Northern Michigan sawmills, in fact, processed so much white pine during that period that, in terms of one-inch boards, it would have covered both peninsulas with enough leftover to build 50 16-foot-wide plank roads from New York to San Francisco. Perhaps even more remarkable is that

the worth of that Michigan white pine rivaled in dollar value all the gold mined in California during the same period.

Today, one of the last remnants of this state's "green gold," 49-acres of virgin white pine, stands at Hartwick Pines State Park. And the area's human history—through artifacts, photographs and displays—comes alive in harmony

(Continued on page 123.)

HARTWICK PINES STATE PARK
(Continued from page 122.)

with its natural beauty.

Brief but stunning glimpses of the great pine forests that blanketed Michigan only a 100 years ago, plus scenic views of four lakes and the east branch of the Au Sable River come from six miles of nature paths plus 17 miles of cross-country skiing and snowmobile trails that network the 9,800-acre park, one of the Lower Peninsula's largest.

The three-mile Au Sable Trail, for example, begins on the northern edge of the park's campground, then crosses the famous trout stream, winds through a mixed hardwood/conifer forest, passes the remains of a logging-era bridge and rises to a scenic overlook before looping back to the campground.

A wheelchair is available for use in exploring the virgin pines and the carefully recreated logging camp—including a bunkhouse, a blacksmith shop, a mess hall and logging equipment—found along the Virgin Pines Foot Trail, a short paved path which begins at the interpretive building. Along this trail a short distance from the interpretive center stands the 300-year-old Monarch, at 45 inches in diameter and 155 feet tall, the largest white pine in the park.

Beginning a short distance down the Virgin Pines Trail is the Mertz Grade Trail, which follows an old narrow-gauge logging railroad spur (the cedar railroad ties are still visible) for two miles through the woods before ending at the interpretive center.

Other trails include the half-mile Hartwick Lake Foot Trail, which leads to that lake from the southeast edge of the campgrounds, and the Whispering Pines Pathway, a short braille trail that begins west of the picnic area. Park rangers also conduct regularly scheduled guided hikes through the virgin pines.

The park's river, lakes and heavily forested hills attract a wide range of animal and plant life. Both a wildflower (including bloom dates) and a birdwatchers' checklist are available at the interpretive building.

Other facilities at Hartwick Pines include a campground, a picnic area and a logging museum.

County: Crawford

City: Grayling

Fees: $2.00 daily vehicle permit or $10.00 annual vehicle permit valid in all state parks.

Schedule: Open daily, 8:00 a.m.-10:00 p.m.

Directions: From I-75 north of Grayling, exit on M-93 and drive east four miles to the park entrance.

Further Information:
Hartwick Pines State Park
Route 3, Box 3840
Grayling MI 49738

---

105 NORTH HIGGINS LAKE STATE PARK

Lumber from the vast stands of white pine that covered much of Michigan in the late 1800s helped to build the nation, but the cost to our state was steep. In their wake, lumbermen left thousand-acre swaths of stumps through wide expanses of northern Michigan. Adding to this bleakness, great fires swept through the trimmings cut from the tall pines and what few trees that were left uncut. The end result was devastation and desolation. Hundreds of thousands of charred acres stretched across portions of Michigan as far as the eye could see.

In 1903 the state of Michigan began the immense job of reforesting the lumbered-out and burned-over lands by building, near northern Michigan's Higgins Lake, its first-ever forest nursery. There, many of the outstanding specimens we see today in Michigan's great forests began as turn-of-the-century seedlings in one of the facility's 700 12-by-four-foot seed beds.

At Higgins Lake State Park, the state is preserving the heritage and history of this great undertaking by restoring the old nursery buildings

County: Crawford

City: Roscommon

Fees: **$2.00 daily vehicle permit or $10.00 annual permit valid in all state parks.**

Directions: **From I-75, take exit 244 and go west approximately 4.5 miles to the park. From US-27, take Military Road east approximately one mile to the park.**

Further Information:
**North Higgins Lake State Park
11511 W. Higgins Lake Dr.
Roscommon MI 48653**

and opening them to the public. Plans also call for the construction of a Civilian Conservation Corps museum. An interpretive brochure to the 1.5-mile Old Nursery Nature Trail is an excellent guide to several buildings—including the ice house, the cone barn (where seeds were extracted) and the state's first iron fire tower—many of which are already open to the public. The trail also winds through a pine plantation (with accompanying explanations in the brochure of reforestation practices and principles) and as a reminder of the past, crosses a field of scarred, burnt stumps.

The 429-acre park's three other hiking trails

(Continued on page 125.)

106 SOUTH HIGGINS LAKE STATE PARK

The recent addition of 700 acres to South Higgins Lake was good news for nature lovers. Previously, the very large 512-site wooded campground and the day-use area had taken up the bulk of the park's 305 acres, and there wasn't much room leftover for hiking or other outdoor activities.

But the near-tripling in size added not only such natural features as Marl Lake, the Cut River and some wetlands to the park's acreage but also 11 miles of hiking and cross-country ski trails on which to explore the new area. The diversity of land in this new parcel also provides habitats for a wide range of plant communities and animal species.

At the day-use area, more than a mile of sandy Lake Higgins shoreline and a gently sloping lake bottom make for excellent swimming. Other facilities at the park include a picnic area and a protected boat basin and launch ramp. Fishing is good for perch, bass, lake trout, rainbow trout and pike.

County: Roscommon

City: Roscommon

Fees: $2.00 daily vehicle permit or $10.00 annual vehicle permit valid in all state parks.

Schedule: Open year round.

Directions: From Roscommon, go west on County Road 100 about nine miles. From US-27, go east on County Road 104 approximately six miles.

Further Information:
South Higgins Lake State Park
Route 2, Box 360
Roscommon MI 48653

NORTH HIGGINS LAKE STATE PARK

(Continued from page 124.)

are the the 6.5-mile Beaver Creek Trail, which extends to the farthest regions of the park; the Bosom Pines Trail, which loops for 3.8 miles through the park's backcountry; and a short fitness trail, located near the parking area. All trails are open and groomed for cross-country skiing in the winter and vary from easy to difficult. A seven-mile snowmobile trail also cuts through the park.

Across County Road 200 from the nursery and trail system, 218 grassy, shady but not very private campsites are divided into east and west sections. Facilities along the park's 1500 feet of Higgins Lake frontage include a good swimming beach, a bath house, a boat-launching site and a pine-sheltered, grassy picnic area.

Higgins Lake, one of the state's largest, is popular with boaters, fishermen, sailboaters and scuba divers.

107   DEAD STREAM SWAMP

Dog-hair-thick white cedar liberally mixed with balsam fir and black spruce coats the Dead Stream Swamp, which, at 30 square miles, is the largest roadless parcel of real estate south of the Straits. Occasionally interrupting and accenting the wide sweep of evergreens in this seemingly endless expanse of the swamp spread across two counties are pockets of red maple, black ash, birch and tag alder.

No roads or even two-tracks completely traverse the heart of the Dead Stream Swamp. You can get a brief, albeit antiseptic, glimpse of this unique ecosystem from the comfort of an air-conditioned car by driving on US-27, which cuts for two miles through the eastern edge of the swamp just north of Houghton Lake. Several county roads follow the edges, and here and there a two-track penetrates the swamp but only for a mile or two. Access is also possible from recent oil-drilling areas on the fringes of the swamp. Several two-tracks and oil-well access

roads lead to the very edge of the wilderness from Boynton Road, reached by going 4.5 miles west of US-27 on M-55. This gravel road, which changes names at almost every curve, heads more or less north for about five miles, then turns in a westerly direction and parallels the southern edge of the swamp. The Addis Creek Trail begins at this road with a dozen names and penetrates the deepest, two miles, into the heart of the swamp, before ending at a foot bridge that crosses Dead Stream. Best access on the north side of the area comes from the Norwich Oil Field Headquarters Road.

An excellent way to enjoy and explore the swamp and surrounding forest is to hike or boat from the Reedsburg Dam Forest Campground, located in the Pere Marquette State Forest. There, 42 well-shaded sites dot a small peninsula that nudges into a 2,000-acre man-made lake created by the Reedsburg Dam on the Muskegon River. The marshy pond stretches upstream for three miles where it touches the southeastern edge of the swamp. Exploration of the backwaters and the miles of flooded, timber-lined shore

(Continued on page 127.)

County: Missaukee & Roscommon

City: Houghton Lake

Fees: None.

Schedule: No posted hours.

Directions: The Reedsburg Dam Forest Campground is 2.2 miles west of US-27 on M-55, then 1.5 miles north on County Road 300.

Further Information:
Michigan Department of Natural Resources
Box 30034
Lansing MI 48909

108 NEITHERCUT WOODLAND

There are four ways to have a meaningful experience at Neithercut Woodland. One: Do what thousands of elementary through college-age students, plus hundreds of teachers and naturalists have done—enroll in one of the many classes that are conducted at the 252-acre site, owned and operated by Central Michigan University. Two: Attend regularly scheduled monthly outdoor programs. Three: Pick up a fistful of helpful interpretive brochures, walk the many trails and informally increase your environmental education. Or, four: Just walk the trails with no particular goal or thoughts in mind and simply enjoy the out-of-doors.

Three trails, totaling 3.25 miles, wander through a varied landscape of hardwood forests, cedar swamps, fields, pine plantations, seasonal spring ponds and marshes. The .75-mile-long self-guiding Brookwood Trail, for example, passes through a beech/maple forest, crosses a creek and wanders beside spring ponds and cedar swamps. An excellent trail guide, available at the beginning of the path, not only interprets the natural setting and phenomena found along this 45-minute walk, but also includes a partial

> **County: Clare**
>
> **City: Farwell**
>
> **Fees: None.**
>
> **Schedule: Open year round, Dawn-Dusk.**
>
> **Directions: On M-115, go 4.5 miles northwest of Farwell.**
>
> **Further Information:**
> **Neithercut Woodland**
> **c/o Department of Biology**
> **Central Michigan University**
> **Mount Pleasant MI 48859**

checklist of the preserve's flora and fauna.

Branching off from the Brookwood Trail, the 2.1-mile Arborvitae Trail passes through a quiet, secluded forest. This trail is also open in the winter for cross-country skiing.

Designed specially for the handicapped, a 1,325-foot-long elevated boardwalk and paved path called the Freedom Trail leads in a roundabout way from the parking lot across a swamp to the interpretive building.

DEAD STREAM SWAMP

(Continued from page 126.)

by boat is easy, as facilities at the campground include both a boat-launching site and boat rental. Also, an extensive system of unmapped, unposted, and unblazed but well-worn trails follow the banks of the river downstream from the dam, head off into the surrounding forest or follow the curving banks of the impoundment.

Several prominent birdwatchers have included the impoundment, forest and swamp in their list of favorite locations. During fall and spring mi-

gration, birds nest and feed in the area in great numbers. At any time of year, drivers, hikers, boaters, canoeists or campers are likely to see a wide variety of species ranging from songbirds and waterfowl to Upland Sandpipers, Osprey, Bald Eagles, bitterns, rails, gallinules, and Black Terns.

Bear, coyote, otter, deer, fox and raccoon are among the wide variety of wildlife that inhabit the swamp, and anglers report good catches of bass, perch, bluegill and pike in the backwaters.

Other facilities at the campground include a day-use picnic area that overlooks the dam.

Once the private hunting preserve of H.M. Jewett, an early automobile tycoon, the Rifle River Recreation Area was purchased in 1945 by the Department of Conservation and served as their field laboratory until 1963 when it became a state park.

Beautiful views of the alternating high, rolling morainal hills, lakes and streams come from a paved one-way road that winds between Grousehaven and Devoe lakes. The road also tunnels through dense forest and, as it circles back to the park entrance, crosses or borders several of the picturesque small streams that lace the park.

More scenic vistas plus close-up looks at the area's natural beauty come from a 12-mile-long foot trail that traverses the 4,329-acre park's length. The trail touches the park's most remote lakes and climbs some of the highest hills to scenic overviews. There are several access points along its full-length route from Grousehaven Lake Campground to Houghton Creek near one of two camping areas on the Rifle River.

Across the road from the modern 80-site campground at Grousehaven Lake, the Pintail Nature Trail makes a mile-long loop around Pintail Pond. Numbered posts keyed to a numbered brochure, available at park headquarters, guide hikers through dense woods, a bog and alongside Gamble Creek. Just north of the campground, on the western side of Grousehaven Lake, is the park's only picnic area.

In addition to the modern campground at Grousehaven Lake and the two small areas on the Rifle River, a 79-site rustic (pit toilets and no electricity) campground at Devoe Lake completes the Rifle River Area's overnight facilities.

Anglers report good takes of bass, bluegills, northern pike and perch from the park's three major and seven smaller lakes, plus brown, brook and rainbow trout from the small creeks that flow through the park's cedar swamps.

County: Ogemaw

City: Lupton

Fees: **$2.00 daily vehicle permit or $10.00 annual vehicle permit valid in all state parks.**

Schedule: **Open year round.**

Directions: **Go 4.7 miles east of Rose City on County Road F-28.**

Further Information:
**Rifle River Recreation Area
Lupton MI 48635**

110 TAWAS POINT STATE PARK

Like a beckoning finger, the peninsula that curves into Lake Huron to shelter Tawas Bay has long drawn tourists to this "Cape Cod of the Midwest." Just the tip of this peninsula attracts more than a quarter million visitors annually and for good reason. The reason is Tawas Point State Park and its 175 scenic acres which have something for just about everyone: campers, hikers, birdwatchers, swimmers, fishermen, picnickers and nature lovers.

Open water, interdunal ponds, sufficient cover, long stretches of beach and the park's location as a landfall for migrating birds crossing Saginaw Bay add up to a great birdwatching area. Spring migration brings flights of warblers (31 different species, according to the park's checklist) and songbirds to the peninsula. Also included in the list of 205 different birds seen here are 17 species of ducks, such as Mallards and Blue-wing Teals, which nest in the ponds, and Merganzers, Shovelers, Wigeons, and Scaup, which often dot the waters of the bay or Lake Huron. Also look for gulls, terns and shorebirds, including Red Knots and Piping Plovers, overhead or along the beach.

One good birding area is back from the tip of the peninsula in the trees and woods that border the park's northern boundary. The best birding, however, comes from the the edges of the ponds and beaches and from the Sandy Hook Nature Trail.

The Sandy Hook Nature Trail begins next to a Coast Guard Lighthouse (built in 1876 to replace the original structure erected in 1853), then borders the shorelines of both Lake Huron and Tawas Bay on its round trip to the tip of the peninsula. Natural points of interest along the trail include two ponds and a good example of plant succession—bare sand, dune grass, low shrubs such as sand cherry and dogwood, and mature hardwood forests—found along Michigan's dunal shoreline. A self-guiding brochure, available at park headquarters, explains many of the significant natural and man-made features, such as a Coast Guard foghorn, found along the trail. Plan to spend a leisurely hour to hour and a half on the round trip. It could take longer, however, especially if you happen to spot some of the park's wildlife such as raccoon, mink, weasel, rabbit, skunk and muskrat.

A 200-site campground, located on a grassy meadow on the bay side of the peninsula, offers little shade or privacy. A small number of camping sites are at water's edge or border the largest of the three ponds found within the park boundaries. Other facilities, a short walk from any point in the park, include a large picnic area and more than two miles of beach, of which some of the most beautiful is at a day-use swimming area facing Lake Huron.

County: Iosco

City: East Tawas

Fees: $2.00 daily vehicle permit or $10.00 annual vehicle permit valid in all state parks.

Schedule: Open year round.

Directions: From US-23 just northeast of East Tawas drive west on Tawas Point Road to the park entrance.

Further Information:
Tawas Point State Park
East Tawas MI 48730

---

111 HOIST LAKES FOOT TRAVEL AREA

Lower Peninsula backpackers who don't want to drive most of the day to find a wilderness camping experience will want to visit the Hoist Lakes Trail system in the Huron National Forest. Backcountry camping, with a few restrictions, is allowed just about anywhere in this large, rugged area, but it's a good idea to carry a compass and a map of the region if you venture very far from either of the two parking areas.

Such freedom does carry with it some responsibilities, however. To minimize man's impact on this wilderness area, camping parties are limited to a maximum of 10 people and must set up no closer than 200 feet to any water or trail. Backpackers are also asked to carry out, not bury, all refuse.

Campers and hikers have a lot of territory to choose from in this more than 10,000-acre parcel. Almost 20 miles of trails wander through second-growth forest, over gently rolling wooded terrain, around marshes, past beaver floodings and across streams. Hikers can also use several two-tracks—barred to motorized traffic—which crisscross the area. Plans call for even more trails and campsites to be developed in the future.

Another added plus for campers and hikers: This section of the Huron National Forest teems with deer, bear, coyote, fox, owls, hawks and songirds, plus turkey, grouse, woodcock and other gamebirds.

Fishing, too, is rated good on the several lakes within the trail system. Bass and panfish are taken in good numbers from Carp, Byron and North Hoist lakes; rainbows have been stocked in South Hoist Lake. Fishermen may carry in light boats or canoes, but motors are banned on all of the lakes.

Originally developed as a cross-country ski area, the area was later opened up to hikers because of the growing demand for places in which to backpack. The trails are open for cross-country skiing in the winter.

County: Alcona

City Harrisville

Fees: None.

Schedule: Open year round.

Directions: From Harrisville on M-72, go west approximately 23 miles to the junction of M-65/M-72; turn south onto M-65 and go less than half a mile to the east parking area and entrance.

To get to the west entrance from the junction of M-65/M-72, turn north (right) onto M-65/M-72 and go approximately five miles (the highway gradually bears west) to where the highway turns sharply north again at Aspen Road; turn south (left) onto Aspen Road and go approximately four miles to the parking area.

Further Information:
Huron National Forest
Harrisville Ranger District
Harrisville MI 48740

112   REID LAKE FOOT TRAVEL AREA

Both novice and veteran backpackers will find the Reid Lake Foot Travel Area a good place to gain experience or test equipment. Here, in the Huron National Forest, you can set up camp in anything from fairly civilized to wilderness conditions. Walk-in camping is permitted anywhere along the 6.1-mile trail system with only one restriction: Camps must not be set up within 200 feet of water or trails. Other rustic campsites, marked by benches, are scattered around Reid Lake itself. And on the northwestern edge of the lake are developed sites, which include pit toilets, fire rings and a well.

The area, opened in 1975, is also an excellent destination for a day hike and picnic. Hiking begins with a single trail which leads southwest from the parking area at M-72 for about a mile to Reid Lake. There, it splits into three adjacent loops. One circles the lake; the other two reach to the east and west around marshes, bogs and a beaver pond. Maps are posted at all loop intersections.

The old fields and open meadows that make up

County: Alcona

City Harrisville

Fees: None.

Schedule: Open year round.

Directions: The parking area is located along M-72 approximately 19 miles west of Harrisville.

Information:
Huron National Forest
Harrisville Ranger District
Harrisville MI 48740

part of the trail system mark the boundaries of an old farm that was worked until it was purchased by the U.S. Forest Service and incorporated into the Huron National Forest in the mid-1960s. Surrounding the farm fields are some of the most imposing hardwoods in the area.

The trails are open in the winter for cross-country skiing.

113   CHIPPEWA HILLS PATHWAY

No matter what your mood, energy level or ability, when you arrive at the Chippewa Hills Pathway you should be able to find a hike to match. Your choice of four trails—.5, 1.3, 2.5 or 4.5 miles long—pass over the hilly, rolling terrain and through the pine-covered valleys of the

Alpena State Forest. The longest trail also skirts a cedar grove and cuts across an old logging trail.

The trails are open in the winter and offer a

(Continued on page 132.)

114 WAH-WAH-TAS-SEE PATHWAY

The Chippewa Indians who roamed the area centuries ago no doubt uttered the word often: *Wah-wah-tas-see*, meaning "in the forest." Today, at the Wah-wah-tas-see Pathway, you can walk in their footsteps along the Thunder Bay River through what is now the Mackinaw State Forest. And if you would really like to absorb the rich Indian lore in the area, stop at any local Department of Natural Resources office and pick up a brochure that describes how the Indians used the many trees and shrubs found along the trail in their daily lives.

The 1.5-mile trail begins next to the boat-launching ramp at the Thunder Bay River State Forest Campground, follows the east bank of the river for about a half mile, dog-legs away, then loops back.

County: Alpena

City: Alpena

Fees: None.

Schedule: Open year round.

Directions: From M-32, 5.5 miles west of Alpena, turn south onto Indian Reserve Road and go three miles to the state-forest campground entrance.

Further Information:
Michigan Department of Natural Resources
Box 30028
Lansing MI 48909

CHIPPEWA HILLS PATHWAY

(Continued from page 131.)

wide variety—with difficulty ranging from novice to expert—of cross-country skiing opportunities. A trail map is available at any local DNR office or the Alpena Visitors Bureau.

County: Alpena

City: Alpena

Fees: None.

Schedule: No posted hours.

Directions: From Alpena take US-23 south about 12 miles to Nicholson Road; turn west (right) onto Nicholson Road and go 11 miles to Kissau Road; turn south (left) onto Kissau Road and go a few hundred feet to a parking area on west side of road.

Further Information:
Convention & Visitors Bureau of Thunder Bay Region
P.O. Box 65
Alpena MI 49707

Northern Lower Peninsula

Grass River Natural Area (page 119)

115 NORWAY RIDGE PATHWAY

Just 10 minutes from the Alpena city limits, more than six miles of easy cross-country skiing and hiking trails crisscross the gently rolling pine-covered terrain of the Mackinaw State Forest. Developed by the Youth Conservation Corp, three loops, ranging from 1.5 to 5.5 miles long, cut swaths through the stand of red Norway pine.

A trail map is available at any local DNR office or the Thunder Bay Region Convention and Visitors Bureau.

County: Alpena

City: Alpena

Fees: None.

Schedule: No posted hours.

Directions: On US-23 approximately one mile south of the Michigan State Police Post in Alpena, turn west onto Werth road and go approximately three miles to the parking area and trailhead.

Further Information:
Convention and Visitors Bureau of the Thunder Bay Region
P.O. Box 65
Alpena MI 49707

116 ALPENA WILDLIFE SANCTUARY

For a "natural" area, the Alpena Wildlife Sanctuary has a rich human history. Prehistoric man, for example, walked here as early as 2000 B.C. Some 3,500 years later, Indians camped along the riverbanks until the coming of the Europeans. And shortly after the Civil War, lumbermen floated white-pine logs down the river to sawmills.

Today, nature lovers, hikers, canoeists and fishermen all seek refuge in this 500-acre sanctuary bordering the Thunder Bay River within the limits of northeast lower Michigan's largest city.

A dam, constructed during the logging era, created a reservoir and, behind it, the sanctuary's large expanse of wetlands. Within the sanctuary, two large islands interrupt the river, which forms most of the sanctuary's border.

A bridge, closed to all but foot or wheelchair traffic, connects the mainland to several trails that traverse or circle the shoreline of the larger island, known as Sportmen's Island or Island Park. Several scattered fishing platforms also jut

(Continued on page 135.)

117 BESSER NATURAL AREA

Nearly a mile of wild, undeveloped Lake Huron shoreline, a ghost town, a sunken ship in a small lagoon, and one of the few remaining stands of virgin white pine left in the state are attractions to this 137-acre preserve.

A stone pier that reaches out into Lake Huron and the name "Bell" (which is still listed on some county maps) are the only reminders of the school, sawmill, store, saloon and several houses that covered the area during the 1880s. Bell was born to serve the lumbering industry, and Bell died along with the lumbering industry.

A one-mile self-guiding trail leads through a magnificent stand of virgin white pine and past the ghost town, a tract of red pine, and a tiny inland lagoon, which serves as the graveyard for an unnamed small vessel, whose date and cause of sinking have long been forgotten. A bronze plaque halfway along the trail honors Jesse Besser who, in 1966, donated this land to the state as a memorial to Michigan's lumbermen.

Just a short, easy walk from the parking area

County: Presque Isle

City: Alpena

Fees: None.

Schedule: No posted hours.

Directions: From US-23 near the Presque Isle County line just north of Lakewood, take Grand Lake Road (also known as County Road 405) north approximately 3.5 miles, jog east (still on County Road 405) and go approximately one mile to the entrance.

Further Information:
Alpena Chamber of Commerce
P.O. Box 65
Alpena MI 49707

---

is the area's 4,500 feet of Lake Huron frontage, including 500 feet of sandy beach.

ALPENA WILDLIFE SANCTUARY
(Continued from page 134.)

out from the shoreline of this recently acquired 17.5-acre addition to the sanctuary, and a viewing platform for the handicapped overlooks the river.

The Michigan Conservation Department first released ducks, geese and swans and also began a feeding program in 1938, the same year the agency, at the urging of local citizens, officially designated this area a wildlife sanctuary. Today, according to the Thunder Bay Audubon Society, 128 different birds have been spotted in the sanctuary. Year-round residents now include Mute Swans, Canadian Geese and Mallards, and spring migration brings Common Goldeneye,

Bufflehead, Scaup, Canvasback, Redhead, Pintail, Gadwall, Widgeon, Black Ducks, Coots and Whistling Swans.

County: Alpena

City: Alpena

Fees: None.

Schedule: Open year round.

Directions: In northwest Alpena on US-23 (Chisholm Street), go just north of 14th Avenue to the entrance, which is on the west side of the highway.

---

118   P.H. HOEFT STATE PARK

One of Lake Huron's finest sections of dunes lines the beautiful one-mile beach at P.H. Hoeft State Park. Although the low Lake Huron dunes lack the size and grandeur of those along Lake Michigan, they do have their own distinct charm. At P. H. Hoeft State Park, the wide belt of low, rolling dunes on an equally wide beach create a seascape ready-made for solitary sunbathing, swimming and beachcombing.

Away from the beach area, 4.5 miles of trails circle through the park's 301 acres. One loop crosses US-23 and leads through a mixed hardwood/conifer forest. Another trail edges

(Continued on page 137.)

County: Presque Isle

City: Rogers City

Fees: $2.00 daily vehicle permit or $10.00 annual permit valid in all state parks.

Schedule: Open year round.

Directions: Go four miles north of Rogers City on US-23.

Further Information:
Hoeft State Park
US-23 North
Rogers City MI 49779

119
OCQUEOC FALLS
BICENTENNIAL PATHWAY

The Lower Peninsula's only major waterfall cascades over a series of two- to six-foot drops and ledges just a few hundred yards from the beginning of the pathway bearing its name.

The Pathway, made up of three loops, winds through the deep woods and over the gently rolling hills of this section of Presque Isle County and the Mackinaw State Forest. All three loops—which measure 3.0, 4.0 and 6.5 miles—border the Ocqueoc (meaning "sacred water") River, and the middle loop bridges the Little Ocqueoc River.

Across M-68 from the trailhead and parking area is a state-forest campground. An unappealing picnic grounds adjacent to the Pathway parking area is little used. Most people picnic, relax and sunbathe on blankets spread on the grassy riverbank next to the falls, which also appear to be a favorite swimming hole for many local residents as well as campers.

> **County: Presque Isle**
> **City: Rogers City**
> **Fees: None.**
> **Schedule: Open year round.**
> **Directions: From Rogers City, go west 11.5 miles on M-68.**
> **Further Information:**
>   **Michigan Department of Natural Resources**
>   **Box 30034**
>   **Lansing MI 48909**

P.H. HOEFT STATE PARK
(Continued from page 136.)

along the back of the dunes, then briefly borders Nagel Creek until the small stream empties into Lake Michigan. Alpine marsh violets, dwarf iris, devils paintbrush and several varieties of orchid are included on the park ranger's list of more than 40 wildflowers that grow along the trails and throughout the park.

Signs of wildlife in the park include the not-so-common summer sound of the Common Loon, regrettably becoming scarce in Michigan because of loss of nesting habitat. A few lucky visitors to the park may also see the Bald Eagles or bobcats that occasionally frequent the area.

Facilities at the park include a picnic area, a playground and a large tree-shaded campground with 144 well-spaced sites. The trails are open in the winter for cross-country skiing.

120 ONAWAY STATE PARK

Fossil, morel-mushroom and wildflower hunters as well as birdwatchers will find plenty to do at Onaway State Park.

Millions of limestone fossils cover the bottom of Black Lake and the park's one-mile stretch of beach on it. The rocky bottom, however, makes for only fair swimming, and sand has been hauled in to provide an acceptable beach area.

Hard and soft maples, beech, oak, ash, birch, pine, spruce and tamarack make up most of the park's 158 heavily wooded acres. Morel mushrooms emerge from the forest floor in the spring, and woodland wildflowers color the area year round. Several short hiking trails, totaling over a mile in length, probe the woods or follow the the lakeshore.

Vireos, warblers, thrushes, flycatchers, wrens, snipes, grebes, teal, loon, terns, bittern, sandpipers and gulls are among the species birdwatchers might spot in the park and the adjoining woods and water.

Fishing is good in Black Lake for bluegills, perch, bass, muskellunge, northern pike and particularly walleye.

Facilities at the park include a playground, a boat-launching site and a well-shaded, fairly private 101-site campground nestled on wooded high ground overlooking the lake.

County: Presque Isle

City: Onaway

Fees: $2.00 daily vehicle permit or $10.00 annual vehicle permit valid in all state parks.

Schedule: Open year round.

Directions: Go six miles north of Onaway on M-211.

Further Information:
Onaway State Park
Route 1, Box 188
Onaway MI 49765

Sinkholes Pathway (page 139.)

121 SINKHOLES PATHWAY

The saying, "the bottom dropped right out from under him," is more than just an expression in certain areas of Presque Isle County and other sections of the northeastern Lower Peninsula. There, the insidiously slow action of underground water on the highly porous, easily dissolvable limestone bedrock gradually creates subterranean caves. When the erosion gets close enough to the thin layer of glacial drift above the rock, the bottom (if you were standing on it) does literally drop out, that is collapse, to form "sinkholes," conical depressions up to several hundred feet across and more than a hundred feet deep.

County: Presque Isle

City: Onaway

Fees: None.

Schedule: Open year round.

Directions: On M-33 drive 10 miles south of Onaway to Tomahawk Lake Highway; turn east onto Tomahawk Lake Highway and follow the signs to Shoepac Lake State Forest Campgrounds; parking for the Sinkholes Pathway is just past state-forest campground, and the hiking trail begins across the road.

Further Information:
Michigan Department of Natural Resources
P.O. Box 30034
Lansing MI 48909

A 1.5-mile trail in the Sinkholes Pathway circles five major sinkholes; a shorter .75-mile loop circles just the first two. The trail passes through jack pine, red pine, aspen and the still-visible signs of a 1939 forest fire as it follows the lip of the holes. For an unusual view, one that you won't get at any of the other areas in this book, peer over the edge of one of the giant thimble-shaped depressions and look down at the tops of the large (10-to 30-foot) trees that have grown in the glacial drift that lines the holes.

Sinkholes drain off water and usually remain dry. But when a creek or stream carries silt or clay into a hole, it can become plugged and form a lake. Across the road from the Pathway trailhead, Shoepac Lake is such a body of water, its shoreline being more than 100 feet above the bone-dry bottom of the trail's first sinkhole, just a quarter mile to the east.

122 CLEAR LAKE STATE PARK

Fossil hunting and a scenic glacial-sculpted landscape are attractions to this moderately used 289-acre park which surrounds nearly half the lake from which it takes its name.

Several scenic views, for example, come from the hilly glacier-created terrain of the multi-looped Clear Lake—Jackson Lake Hiking Trail. Blue dots and blue-and-white pathway signs mark the interconnected loops which link the Clear Lake State Park campground, on the lake's northern shore, to the Jackson Lake State Forest Campground, three miles south on the shores of Jackson Lake. At about the halfway point between the two campgrounds, a short branch circuit leads to a state roadside picnic area on M-33. Fossil hunters will find an abundance of limestone fossils, including Petoskey Stones, in a gravel pit just off the trail on the east side of Clear Lake.

A self-guiding brochure, which includes a map, points out these and other natural and scenic points of interest such as a jack-pine planta-tion, started in the 1930s by the Civilian Conservation Corps, and the site of the once-flourishing lumber town of Valentine, which vanished with the area's white pine. Twenty-five numbered stops along the trail correspond to the numbered descriptions in the brochure, which is available at park headquarters.

Other facilities at Clear Lake State Park include a 200-site shaded campground, a large picnic area, a boat-launching ramp, and a sandy swimming beach with a shallow, gently sloping lake bottom ideal for children.

County: Montmorency

City: Atlanta

Fees: **$2.00 daily vehicle permit or $10.00 annual vehicle permit valid in all state parks.**

Schedule: **Open year round.**

Directions: **Go 12 miles north of Atlanta on M-13.**

Further Information:
  Clear Lake State Park
  Route 1, Box 51
  Atlanta MI 49709

123

PIGEON RIVER COUNTRY STATE FOREST

At the mention of Pigeon River Country, two thoughts probably come to mind: Elk and controversy.

The Pigeon River Country State Forest, a 93,000-acre parcel in the Mackinaw State Forest, is a good example of how the state attempts to balance land use between recreation and the harvesting of natural resources. That responsibility is awesome when you consider that nearly half of Michigan, more than 18 million acres, is wooded land and that nearly four million of those acres make up the largest dedicated state-forest system in the continental United States. That responsibility can also generate controversy, as evidenced by the public outcry and protest over the granting of carefully monitored oil and natural-gas drilling rights in the Pigeon River Country within range of Michigan's only elk herd. Most outdoor purists will find, however, that the drilling has, so far, had little impact on the area.

Oil and gas aren't the first natural resources to be removed from the Pigeon River Country. Lumbermen ravaged the area between 1860 and 1900, and in their wake, the seemingly inevitable forest fires left the land scarred and barren. When farmers failed and left the land, the state, in 1919, created the Pigeon River State Forest.

And the state planted something other than just seedling trees. In 1918, seven elk—once numerous in Michigan but long gone with the destruction of their habitat—were released in the area. Today the herd of over a thousand elk are without a doubt the forest's major tourist attraction.

According to the DNR, the best chance of seeing the imposing animals comes from an area near the corner of Osmun and Clark Bridge

County: Otsego

City: Vanderbilt

Schedule: Open year round.

Directions: The Pigeon River State Forest begins 10 miles east of Vanderbilt on the Sturgeon River Road. To reach the intersection of Clark Bridge and Osmun roads: On Sturgeon Valley Road, go east from the Pigeon Bridge Forest Campground about a mile to Osmun Road; turn north (left) and go approximately 4.5 miles.

Further Information:
Michigan Department of Natural Resources
Box 30028
Lansing MI 48909

roads (see *Directions*, above). South of that intersection, a half-mile path leads from a parking lot on the west side of Osmun Road up gently rising ground to Inspiration Point, a high hill overlooking broad meadows and the Cornwall Creek Floodings. Elk often graze in the meadows spread around the bottom of the hill. A sweeping view of another large meadow where elk come to feed comes from a parking area on the east side of Osmun Road, just north of the same intersection with Clark Bridge Road. Early morning and early evening are the best times to spot the magnificent creatures.

And elk aren't the only wildlife that roams the

(Continued on page 142.)

124 YOUNG STATE PARK

Five hundred sixty-three acres of natural beauty, a mile frontage on Lake Charlevoix, an abundance of wildflowers and wildlife, plus good hiking, camping and fishing attract nearly 150,000 visitors to Young State Park each year.

Two nature trails wind through the dense hardwood/conifer forest and skirt the lake in this largely undeveloped park. The woods and lakeshore shelter an abundance of animals including raccoons, squirrels, deer, ducks, and an occasional swan, weasel or flying squirrel. A variety of plantlife — including special wildflowers such as the showy lady's-slipper, yellow lady's-slipper, mocassin flower, pitcher plants, trailing arbutus and Michigan lily — also thrives here. Mushrooming is good for morels in the spring and shaggy-manes in the fall. Fishing on Lake Charlevoix is reported good for for bass, pike and perch.

Facilities in the developed western edge of the park include 293 shaded sites at three camp-

County: Charlevoix

City: Boyne City

Fees: $2.00 daily vehicle permit or $10.00 annual vehicle permit valid at all state parks.

Schedule: Open daily, 8:00 a.m.-10:00 p.m.

Directions: On Boyne City Road, go 1.5 miles northwest of Boyne City to the park entrance.

Further Information:
Young State Park
Box 3651
Boyne City MI 49712

grounds, a picnic area and a beautiful, sandy swimming beach.

PIGEON RIVER COUNTRY STATE FOREST

(Continued from page 141.)

area. Deer are so numerous they are often spotted along the roads. Bear, coyote, bobcat, grouse, beaver, otter and muskrat also inhabit the forest, but most are more elusive and difficult to spot than deer and elk. Good chances of spotting wildlife come from the forest's many good dirt roads, which also make pleasant scenic drives.

Hiking trails, too, traverse some of the most beautiful parts of the country. The Shingle Mill Pathway, with five loops ranging in length from .75 miles to 11 miles, passes through deep woods, borders the Pigeon River, and on the

longer northern loops, crosses rolling, hilly terrain. The Pathway begins at either the Pigeon Bridge Forest Campground or just off Sturgeon Valley Road 11 miles east of Vanderbilt.

Eleven heavily shaded sites at the Pigeon Bridge Forest Campground border the river, and 2.5 miles uptrail are 19 more sites at the Pigeon River Forest Campground. Hikers walking Shingle Mill Pathway's 6.0-, 10- or 11-mile loops will pass the campground, which can also be reached by car from Osmun Road.

The Pigeon River Country State Forest field office is a mile north of Sturgeon Valley Road on Osmun Road. Maps of the Pigeon River Country are available there, as is friendly advice and directions from forest-service personnel.

Fisherman's Island State Park (page 144)

125 FISHERMAN'S ISLAND STATE PARK

Nearly deserted beaches, breathtaking vistas of Lake Michigan, rugged hiking trails, serene forests and some of the most significant archaeological finds in the Northeast are reasons to visit Fisherman's Island State Park, an undiscovered gem in the Michigan state-park system.

Over six miles of undeveloped, natural shoreline form the park's northeast edge. Beachcombers will find plenty of Petoskey Stones along this stretch of sandbars, old beach ridges and low dunes. Swimmers and waders will like the gently sloping lake bottom and—with the exception of a few rocky and gravel-strewn sections—the beautiful soft sand.

Thick second-growth aspen and birch forest, cedar swamps and a scattering of northern hardwoods cover the inland portion of the park's 2,762 acres. As one of Michigan's newest (just a little over 10 years old) and least-developed state parks, Fisherman's Island has only two miles of designated hiking trails. However, hikers and cross-country skiers can also use almost 20 miles of unposted, unmapped but well-worn two-tracks that web the area. And hikers here will find that they share this fine corner of the out-of-doors with few people but many deer, waterfowl, rabbits, fox and bobcats.

Fisherman's Island is divided into two almost equal halves by a stretch of private property. The southern half is completely undeveloped, which is probably why it is also the least-visited half of the park. To even reach the area you must either take a 2.3-mile two-track to a parking area at Whiskey Creek or park at one of several pulloffs along the rugged road and walk to the creek. This road has every potential for being a muffler mangler, so check it's current condition with rangers at the northern park entrance before proceeding.

But no matter what it takes to get here, the trip is well worth the effort. Miles of pristine, open sandy beaches stretch in either direction. And hikers, after wading or jumping picturesque Whiskey Creek at its outlet on the beach, have their choice of several trails that wind back into the woods and parallel the shore. An especially scenic path borders Whiskey Creek as it penetrates deep into the forest.

In the comparatively "civilized" northern half of the park, only one posted hiking trail travels

County: Charlevoix

City: Charlevoix

Fees: $2.00 daily vehicle permit or $10.00 annual vehicle permit valid in all state parks.

Schedule: Open year round.

Directions: Go five miles south of Charlevoix on US-31 to Bell's Bay Road; turn west (right) onto Bell's Bay Road and go approximately 2.5 miles to the park's northern entrance.

To get to the Whiskey Creek parking area in the southern half, from US-31 approximately 11 miles south of Charlevoix, take Norwood Road into the village of Norwood to Norwood Township Park. The two-track to Whiskey Creek begins at the back of the park.

Further Information:
Fisherman's Island State Park
P.O. Box 456
Charlevoix MI 49720

(Continued on page 145.)

126 CHARLES A. RANSOM PRESERVE

On clear days from this 80-acre preserve perched 320 feet above Lake Michigan, you can see more than 20 miles in either direction—south to the Leelanau Peninsula and north to Beaver Island. On just about any day, you will not be disappointed with the panoramic view of Lake Michigan plus the city of and Lake Charlevoix. And you don't even have to leave the parking lot—or, if you're handicapped, the car—to enjoy the view.

But those who are able should leave their vehicles and take a mile-long nature trail down the hill, through woods and a small forest clearing, back up the moderately steep banks and along the edge of a large meadow. Or, hike an even shorter path which loops for less than half a mile through the woods before crossing the big meadow and returning to the parking area. In spring the large meadow is blanketed with wildflowers. The forest floor, too, before its leafy canopy restricts the sunlight, comes to life with wildflowers. In summer, ferns replace wildflowers in the shade of impressive specimens of birch, beech, sugar maple and aspen. Maps to both trails are included in a numbered self-guiding interpretive pamphlet, available from a box just inside the treeline near the

County: Charlevoix

City: Charlevoix

Fees: None.

Schedule: No posted hours.

Directions: From US-31 3.5 miles southwest of Bay Shore (between Charlevoix and Petoskey), take Burgess Road south 3.5 miles to Quarterline Road; turn east (left) onto Quarterline Road and go one mile to Maple Grove Road; turn north (left) onto Maple Grove Road and go .75 miles to the preserve.

Further Information:
Little Traverse Conservancy
3264 Powell Road
Harbor Springs MI 49740

trailhead.

The Charles A. Ransom preserve is one of 20 owned and managed by the Little Traverse Conservancy, a private, non-profit organization devoted to protecting and preserving natural areas in northern Michigan.

FISHERMAN'S ISLAND STATE PARK
(Continued from page 144.)

(Continued from page 144.)

from near the park's entrance gate through the back country to the southernmost of this section's two small camping areas. Ninety sites at the two loops—both located across the park road from the beach and separated by about a mile—are rustic, private and shaded. Other facilities in the northern section include a small picnic area on the beach.

Prehistoric visitors were also attracted to this area, as evidenced by some of the most important Michigan archaeological sites—dating from 1,200 B.C. to one as early as 8,000 B.C.—relating to the Woodland Indian culture. All stone tools and weapons for the entire northeastern Woodland Indian culture, for example, came from a chert quarry located near the beach in the southern section of the park. In the northern half of the park, the Inwood Creek site, which is listed on the National Register of Historic Places, has yielded pieces of stone tools plus utensils and pottery fragments.

127 PETOSKEY STATE PARK

Nestled in the dunes of Little Traverse Bay, the campground at Petoskey State Park is one of the most attractive and cozy spots in the state. Many of the 90 campsites here are picturesquely framed on three sides by precipitous dunes and retaining walls that keep the sand from covering the trailer or tent lots. Mature pine and cedar cover the grounds, most sites are grassy, all provide some shade, and many offer a degree of privacy not usually found in state-park campgrounds.

Just a short, easy walk over the sheltering dunes is 1.25 miles of wide, sandy swimming beach. Facilities there include a modern bathhouse, a children's playground and a small, secluded picnic area lying in the low dunes back from the beach.

Two foot trails, which begin at the back of the campground, probe the outer regions of the 34-acre park. The 2/3-mile-long Old Baldy Trail, which includes a long series of stairs, climbs to the top one of the park's higher dunes and a commanding view of Little Traverse Bay. The assent involves some moderate exercise, and the round trip takes at least a half hour to complete. The 2.8-mile Portage Trail, which takes about

---

County: Emmet

City: Petoskey

Fees: **$2.00 daily vehicle permit or $10.00 annual vehicle permit valid in all state parks.**

Schedule: **Open year round.**

Directions: **On US-31 go north of Petoskey approximately three miles to M-119; turn north (left) onto M-119 and go approximately 1.5 miles to the park entrance.**

Further Information:
**Petoskey State Park
2475 Harbor-Petoskey Rd.
Petoskey MI 49770**

1.5 hours to to walk, leads to Lake Michigan and a small inland lake, climbs the barrier dunes in back of the beach and extends to the park's southern boundary.

An added plus for nature lovers: The Round Lake Nature Preserve is located directly across the highway.

128 ROUND LAKE NATURE PRESERVE

"Double your pleasure, double your fun," as the commercial goes, pretty accurately describes what awaits visitors to the Round Lake Nature Preserve. Complementing the preserve and lo-

cated directly across M-119 is Petoskey State Park. So simply by crossing Michigan's least-

(Continued on page 147.)

ROUND LAKE NATURE PRESERVE
(Continued from page 146.)

traveled state highway from either place, hikers can nearly double trail mileage and birdwatchers and wildflower enthusiasts can explore a larger variety of habitat.

The habitat at Round Lake Nature Preserve is composed of a mixed hardwood/conifer forest, swamp, dense vegetation and 500 feet of frontage on the northwest corner of the lake from which the preserve takes its name. Under the canopy of some fine white pine, red maple, cedar and hemlock specimens is dense vegetation, especially near the lakeshore and swampy area. Marsh marigolds and trillium are among the many spring wildflowers native to the preserve, and the good cover and variety of habitats attract numerous birds and other animal life.

A well-trodden path cuts through the heart of the preserve; a side trail branches off toward the lakeshore.

The Little Traverse Conservancy, which owns Round Lake Nature Preserve, recently moved its headquarters to a building on the northern edge

County: Emmet

City: Harbor Springs

Fees: None.

Schedule: Open year round.

Directions: On US-31 go north from Petoskey approximately three miles to M-119; turn north (left) onto M-119 and drive about two miles (just past Petoskey State Park) to Powell Road; turn east (right) onto Powell Road and go a few hundred feet to the preserve entrance, on the right.

Further Information:
Little Traverse Conservancy
3264 Powell Rd.
Harbor Springs MI 49740

of the property. Information—including pamphlets, brochures and maps—on this and more than 30 other preserves owned by the organization is available at that office.

Fisherman's Island State Park (page 144)

129 THORNE SWIFT NATURE PRESERVE

A cedar swamp even Steven Spielberg would have trouble re-creating and a picture-postcard view of Lake Michigan shoreline are two very good scenic reasons to visit the Thorne Swift Nature Preserve.

The shallow-rooted, sweet-smelling cedars in the swamp here are easily toppled and, as a result, become crazily canted in all directions. Even after being completely blown over, the trees seem to defy destruction, and their trunks make bends contortionists would envy as they strain to reach for sunlight and life. Wildflowers and ferns color this eerie, unworldly landscape, and birds add surrealistic charm.

Three short nature trails, some with extensive sections of boardwalks, lead into the swamp area as well as through an evergreen woodland, around a pond and to the beach.

The preserve's nearly 1,000-foot-long sandy Lake Michigan beach and low dunes are divided into two areas. The largest section, about two-thirds of the shoreline, is off limits to foot traffic. One of the trails, however, leads to an observation platform which extends from the edge of the restricted area out onto a low dune. From the dune, a grand panorma of water and shoreline stretches for several miles in both directions. The platform also allows close-up inspection of the untrammeled dune and the plants

trying to colonize the barren sand. At the smaller public-use shoreline area, also reached by the trails, a 300-foot-long swimming beach is a fine alternative to crowded public Lake Michigan beaches in the area.

The 30-acre preserve is home to a wide variety of plant and animal life. The abundance of wildflowers includes orchids and two of Michigan's threatened plant species, pitcher's thistle and Lake Huron tansy. The park's birdwatchers' checklist identifies 74 species, including 19 varieties of warblers and five different kinds of woodpeckers (including Pileated).

Guided walks begin at the preserve's nature center, which itself houses interpretive displays and exhibits. A park naturalist is usually on duty to welcome visitors, answer questions and highlight seasonal points of interest.

The Little Traverse Conservancy and West Traverse Township cooperatively developed this small but singularly beautful natural area.

County: Emmet

City: Harbor Springs

Fees: Township residents, free; All other visitors, $2.00 per car.

Schedule: Open daily Memorial Day to Labor Day, 10:00 a.m.-one half hour after sunset.

Directions: From Harbor Springs go 3.5 miles west on M-119 to Lower Shore Drive; turn left onto Lower Shore Drive and go one-half mile to the preserve entrance.

Further Information:
Thorne Swift Nature Preserve
Lower Shore Drive
Harbor Springs MI 49740

130
AGNES ANDREAE NATURE PRESERVE

Two thousand feet of frontage on the swift and turbulent Pigeon River is the main attraction to this beautiful, secluded 27-acre preserve. Ten to 15 feet above the state-designated Wild Scenic River, a picturesque suspension bridge reaches from bluff to bluff to connect wild and untamed park property on both banks.

On the west side of the river, where the great majority of the park's property is located, lowland stands of cedar bordering the river bank rise to high bluffs covered by a dense hardwoods and conifers—many of imposing size—which eventually give way to a blueberry plain. No designated trails probe the area, but a well-worn two-track leads from the parking area to a large old log cabin that overlooks the bridge and the fast-moving water. Other faint trails border the river both upstream and downstream.

The much smaller eastern section of the preserve covers a densely wooded high bluff.

The Little Traverse Conservancy, which acquired this small but picturesque preserve in 1983, encourages visitors to roam the entire area but not trespass on neighboring private property, which is well marked. Cross-country skiers are welcome in the winter. Overnight camping with permission from the conservancy is also allowed.

County: Cheboygan

City: Indian River

Fees: None.

Schedule: Open year round.

Directions: On M-68, drive five miles east of Indian River to Onaway Street Road; turn north (left) onto Onaway Street Road and drive 1.5 miles to River Woods Road; turn east (right) onto River Woods Road and go less than a mile to Big Sky Trail. Park on the west side of Big Sky Trail.

Further Information:
   Little Traverse Conservancy
   3264 Powell Rd.
   Harbor Springs MI 49740

131   BURT LAKE STATE PARK

Boaters who put in at one of Burt Lake State Park's two launching sites have a unique opportunity to enjoy the inland beauty of the northern Lower Peninsula. Burt Lake is almost in the middle of a 40-mile, near coast-to-coast string of interconnected lakes and rivers. So boaters from here can go northeast to Cheboygan and Lake Huron or go west to Conway, which is a mere 2.5 miles from Petoskey and Lake Michigan. The park—centrally located near the northern tip of the Lower Peninsula less than 30 miles from Petoskey, Charlevoix, the Straits of Mackinac and the Pigeon River State Forest—is also a good base camp for motor-vehicle exploring.

But that doesn't mean you have to leave Burt Lake State Park to enjoy a variety of scenic beauty or activities. The park certainly holds its own in both areas. Located on the south shore of

Burt Lake and bordered on one side by the Sturgeon River, almost 100 of the park's 405 acres are undeveloped. No marked trails enter this natural area, on the southeast side of Old US-27, but casual hikers, mushroom hunters, birdwatchers and wildflower enthusiasts will find it easy to wander the woods.

For swimmers and sunbathers, a beautiful sandy beach (with a bathhouse) stretches for almost the entire length of the park. Set back from the beach, a stately stand of mature hardwoods and evergreens engulfs a large, pleasant picnic area. Other facilities include a grass-covered campground whose 360 modern sites are shaded but very small and cramped together.

Many anglers rate Burt Lake as the best walleye fishing hole in the state. Fishing is also good for pike and perch.

County: **Cheboygan**

City: **Indian River**

Fees: **$2.00 daily vehicle permit or $10.00 annual vehicle permit valid at all state parks.**

Schedule: **Open year round.**

Directions: **From I-75, take the Indian River exit (310), then drive west a half mile to Old US-27; turn south onto Old US-27 and go less than a mile to the park entrance.**

Further Information:
**Burt Lake State Park
P.O. Box 609
Indian River MI 49749**

132 COLONIAL POINT FOREST

Somehow by chance and luck over the last century and a half, both loggers and forest fires spared heavily wooded Colonial Point. As a result, this peninsula, which protrudes into Burt Lake like an old witch's nose, embraces a valuable and unique natural treasure: a 100- to 150-year-old hardwood forest that includes the largest stand of old-growth red oaks south of the Straits. Scattered among these telephone-pole-straight, towering oaks are equally impressive specimens of maple, beech, white pine, basswood, white ash and black cherry.

This unique piece of Michigan's natural heritage did almost run out of luck in the 1980s, however. A sawmill purchased the tract from its long-time owner, a family trust, then scheduled the area for harvesting.

Fortunately, the Little Traverse Conservancy, the Nature Conservancy and the University of Michigan Biological Station joined forces to save the 283-acre tract. The sawmill agreed to stay the harvesting while the nature organizations, with the help of public donations, began raising the $1.25 million required to buy all of the land. The purchase agreement allowed the groups to obtain 13 separate parcels over a 36-month period, and as long as payments were made on time, no logging would be done. The last payment is due October 1987, when the entire tract will then be managed by the Little Traverse Conservancy for nature study, recreation and research.

The immediacy of this near disaster is forcefully brought home when you wander through the forest and see the great trees tagged for cutting. The logging of these regal giants would have been especially tragic because, for all their imposing size, they are relatively young. Forestry experts, in fact, estimate that many of the trees could live another 200 years.

County: Cheboygan

City: Brutus

Fees: None.

Schedule: No posted hours.

Directions: From US-31 in Brutus, turn east onto Brutus Road and go about 4.5 miles to where the road curves sharply to the north; leave the blacktop and continue east on Brutus Road a short distance to Lathers Road, a two-track which heads south into the forest; park on Brutus Road near Lathers Road.

Further Information:
Little Traverse Conservancy
3264 Powell Rd.
Harbor Springs MI 49740

A walk into this peaceful, beautiful woodland is just about guaranteed to leave you with a feeling of awe and reverence. Though no designated trails mark the area, hikers can use a two-track which cuts though the heart of the preserve from north to south or a foot path that crosses it from east to west. From Lathers Road (itself a two-track that marks part of the preserve's western boundary), both a footpath and another two-track angle east to the area of the largest oaks.

Before visiting, stop at the Little Traverse Conservancy office in Harbor Springs and pick up a map which will show those portions of the preserve currently open to the public.

133 GRASS BAY PRESERVE

Grass Bay Preserve is one of the finest examples of original Great Lakes interdunal wetland habitat—characterized by beach pools, marshes, flats and wetlands, all separated from the lakes by low dunes—found anywhere around the five Great Lakes.

This delicate ecosystem hosts an extraordinary diversity of plant life, including over 300 species of vascular plants, 25 species of orchids and 11 types of conifers. Four of the plants—dwarf lake iris, Lake Huron tansy, pitcher's thistle and Houghton's goldenrod—grow only on the shores of lakes Huron and Michigan. Five plants included on a federally threatened species list and two on a similar state list also thrive here.

From May to September, wildflowers of every description and size literally grow underfoot in the sanctuary. Grass Bay is particularly noted for its abundance of carnivorous plants, including yellow bladderworts, pitcher plants and sun-

dews. Other interesting flowers here include ram's head, lady's-slipper, showy lady's-slipper, Indian paintbrush, blue harebell and orange hawkweed.

The best way to view them is from one or both of the park's two short trails. One descends from US-23 for a half mile through an aspen/birch forest and across a succession of old shoreline ridges to the beach. The other parallels the shoreline. The walk to the beach and back can easily be accomplished in 45 minutes; it's just as easy to get distracted for half a day.

The Nature Conservancy, a private, non-profit organization dedicated to the preservation of natural areas nationwide, considers Grass Bay the *creme de la creme* of the Michigan areas they own. The group's original 80-acre purchase here has—through the generous support of the Feder-

(Continued on page 153.)

134 CHEBOYGAN STATE PARK

Solitude is just about guaranteed along this park's hiking trails and portions of its 4.5 miles of Lake Huron shoreline. Fewer than 50,000 visitors come to this area on Duncan Bay each year, and fewer still explore much of its 1,200 acres. Why? Probably because all trails begin at a campground which is located more than four miles by road from the day-use area. The size of the campground, only 78 sites, also contributes to the less than expected use.

Those who do take the five miles of trails through woodland and along more than two miles of uncrowded lakeshore are rewarded not only with quiet, but also some spectacular views of wildflowers, many of them rare and only found in this type of lakeshore habitat.

Facilities at the day-use area include an excel-

County: Cheboygan

City: Cheboygan

Fees: $2.00 daily vehicle permit or $10.00 annual vehicle vehicle permit valid in all state parks.

Schedule: Open year round.

Directions: Go approximately 3.5 miles south of Cheboygan on US-23.

Further Information:
Cheboygan State Park
4490 Beach Rd.
Cheboygan MI 49721

lent swimming beach. Fishing is good both on the bay and at Little Billy Elliot's Creek.

GRASS BAY PRESERVE
(Continued from page 152.)

ated Garden Clubs of Michigan, who have donated more that $100,000—grown to 400 acres, including a mile of Lake Huron shoreline.

Visitors should be aware that, although they are welcome, this is not only private, but also fragile land. For those reasons the Conservancy asks all visitors to adhere to the following suggestions when visiting this or any other of their preserves:

1. Use trails, where present, to avoid trampling vegetation;

2. Avoid walking in boggy areas due to their sensitivity;

3. Do not remove any poles, stakes, signs or other objects; they may be part of a research project.

County: Cheboygan

City: Cheboygan

Fees: None.

Schedule: Open year round.

Directions: On southbound US-23, drive five miles from Cheboygan to the Nordic Inn; park in the inn's lot after requesting permission (The inn, itself, furnishes informational brochures, which describe points of interest in the preserve and their significance.) the trail starts .1 mile south of the inn on the east side of US-23 near a white road post.

Further Information:
Nature Conservancy
531 N. Clippert St.
Lansing MI 48912

135

OLD MILL CREEK
STATE HISTORICAL PARK

A fascinating glimpse into Michigan's past, scenic views of the Straits, and a 550-acre natural setting that includes one of the few waterfalls in the Lower Peninsula are reasons to visit Michigan's newest state park.

Archaeologists discovered the site of northern Michigan's first industrial settlement here in 1972. Today, while their digs into the past continue, an authentically reconstructed water-powered sawmill, a mill dam, demonstrations and a museum also bring that early Michigan history alive. The sawmill, for example, is an exact duplicate of one located on exactly the same spot on Mill Creek that produced lumber for construction throughout the area from the 1780s to 1839. Artifacts recovered from archaeological digs here, plus exhibits which explain the historical significance of the settlement are displayed in a museum.

A half-mile interpretive nature trail borders Mill Creek, and another makes a one-mile round

County: Cheboygan

City: Mackinaw City

Fees: Adults, $2.00; Children under 13, free.

Schedule: Open daily June 15 through Labor Day, 10:00 a.m.-6:00 p.m.

Directions: Go four miles south of Mackinaw City on US-23.

Further Information:
Old Mill Creek
State Historic Park
Mackinaw City MI 49701

trip to a beaver pond. One of the few waterfalls in the Lower Peninsula adds to the beauty of this natural setting.

Other facilities at the park include a picnic grounds, a concession stand and restrooms.

136 WILDERNESS STATE PARK

For hikers, backpackers, sunbathers, birdwatchers, beachcombers or anyone else who longs to escape urban gridlock and suburban sprawl, it's hard to find a better place to do it than at Wilderness State Park. Located on the western edge of the Straits of Mackinac, 8,000 acres of almost untouched wilderness—including 30 miles of isolated shoreline and a string of unin-

(Continued on page 155.)

WILDERNESS STATE PARK
(Continued from page 154.)

habited islands—reach out into Lake Michigan to separate the Straits from Sturgeon Bay. From the tip of this peninsula, named Waugoshance Point, rugged, rocky outcroppings gradually break down on either side to long expanses of sandy beach. Inland, a pine forest covers one of the largest tracts of wilderness left in the Lower Peninsula.

A network of foot trails—from short nature paths to demanding overnight trips—webs the park. From the eastern end of the road on the park's north side, for example, three trails cut south through the forest until they intersect with the South Boundary Trail, which, as its name suggests, traverses the park's southern limits. Near the western end of that east-west path, the Sturgeon Bay Trail branches off, heads north, and returns to the western end of the park road. Short branch trails shoot off in all directions including to some remote beaches, with several more potential miles of walking.

Several short hiking and nature trails originate near two picturesque campgrounds located on Big Stone Bay. The park's 210 sites are divided between Lakeshore Campground, which stretches along the shore of the bay, and Pines Campground, which stands in a grove of mature pines across the road from the Lakeshore site. A couple of hundred yards east of the Pines Campground, the Pondside Trail—a less than half-mile-long, self-guided (brochure available at park headquarters) nature path—circles a pond. At a dam on the northeast side of the pond, two other trails branch off from the Pondside Trail. The Big Stone Trail splits off at the north side of the dam, then follows a creek for about a mile to where it empties into Lake Michigan. The 2.5-mile Red Pine Trail starts at the south side of the dam, then heads east, circles a large hill named Mt. Nebo, and returns to the campground via the park road.

Those who want to spend more than a day in the backcountry away from civilization, can use one of five overnight cabins or a trail shelter that are scattered along the park's shoreline and perimeter trails. Dirt roads lead to three of the cabins, but the other two as well as the shelter can be reached only by two-mile hikes either down Nebo Trail or along the Lake Michigan shoreline to the tip of Waugoshance Point. If you plan to use these facilities, make reservations far in advance.

The wide range of habitat and good cover at Wilderness State Park make for especially good birdwatching. Over 100 species, including a large number of nesters, have been sighted here, with spring and fall migrations bringing exceptional numbers of songbirds, warblers and hawks. (While Waugoshance Point is the best place to sight large numbers of warblers and songbirds, the best chances for spotting hawks or even a rare Bald Eagle come from the narrowest part of the Straits area near the Mackinac Bridge.) Waterfowl congregate offshore, and the beaches attract numerous shorebirds, including the rare Piping Plover.

Beaver, deer, black bear and the usual diversity of other wildlife found in northern Michigan forests also all roam the peninsula. Numerous native Michigan orchids, including the rare calypso orchid, are among the profusion of wildflowers that grow within the state-park area.

County: Emmet

City: Mackinaw City

Fees: $2.00 daily vehicle permit or $10.00 annual vehicle permit valid in all state parks.

Schedule: Open year round.

Directions: Go 12 miles west of Mackinaw City on Wilderness Park Road.

Further Information:
Wilderness State Park
Box 380
Carp Lake MI 49718

Upper Peninsula

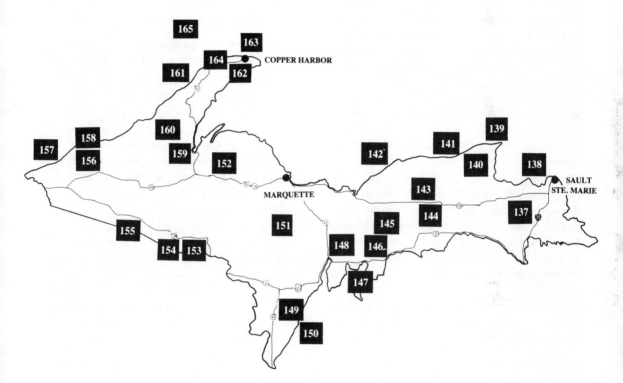

COPPER HARBOR

MARQUETTE

SAULT
STE. MARIE

137
SANDHILL CRANE FEEDING GROUNDS

The magnificent Sandhill Crane, one of Michigan's largest birds, nests in pairs throughout the eastern Upper Peninsula during the summer and, like many Michiganians, spends the winter in Florida. In late summer/early fall, the birds gather in the Rudyard area, about midway between Sault Ste. Marie and the Straits, before beginning their long flight south. It's not surprising, then, that for years from mid-August to mid-September, birdwatchers, too, have flocked to this area.

In 1968, Mr. and Mrs. Kermit Cartwright, working with the Michigan Nature Association, began a project which pleased both cranes and crane watchers. The Cartwrights, by planting part of their grain acreage as food for the birds, created a feeding grounds and refuge for the Sandhill Crane on their farm. For a small fee, birdwatchers can ride a tractor with the Cartwrights into the refuge at feeding times, 6:00 a.m. and 5:00 p.m.

The cranes are no longer bothered by the farm equipment, so by staying on the tractor it is possible to get within 75 feet of the impressive

County: Chippewa

City: Rudyard

Fees: Not available.

Schedule: Mid-August to mid-September, 5:00 a.m. and 6:00 p.m.

Directions: From I-75 about 26 miles north of the Straits, take the Rudyard exit (373); go through town and continue west on County Road H40 to Dayburg; go one mile past Dayburg, then turn north to the Cartwright farm, on the righthand side of the road.

Further Information:
Michigan Nature Association
P.O. Box 102
Avoca MI 48006

birds, some standing nearly five feet tall with a wingspans of six to seven feet. The largest flocks, sometimes totaling as many as 500 cranes, usually arrive later in the season.

138 BRIMLEY STATE PARK

For some beautiful views of the Canadian highlands across Whitefish Bay and Great Lake freighters making their way to the Soo Locks, stop at Brimley State Park, located west of Sault Ste. Marie.

Only one marked path, a one-mile cross-country ski route, probes the park's 151 acres, but several unmarked trails parallel the shoreline

(Continued on page 159.)

139 WHITEFISH POINT

Jutting out into Lake Superior and pointing to Canadian bluffs, Whitefish Point and its adjacent waters during spring migration is one of Michigan's best birdwatching sites. Birdwatchers from at least 14 states and four countries have recorded sightings of 230 species, including Golden and Bald Eagles, plus unusual birds such as the Arctic Tern, Iceland Gull, Arctic Loon, Parasitic Jaeger, Willet, Black Scoter and Surf Scoter. And Whitefish Point is undoubtedly *the* best place in Michigan to spot migrating birds of prey. More than 10,000 hawks, for example, are among the 15,000-20,000 birds of prey that pass through the area each spring.

Why here? Most birds do not like to cross large bodies of water on their long migration flights and will follow shorelines until land runs out and they are forced over open water. So Whitefish Point, the northernmost piece of land in the eastern Upper Peninsula, acts like a giant funnel, channeling birds to the tip, then across Whitefish Bay.

In April, winter finches and hawks lead the migrating hordes, which build steadily through May, then taper off and end in mid-June. April is the best month to spot birds of prey; loons, grebes and ducks arrive in late April and May; and songbirds make their appearance throughout May and in early June.

Since 1978 the Whitefish Point Bird Observatory, an independent non-profit group supported by the Michigan Audubon Society and other or-

(Continued on page 160.)

BRIMLEY STATE PARK
(Continued from page 158.)

or wander through the wooded area south of the modern 270-site campground. A variety of hardwoods, spruce, balsam and tamarack, plus many wildflowers cover the park grounds. And, in season, strawberries, raspberries and thimbleberries will fill the pails of pickers.

Due to the shallow waters of the bay and the shelving of the beach, probably the warmest waters anywhere along Lake Superior roll up onto the sandy shore here. Other facilities include a large picnic area. The cross-country ski trail, suitable for both beginning and intermediate skiers, is groomed weekly.

But except for the fine beach and the beautiful view of Lake Superior, Brimley State Park does not have much to recommend itself to nature lovers. It does, however, make a good stopover or base camp for exploring the northeastern end of the Upper Peninsula and the Sault area of Canada.

County: Chippewa

City: Brimley

Fees: $2.00 daily vehicle permit or $10.00 annual vehicle permit valid in all state parks.

Schedule: Open year round.

Directions: From I-75 about eight miles south of Sault Ste. Marie, exit on M-28 and go west about seven miles to M-221; turn north (right) onto M-221 and go three miles to 6 Mile Road in Brimley; turn east onto 6 Mile Road and go one mile.

Further Information:
Brimley State Park
Route #1, Box 202
Brimley MI 49715

WHITEFISH POINT

(Continued from page 159.)

ganizations, has studied the great flights of birds that have passed through here. Those studies include annual spring bird-banding projects. In 1984, for example, trained banders using mist nets captured, tagged and released 3,069 birds, including 36 Great Horned Owls, 38 Barred Owls, 11 Great Gray Owls, 25 Long-eared Owls, 1,293 Sharp-shinned Hawks and 13 Red-tailed Hawks. If you happen to be there during banding activities, you may, with permission, take photographs. The Observatory also requests that all birdwatchers at Whitefish Point turn in their sighting information to help in the group's studies.

Whitefish Point has not only sheltered birds, but also ships plying the waters of the world's largest freshwater lake. Offering protection from the great storms that sweep across Superior, the point has long been one of the lake's most important landmarks for sailors. A beacon has shown them the way since 1849.

But because countless craft have not quite made it into Whitefish Bay's sheltered waters, it is also known as the "Graveyard of the Great Lakes." The earliest known wreck is that of the schooner *Invincible*, which sank in 1816. The most recent: the already legendary *Edmund Fitzgerald*, which went down in 1975 just 15

County: Chippewa

City: Paradise

Fees: None.

Schedule: No posted hours.

Directions: Go 11 miles north of Paradise on Wire Road.

Further Information:
Whitefish Point Bird Observatory
c/o Michigan Audubon Society
7000 N. Westnedge Ave.
Kalamazoo MI 49007
or
Great Lakes Shipwreck Historical Society
Route 2, Box 279A
Sault Ste. Marie MI 49783

---

miles northwest of the point with all 29 hands aboard. A unique "iron pile" lighthouse—constructed in 1861 to replace the original beacon and now listed in the National Register of Historic Places—is the centerpiece of a museum dedicated by the Great Lakes Shipwreck Historical Society to the memory of all Great Lakes sailors.

Beachcombers and rock hounds will like the long sand, pebble, rock and driftwood-strewn beach.

Pictured Rocks National Lakeshore (page 165)

140 TAHQUAMENON FALLS STATE PARK

Second to the Mackinac Bridge, upper Tahquamenon Falls is probably Michigan's best-known landmark. Two hundred feet across with a sheer drop of nearly 50 feet, this waterfall is the second-largest east of the Mississippi River. At maximum flow, 50,000 gallons of the Tahquamenon River roar over the precipice every second.

Four miles downstream, the less-well-known lower falls—a series of cascading drops and rapids separated into two channels by a large mid-river island—lower the river another 22 feet on its downhill run to Whitefish Bay.

The upper falls overpower; the lower falls

charm. Both are part of a larger scene of spectacular beauty and enchantment that should not be missed by photographers, nature lovers, hikers or sightseers.

A quarter-mile blacktop trail leads from the upper falls parking area through a magnificent beech/maple forest to the upper falls and another paved quarter-mile path, which borders the top of the river gorge. Long flights of stairs descend at one end of this gorge trail to the lip of the falls and at the other end to the base of the falls. Several outstanding views of the falls come from

(Continued on page 163.)

Upper Peninsula

TAHQUAMENON FALLS STATE PARK

(Continued from page 162.)

both trails which, except for the stairs, are easily accessible by wheelchair.

Good views of both channels of the lower falls come from an overlook reached via a short, paved path from the lower falls parking area. Wheelchair access to the overlook is possible if one can manage two or three steps or a short detour by dirt trail around them at the trail's beginning. More intimate views of the lower falls come from a half-mile dirt path which leaves from the overlook, borders the northern riverbank, then leads practically onto the falls. For a different perspective and a close-up view of the falls in both channels, take a rented rowboat to the midriver island and walk the trails that circle it.

Backcountry trails penetrate the 35,000-acre state park, Michigan's second-largest, even deeper and offer a quiet solitude not found near the main attractions. Three loops—Giant Pine (3.7 miles), Wilderness (8.5 miles) and Clark Lake (13 miles)—make up the park's 13-mile Natural Area Pathway. The Clark Lake Loop follows a route used by Indians since the first half of the 1800s or earlier. Other loops pass the remains of an old logging camp and logging railroad grades.

The Pathway begins at the upper falls parking lot, then passes through a variety of habitat including a beech/maple climax forest, with trees over 300 years old, plus a characteristic far-north landscape of pines, muskeg, shallow bog lakes and sandy ridges. And the majestic Tahquamenon River itself flows through the heart of the 13-mile-long park.

Unfortunately, because of state budget cuts, two of the park's trails are closed. Nearly one third of the fulltime park personnel throughout Michigan, including several at Tahquamenon, have been laid off or released since the 1970s. As a result of lack of maintenance, then, both the Climax Forest Interpretive Nature Trail at the upper falls and the trail along the river between the upper and lower falls have been closed.

Other attractions to the park include camping, fishing and picnicking. In late spring and early summer, black flies and mosquitoes can be especially bothersome, so bring a good insect repellant.

County: Chippewa

City: Paradise

Fees: $2.00 daily vehicle permit or $10.00 annual vehicle permit valid in all state parks.

Schedule: Open year round.

Directions: Lower Falls—From Paradise go 12 miles west on M-123. Upper Falls—From Paradise go 14 miles west on M-123.

Further Information:
Tahquamenon Falls State Park
Star Route 48 Box 225
Paradise MI 49768

141 MUSKALLONGE LAKE STATE PARK

Serious hikers and backpackers dream about an area like Muskallonge State Park. A completed portion of the North Country Trail, which will eventually link the Appalachian Trail in Maine to the Lewis and Clark Trail in North Dakota, passes through the 217-acre park as it connects Whitefish Bay, at the mouth of the Tahquamenon River, to Munising, 80 miles to the west at the western end of Pictured Rocks National Lakeshore. Located just about at the halfway point on that section of the North Country Trail, the park is a base for some of the most scenic hiking in the state, for several hours to several days in either direction. Novice backpackers can test their endurance and equipment here, and experts can leave civilization behind for days.

The remote but never-too-far-from-help route to Lake Superior State Forest Campground, five miles west of Muskallonge, for example, makes a good shake-down hike for novice backpackers. From the campground, backpackers can then either return to the state park the same day or camp overnight and explore the complex of trails around the Blind Sucker River before returning the next day. Fifteen miles farther west along the trail is Grand Marais and the eastern entrance to Pictured Rocks National Lakeshore.

East from the state park, the North Country Trail leads 10 miles along the Lake Superior shore to the mouth of the Two Hearted River and the state-forest campground located there. Unlike the trail to the west, hikers along this route, have few if any choices. You're often several miles from any improved road so there's little chance of packing it in and hitching a ride back to the state park. And once at the Two Hearted River State Forest Campground, there's usually no time to return to Muskallonge Lake until the next day. Experienced backpackers, with proper planning, can continue east, then south to Tahquamenon Falls State Park, a journey of approximately 30 miles.

Recreational hikers, on the other hand, don't have to leave the park's boundaries. There's plenty of room to roam on this 1,500-foot-wide strip of land nestled between the shores of Lake Superior and Muskallonge Lake. Beachcombers can stroll the mile of Muskallonge Lake shoreline included in the park, and rockhounds will find agates and other colorful stones along the park's mile of Lake Superior frontage. A 1.5-mile trail from the 179-site campground follows the Lake Superior shore, then circles back through the forest.

In addition to the shaded, somewhat private campsites, other facilities on the north shore of Muskallonge Lake include a swimming beach, a picnic area and a boat ramp. Fishing in the 800-acre lake is good for northern pike and bass. On the Lake Superior side, some old pilings and a few hills of sawdust hint at the existence of a lumbering town that once stood there.

County: Luce

City: Deer Park

Fees: $2.00 daily vehicle permit or $10.00 annual vehicle permit valid in all state parks.

Schedule: Open spring through fall.

Directions: Go 28 miles north of Newberry on County Road H37.

Further Information:
Muskallonge Lake State Park
Route 1, Box 205
Newberry MI 49868

142
PICTURED ROCKS
NATIONAL SHORELINE

The word *spectacular* can hardly be overused in describing the sheer cliffs, waterfalls, beaches, dunes, lakes, streams and forests embraced by Pictured Rocks National Lakeshore. Even the federal government—not particularly noted for overstatements—used the word. "Unique and *spectacular* scenery unmatched elsewhere in the Great Lakes," pronounced a federal report that, in the 1950s, singled out this

County: Alger

City: Munising

Fees: None.

Schedule: During the summer the visitors centers at Grand Sable and Munising are open during the day seven days a week. In the fall, winter and spring seasons, Grand Sable is closed and Munising is open only on weekends from 9:00 a.m. to 5:30 p.m.. Lakeshore headquarters, on Sand Point Road just north of Munising, is open year round, Monday through Friday 7:45 a.m. to 5:15 p.m.

Directions: Take County Road H58 east of Munising or west of Grand Marais.

Further Information:
Pictured Rocks National Lakeshore
P.O. Box 40, Sand Point
Munising MI 49862-0040

section of Lake Superior shoreline from all the Great Lakes coastline for designation as a national park. In 1966, Pictured Rocks—one of the scenic wonders of the nation—became America's first National Lakeshore.

Fifteen miles of 500-million-year-old sandstone cliffs rising 50-200 feet above Lake Superior dominate the western end of this 43-mile-long, three-mile-wide park. During the past hundreds of centuries, wind and water have molded the rock into pillars, arches and caves with such distinct character that they have acquired names such as Lovers Leap, Rainbow Cave, Lower Vase, Miners Castle, Chapel Rock and the Battleships. In two places, waterfalls plummet from the top of the escarpment directly into the blue waters of the world's largest freshwater lake. And, as sunlight plays across its face, the green, red and brown colors of the rock constantly change shade and mood.

Marking the easternmost five miles of the

(Continued on page 166.)

PICTURED ROCKS
(Continued from page 165.)

park, near Grand Marais, are the Grand Sable Banks and Grand Sable Dunes. The Grand Sable Banks, a sand/gravel mixture left by receding glaciers, rise at an angle of 35 degrees to heights of 275 feet above the shoreline. Sitting on top of these banks are the Grand Sable Dunes, five square miles of constantly shifting 80-foot-tall sand mounds.

Stretched between the majestic dunes on the east and the legendary cliffs on the west is a beautiful, unbroken expanse of sand and gravel named 12-Mile Beach.

Hikers and backpackers can walk all or parts of the Lakeshore Trail, a 42.8-mile route that follows the park's entire shoreline. Overnight camping is permitted at several backcountry sites, but those planning to stay overnight along the trail should obtain permits at either of the park's two visitors centers, located in Munising and a few miles west of Grand Marais. If you don't have the desire, time, equipment or stamina to hike the entire trail, you can reach it by automobile at several points and take shorter walks.

Many short trails throughout the park lead to a variety of sights found nowhere else in the state. From the west, the first of these short trails leads from the Munising visitors center to 50-foot-high Munising Falls. Hikers who use this trail can go not only *to* the falls, but because of the large overhang of bedrock that creates them, also pass completely *behind* the cascading water without getting wet. A view of the falls is also accessible by wheelchair.

The second trail is reached by taking County Road H58 approximately four miles east of the visitors center, then Miners Castle Road north four miles to the trailhead. Two miles farther north on Miners Castle Road, a mile path leads from the road through the woods to Miners Falls. At the end of Miners Castle Road, one of the best and certainly easiest-reached views of the cliff line comes from Miners Castle, a nine-story-tall monolithic rock which rises directly from the lake. Legend has it that Father Marquette stood on the point and preached to a large gathering of Indians.

Farther east on H58, which runs the entire length of the park, an easy day hike winds from the parking area at the end Chapel Road to 90-foot-high Chapel Falls, Chapel Rock and a secluded beach on the Lakeshore Trail. Even farther east on H58, several wooded trails circle three small lakes near Little Beaver Lake Campground.

About 15 miles west of Grand Marais, an approach road from H58 passes through a stunning stand of white birch before reaching 12-Mile Beach and its seemingly limitless space for picnicking and beachcombing.

East of 12-Mile Beach, the coastline is treacherous to ships, as evidenced by the remains of several wrecks, but hiking is easy along a 1.5-mile section of the Lakeshore Trail from Hurricane River Campground to the AuSable Lighthouse. The beacon, which is listed in the

(Continued on page 167.)

PICTURED ROCKS
(Continued from page 166.)

National Register of Historic Places, has been cited as one of the finest examples of late-19th-century lighthouse architecture in the country.

Two and a half miles east of the lighthouse and reached either by a somewhat rougher section of the foot trail or by car from H58 is the Log Slide. One of the best panoramic views of the Grand Sable Banks comes from this area where late-19th-century lumberjacks slid logs down the banks to waiting ships. To get a closer look at the Banks and Grand Sable Dunes, take either of two half-mile trails from the parking lot just inside the park entrance west of Grand Marais. One trail climbs to the dune area; the other drops into the gorge of Sable Creek and passes beside cascading Sable Falls.

The Lakeshore Trail and most of the branches mentioned here are open in the winter for snowshoeing, cross-country skiing and cold-weather camping.

Sites at three campgrounds—Hurricane River, 12-Mile Beach and Little Beaver Lake—are primitive but accessible by by car. Camping is free and available on a first-come, first-served basis. Throughout the summer at the campgrounds, park rangers present "Pictured Rocks—Its Place in History," "The First Residents—Native Americans," "Lighthouse and Shipwrecks Walk" and other interpretive programs.

Information on hiking, camping, programs, trail maps and much more is available at the two visitors centers.

143 FOX RIVER PATHWAY

Ernest Hemingway liked this area so much that he wrote a short story about it. Today, on the little-known and seldom-used Fox River Pathway, experienced backpackers can enjoy beautiful scenery and adventure little changed from when the famous author visited 60 years ago.

Hemingway made his backpacking, trout-fishing trip to the Fox River in 1919 or 1920, while he recovered from war wounds. The trip provided the inspiration for one of his famous Nick Adams stories, "The Big Two-hearted River." The fact that there is a Two Hearted River not too far from the Fox confused Hemingway fans for awhile, but the author, in a letter to his father in 1925, identified the Fox River trip as the source of his story.

The area had gained some notoriety even before Hemingway's story. During the white-pine boom of the late 1800s, Seney—largely because of a national (and at least partially fabricated) expose of the city's prostitution, white-slavery operations, saloons and shady boom-town characters—became known as "Hell Town U.S.A." The main street of Seney was, in fact, at the time lined with 21 saloons and punctuated at both ends with competing brothels.

Today, the 27.5-mile Fox River Pathway begins near Seney, but backpackers passing through the peaceful village can only try to conjure up a mental image of the Seney of the last century.

The strenuous three- to four-day hike to Kingston Lake State Forest Campground, four miles short of Pictured Rocks National Lakeshore, begins at the Seney Township Campground, on the Fox River just north of town. Twenty-one numbered stops along the route mark out forest-management projects, remnants of the logging era and other points of interest. Still visible along the Pathway, for example, are the foundations of a lumber camp, an abandoned logging railroad, traces of a winter ice road and ruts left by the big wheels used to move logs during the summer months. Farther up the trail, a turn-of-the-century logging dam still holds back the waters of Stanley Lake. And near the end of the trail on the Kingston Plains, hundreds of white-pine stumps jut from the ground as a memorial to the great trees.

The path never wanders far from the Fox River, which, as Hemingway discovered, is an excellent trout stream. Numerous stands of jack pine—a natural-succession tree left in the wake of lumbering and the almost inevitable forest fires of that era—line the trail. The path also passes by red-pine plantations and, near Stanley Lake, a wild-blueberry management area which is regularly burned to stimulate new growth and improve picking. Between the two ends of the Pathway, camping is permitted at both the Stanley Lake and Fox River State Forest campgrounds.

County: Schoolcraft

City: Seney

Fees: None.

Schedule: Open all summer.

Directions: Drive north of Seney about one mile on Fox River Road to Seney Township Park.

Further Information:
Michigan Department of Natural Resources
Box 30034
Lansing MI 48909

144
SENEY NATIONAL WILDLIFE REFUGE

About 100 years ago, humans began assaulting the vast Upper Peninsula area of marshes, rivers, pools, creeks, sandy ridges and bogs known as the Great Manistique swamp. After nearly 50 years of exploitation, parcel after disfigured parcel was then abandoned. But careful and patient reconstruction and rehabilitation by state and federal agencies brought the area back to life, then returned it to nature's grand design as the Seney Wildlife Refuge.

And life has been more than just restored at Seney—it thrives there. Over 200 species of birds, for example, have been spotted in the 95,000-acre refuge. It is now recognized as one of the best birding spots in the Upper Peninsula and *the* best woodcock habitat in the nation. Mallards, Black Ducks, Ring-necked Ducks, Common and Hooded Mergansers, Blue-winged Teal and Wood Ducks nest in the area, and snipe regularly feed along the pool edges. Pileated

(Continued on page 170.)

SENEY NATIONAL WILDLIFE REFUGE

(Continued from page 169.)

Woodpeckers, warblers, sparrows, Kingfishers and several species of grouse, also help fill the bird checklist available at the Visitor's Center. And beaver, black bear, otter, muskrat, fox, mink, coyote and the rare Eastern timber wolf are among 50 species of mammals that call the refuge home.

In short, Seney today is much like it was for centuries before lumbermen invaded the area in the late 19th century and nearly clear-cut the magnificent stands of white pine. Deliberate and accidental fires razed the timber barons' slashings, and a development company later drained the land and sold it to farmers. But nothing grew in the poor soil, so parcel by parcel, as discouraged farmers failed to pay their taxes and left, the land reverted to the state.

In 1935, at the urging of the Michigan Conservation Department, the federal government took over the land and created the Seney National Wildlife Refuge. Crews from the Civilian Conservation Corps and other Depression-era agencies moved in to begin the extensive restoration work. They constructed roads, drainage ditches, dikes and an elaborate water-control system, all of which in turn created 7,000 acres of open water in 21 major pools to attract and shelter waterfowl.

A captive flock of Canadian Geese were released, and the goslings born to them were allowed to migrate south in the fall. The next spring, they returned. In 1936, for the first time in decades, geese had come back to Seney, and they have done so each spring since. By 1944 a firmly established flock thrived in the refuge, and today their descendants—adults and goslings, both looking for handouts—act as unofficial hosts at the Visitors Center parking lot.

Man did not perform restorative surgery on the entire parcel, however, and 25,000 acres have remained untouched since the logging era. Within this wilderness area, low sandy dunes created by prehistoric glaciers have been formed by the wind into long ribbon-like ridges. Lines of these brush- and tree-covered ridges run like parallel islands through the sections of the wilderness but particularly at 9,500 acres known as Strangmoor Bog, which, because of its unique character, has been designated a Registered National Landmark.

Man and nature together, then, created one of only two national wildlife refuges in the state (the other is Shiawassee, in Saginaw County). This living tourist attraction draws 50,000 people a year, many of whom go out of their way to see this fascinating area.

Plan to spend two hours to a full day here. A good place to start is on the Marshland Wildlife Drive, a seven-mile auto tour that begins near the Visitors Center, then winds through the eastern edge of the refuge on one-way roads past panoramic views of the marshland and man-made pools. Feel free to park your car anywhere along the drive where there is room to pull off. And you may want to do it often, as excellent views of Great Blue Herons, Sandhill Cranes and many other shorebirds and waterfowl seem to come at every turn. Bald Eagles, too, nest in the refuge, and during the drive you normally can spot the one of at least two nests that is usually

County: Schoolcraft

City: Seney

Fees: None.

Schedule: Visitors Center—Open mid-May to September 30 during daylight hours.
Marshland Auto Tour—Open mid-June to September 30.

Directions: Drive three miles north of Germfask on M-77.

Further Information:
Seney National Wildlife Refuge
Seney MI 49883

(Continued on page 171.)

SENEY NATIONAL WILDLIFE REFUGE

(Continued from page 170.)

active. Plan to spend at least an hour on the drive and pick up a self-guiding brochure at either the Visitors Center or the beginning of the tour. Significant points of interest along the drive are marked by numbered posts which correspond to numbered descriptions in the pamphlet.

You can get more intimate views of the refuge from two nature trails. The 1.4-mile Pine Ridge Nature Trail, for example, starts to the right of the Visitors Center, circles one of the smaller pools, passes through a wooded area, then skirts a larger pool before returning to the parking lot. A half-mile path connects this trail with the Wigwam Picnic Area and, a half mile south, the Visitors Center. The one-mile Driggs River Nature Trail, located eight miles west of the village of Seney at the Driggs Picnic Area, heads south into the refuge from M-28. The wilderness area is open to limited hiking and study from August 1 through September 14 only. Irisis, wild roses, lady's-slippers, bunch flowers and other wildflowers line the trails and the auto route in early spring and summer.

Exhibits and displays at the Visitors Center (almost worth a trip in itself) illustrate and explain the history of northern forests and the refuge as well as the principles and purposes of wildlife management at Seney. Each week a different nature film is shown hourly in the auditorium.

Facilities at the two picnic areas include tables, fireplaces, toilets and water.

145　PALMS BOOK STATE PARK

At Palms Book State Park near Indian Lake, 20 separate inlets constantly bubble underground water through grey-white sand to form the state's largest spring. Called Kitch-iti-ki-pi (big cold water), the large elliptical pond measures 300 feet long, 175 feet wide and 40 feet deep.

This beautifully clear pool, its precipitous sides covered with moss and sunken trees and its shore fringed with pines, is one of the most picturesque spots in the state. If you drop a penny into the crystal-clear waters, you can watch it disappear into the roiling sand 40 feet below. You can also see huge trout swimming near the bottom as well as in the shallows near shore.

For the best views (and a bit of exercise), take a raft ride across the pool. A large iron cable strung from shore to shore passes through two guides at each end of the 15-by-15-foot raft, and passengers have to winch themselves across the pond. But the effort is well worthwhile, and the quiet beauty of the scene seems to effect all visitors. Voices from the raft are almost always rev-

County: Schoolcraft

City: Manistique

Fees: $2.00 daily vehicle permit or $10.00 annual state park vehicle permit valid in all state parks.

Schedule: Open all summer.

Directions: From US-2 six miles west of Manistique, take M-149 north approximately eight miles to the park.

Further Information:
Michigan Department of Natural Resources
P.O. Box 30034
Lansing MI 48909

erently hushed.

Facilities here, located away from the main attraction, include a picnic area and a park store that sells souvenirs and snacks.

146　INDIAN LAKE STATE PARK

Indian Lake Park's split personality doubles the possibilities for all outdoor lovers, but especially campers and swimmers. The park's mile of beachfront on the warm, shallow Upper Peninsula lake plus its inland area are divided between a south-shore and a west-shore unit. Together the parcels add up to 847 acres.

At the center of the older south-shore unit, the rich heritage and way of life of the Indians who resided on the shores of Indian Lake as late as the 1850s lives on in a museum and an interpretive trail. How the Indians used a wide variety of

(Continued on page 173.)

Upper Peninsula

147 FAYETTE STATE PARK

Born 1867. Died circa 1891. Reborn in the 1960s as a state park, the town of Fayette—through careful restoration of 19 of its rugged, durable original structures—has become Michigan's only completely restored ghost town and a living Victorian America industrial museum.

The fascinating historic townsite is only one of many reasons to visit this 711-acre park located on the beautiful, noncommercialized, and aptly named Garden Peninsula. The village's natural setting on Snail Shell Harbor—with 90-foot-high cliffs that look like they were hand-chiseled out of the white limestone—is one of the most picturesque in the state. And stretched along the Big Bay De Noc shoreline south of the village are an 80-site campground, a magnificent sandy swimming beach and a picnic area. Back from the scenic shoreline, maple, beech, birch, ash, pine and spruce cover most of the park's acreage.

Two trails, both slightly more than a mile long, wind through the beautiful surroundings of this out-of-the-way corner of Michigan. One circles through woods filled with Dutchman's britches, trillium, violets and other spring flowers. Many excellent scenic photographic opportunities come from the other trail, a shoreline route which connects the beach, picnic area, campground and ghost town.

But for most of the approximately 100,000 visitors who come here each year, the ghost town is

(Continued on page 174.)

INDIAN LAKE STATE PARK

(Continued from page 172.)

common plants for food, medicine, tools and construction, for example, is explained in the self-guiding brochure for the short Chippewa Trail, which begins and ends at the artifact-filled museum.

Another short (one-mile-long) hiking trail begins at the south shore's picnic area, then winds through the western end of the unit, crosses Dufour Creek, and returns to the park road near the entrance. Other facilities at the south-shore unit include a boat ramp and 157 grassy, lightly shaded campsites strung along the shoreline.

At the newer (opened in the mid-1960s) and smaller west-shore unit, a heavily wooded 144-site campground has more shade and privacy, but it is several hundred yards from the lake.

Because Indian Lake is exceptionally shallow, it is an unusually warm lake for the Upper Peninsula. Over 90 percent of its 8,400 acres are less than 15 feet deep, and its maximum depth is only 18 feet. As a result, the park's mile of sandy beach slopes gently far out into the lake.

County: Schoolcraft

City: Manistique

Fees: $2.00 daily vehicle permit or $10.00 annual vehicle permit valid in all state parks.

Schedule: Open all summer.

Directions: South-shore Unit—Go five miles west of Manistique on County Road 442.
West-shore Unit—Go west and north of the south-shore unit on County Road 455.

Further Information:
Indian Lake State Park
Route 2 Box 2500
Manistique MI 49854

FAYETTE STATE PARK

(Continued from page 173.)

the main attraction. In 1867 the Jackson Mining Company founded the town (and named it after one of their managers, Fayette Brown) for the sole purpose of producing pig iron from ore mined by the company at Negaunee. The site at a natural harbor on Big Bay De Noc was ideal for the operation because it also had an abundance of two other essential ingredients for smelting iron: lime, plus hardwood for charcoal. Fayette produced high-quality pig iron for more than 20 years, and at the height of its prosperity, more than 500 people lived in the busy company town.

But the increasingly costly charcoal process couldn't compete with the coal-fired smelters in the east. When the company could no longer turn a profit, jobs and people disappeared, and the town quickly withered and died. Except for a brief interlude as a resort town, Fayette was abandoned until the 1960s when it was acquired by the state. Today 19 buildings still stand, including the hotel, opera house, superintendent's home, doctor's office and house, machine shop

County: Delta

City: Garden

Fees: $2.00 daily vehicle permit or $10.00 annual vehicle permit valid in all state parks.

Schedule: Spring and fall, 9:00 a.m.-10:00 p.m.; Summer, 9:00 a.m.-8:00 p.m.

Directions: From US-2 approximately 16 miles west of Manistique, turn south on Delta County Road 483 and go approximately 15 miles south.

Further Information: Fayette State Park 13700 13.25 Lane Garden MI 49835

and a large portion of the furnace complex. Many of the buildings have been fully restored inside and out and are open to the public.

148

BAY DE NOC—GRAND ISLAND TRAIL

The Bay De Noc—Grand Island Trail follows an old Chippewa Indian portage which connected Lake Superior to Lake Michigan. Indians and early explorers used this trail to transport canoes, supplies and trade-goods between the two lakes.

The trail, which begins just west of Rapid River near the head of Little Bay De Noc, follows the valley of the Whitefish River for most of its 36-mile length and never strays far from County Road 509. Blazed with dash-and-dot marks on trees, the trail meanders through stands of jack pine, red pine and ash in the southern half of its south-to-north route. In the

(Continued on page 175.)

149   CEDAR RIVER PATHWAY

Four loops, from two to seven miles long, make up the more than seven miles of hiking and cross-country ski trails of the Cedar River Pathway, located in the Escanaba River State Forest. The first three loops border the Cedar River for much of their length, and the fourth and longest circuit crosses River Road before returning to the trailhead at the state-forest campground on the banks of the Cedar River .75 miles east of River Road.

The winter starting point for cross-country skiers is on River Road six miles north of M-53.

County: Menominee

City: Cedar River

Fees: None.

Schedule: Open year round.

Directions: Go two miles northeast of Cedar River on M-35 to River Road, turn north (left) onto River Road and drive six miles to the entrance to Cedar River Forest Campground.

Further Information:
Michigan Department of Natural Resources
Box 30028
Lansing MI 48909

BAY DE NOC—GRAND ISLAND TRAIL
(Continued from page 174.)

northern half, it zig-zags across CR 509 and winds over maple- and birch-covered hills before ending at M-94 approximately 10 miles short of Munising and Lake Superior. Plans call for the trail to be both widened (for horseback riding) and lengthened to eventually reach Lake Superior across from Grand Island.

Backcountry camping is permitted anywhere along the trail. Also, about seven miles north of the trailhead just after crossing Haymeadow Creek, you can reach Haymeadow Creek State Forest Campground (and the only potable water on the entire trail) by taking the first two-track half a mile east, then CR509 a half mile north. Facilities at the 17-site campground include pit toilets.

Bay De Noc—Grand Island trail is open in the winter for cross-country skiing.

County: Delta

City: Rapid River

Fees: None

Schedule: No posted hours.

Directions: From US-2 approximately two miles east of Rapid River, turn north onto County Road 509 (identified on state road maps as H-05) and go two miles north to the trail parking area.

Further Information:
Michigan Department of Natural Resources
Box 30028
Lansing MI 48909

150 J. W. WELLS STATE PARK

Four trails wind through extensive tracts of virgin pine, beech and hemlock, plus dense stands of cedar and spruce that stretch for three miles along the shore of Green Bay. The longest trail, the three-mile Picnic Area Loop, circles the southern, more heavily used area of the park. The 1.1-mile Evergreen Trail and the 1.3-mile Timber Trail wind through more isolated sections of the 974-acre park north of the campground. And the 1.6-mile Cedar River Trail heads north to the park's 1,400 feet of banks on the Cedar River.

Numerous wildflowers line the trails, and wildlife spotted here includes birds, small game and a few white-tailed deer. Three shelters are spaced along the trails.

Hikers or beachcombers can also walk the park's three miles of fine, sandy Green Bay beach. Facilities near the beach include a playground, a bathhouse and a large picnic area.

The campground—162 grass-covered, well-shaded sites, including 32 with beach frontage—

County: Menominee

City: Cedar River

Fees: **$2.00 daily vehicle permit or $10.00 annual vehicle permit valid in all state parks.**

Schedule: **Open year round.**

Directions: **Go 30 miles south of Escanaba on M-35.**

Further Information:
**J.W. Wells State Park
M-35
Cedar River MI 49812**

also hugs the bay. Amenities at each of five rentable, rustic frontier cabins, located a mile north of the campground, include nine double bunks, a barrel stove, firewood and a saw.

In the winter, the seven miles of trails are open and groomed weekly for cross-country skiing.

151 ANDERSON LAKE PATHWAY

Short and varied hikes are the calling card to the Anderson Lake Pathway, located in the heart of the Escanaba River State Forest. The more than 4.3 miles of hiking and cross-country skiing trails here are divided into three loops. The shortest, 2.5 miles long, circles low swampy areas and the twin Flacks Lakes. A second loop makes a 3.5-mile circuit, and the longest swings the full 4.3 miles through the area.

The summer starting point is on Anderson Lake's northwest shore just north of the Anderson Lake State Forest Campground. In the winter, cross-country skiers must start at the campground entrance road on County Road 557.

County: Marquette

City: Gwinn

Fees: None.

Schedule: Open year round.

Directions: From the junction of M-53 and County Road 557 about three miles east of Gwinn, go south on CR557 and drive five miles to the entrance to the state-forest campground.

Further Information:
Michigan Department of Natural Resources
Box 30028
Lansing MI 48909

152 VAN RIPER STATE PARK

Several miles of trails at this 1,044-acre park, which embraces the eastern end of Lake Michigamme in western Marquette County, lead to a beaver pond, pass old mine shafts, briefly border the Peshekee River and climb hills to several scenic overlooks of the lake and the hilly tree-covered terrain. All trails are on the north side of US-41, which bisects the park from east to west.

Facilities at Lake Michigamme, which is on the south side of the highway, include a 226-site campground, a swimming beach, a boat-launching ramp and a large picnic area. Anglers report good takes of perch, pike, whitefish, muskies and walleye from the lake.

County: Marquette

City: Champion

Fees: $2.00 daily vehicle permit or $10.00 annual vehicle permit valid in all state parks.

Schedule: Open spring through fall.

Directions: Go about a mile west of Champion on US-41.

Further Information:
Van Riper State Park
Champion MI 49814

153 BEWABIC STATE PARK

You get four for one when you visit Bewabic State Park, nestled on the northwestern shore of Fortune Lake. Bewabic's Fortune Lake, you see, is one in a chain of four lakes, all interconnected and all named Fortune Lake. Hikers, unfortunately, can't reach all four lakes, but canoeists can.

Hikers can circle one Fortune Lake, however, by taking an hour-long walk along a trail which heads south from the park's campground, then winds back north along the lakeshore before ending at the day-use area. Ruffled Grouse and Pileated Woodpeckers are just two of the many fascinating birds you might spot in the heavily wooded area of the 275-acre park. And while resting on one of the many benches spaced along the trail, you might hear the forlorn sound of a loon or even see one the increasingly rare birds in the park's waters.

At the campground, 144 modern sites are scattered in a wooded area of mixed hardwoods and evergreens. Wooded buffer strips separate most

County: Iron

City: Crystal Falls

Fees: **$2.00 daily vehicle permit or $10.00 annual vehicle permit valid in all state parks.**

Schedule: **Open spring, summer and fall.**

Directions: **Go four miles west of Crystal Falls on US-2.**

Further Information:
**Bewabic State Park
1933 US-2 West
Crystal Falls MI 49920**

sites, giving each camper a degree of privacy regrettably lacking at most other state-park campgrounds.

Facilities at the day-use area include a picnic area, a beach and a playground.

154 LAKE OTTAWA RECREATION AREA

More than 14 miles of hiking trails are the main draw to this parcel of Ottawa National Forest land. Birdwatchers, wildflower enthusiasts, photographers and other outdoor lovers will all find something to hold their interest on the varied routes, which wind over steep hills, through hardwood forests and across gently rolling countryside with many panoramic views from the higher elevations.

The trail mileage is divided almost equally between two systems. The Ge-Che trail System's six loops web the south shore of Lake Ottawa.

(Continued on page 179.)

LAKE OTTAWA RECREATION AREA

(Continued from page 178.)

Connected to the Ge-Che system on its west end is another series of loops, the Hagerman-Brule Lake Trail System, which probes the land west of Hagerman Lake. Parts of both trails are open in the winter for cross-country skiing.

Facilities and activities at Lake Ottawa include a 32-site lakeshore campground, a short interpretive trail, boat access, swimming, fishing and a large picnic area.

County: Iron

City: Iron River

Fees: None.

Schedule: No posted hours.

Directions: From Iron River go west on US-2 approximately one mile to M-73; turn south (left) onto M-73 and go less than a mile to USFS Road 101; turn west (right) onto USFS 101 and go about five miles to Lake Ottawa Recreation Area.

Further Information:
Ottawa National Forest
Watersmeet MI 49969

155 SYLVANIA RECREATION AREA

Twenty-nine secluded backcountry campgrounds plus 26 miles of scenic trails through 21,000 acres of pristine wilderness add up to a wealth of potentially outstanding hiking and camping experiences.

The list of other plusses for this section of the Ottawa National Forest on the Wisconsin/Michigan border in the far western Upper Peninsula is impressive. Countless crystal-clear lakes host bass, lake trout, pike and walleye. Motorized traffic on land is prohibited, and boats with motors are allowed on only two lakes. Canoeing is permitted on all lakes, and paddlers can take extensive canoe camping trips by using the many marked portages and lakeside campsites. Wildlife is abundant. Deer, coyote, fox, mink, porcupine and bear are commonly seen here, and two relatively rare birds in Michigan, the Bald Eagle and the Loon, nest in the area. Maple, birch, hemlock, spruce and fir, much of it virgin timber, cover the area, and fall color here is spectacular.

Twenty-six miles of trails network the lakes and forests of the Sylvania Recreation Area, which was purchased by the government in 1966 from a hunting and fishing club. Hikers can plan anything from a scenic day-hike to a several-day-long backcountry expedition. The trails are also open in the winter for cross-country skiing.

A 48-unit tent/trailer campground accessible from Forest Road 535, makes a good base camp. Overnight hikers can stay at any of 84 wilderness-type campsites at 29 backcountry campgrounds. To ensure low human impact on the area (and guarantee relative seclusion), each backcountry campground has only three sites, each with tent space, a table and a fire ring.

Other facilities at Sylvania include a picnic area, plus a sandy swimming beach accessible by car at the north end of Clark Lake, west of the tent/trailer campground.

Exhibits, slide shows and summer evening nature programs are activities at the Ottawa National Forest Visitors Information Center, a quarter mile east of the junction of US-45 and US-2 in Watersmeet. Information about the Sylvania Recreation Area and the entire Ottawa National Forest is available there, and a quarter-mile self-guided nature trail winds through a few of the Center's 25 acres. The interpretive building is open from 8:00 a.m. to 5:00 p.m., April through October.

County: Gogebic

City: Watersmeet

Fees: None.

Schedule: Open year round.

Directions: On US-2 from Watersmeet, drive west four miles to County Road 535 (Thousand Island Lake Road); turn south (left) onto CR 535 and go approximately four miles to the visitor information station.

Further Information:
District Forest Ranger
Ottawa National Forest
Watersmeet MI 49969

156

GOGEBIC RIDGE HIKING TRAIL
and
NORTH COUNTRY TRAIL
(Bergland Section)

One completed Michigan portion of the North Country Trail, which will eventually link the Appalachian Trail in Maine to the Lewis and Clark Trail in North Dakota, connects Porcupine Mountains State Park to Norwich. Called the Bergland Section, this 25-mile stretch holds the potential for a true wilderness experience, including some of the most rugged, remote and scenic hiking in the state. Backcountry camping is permitted anywhere along the route, most streams and rivers are unbridged, contact with other people is rare, and, for most of its length, the trail is several miles from the nearest road. Hikers embarking on this section, then, should be in good physical condition and should carry a

---

County: Ontonagon

City: Merriweather

Fees: None.

Schedule: Open year round.

Directions: From M-28 at Merriweather, turn north onto FR 789 and go one mile to the trailhead.

Further Information:
District Ranger
Ottawa National Forest
Bergland MI 49910

---

map available from Ottawa National Forest headquarters.

Neatly intersecting the Bergland Section at almost its halfway point is the Gogebic Ridge Trail, a relatively new 8.7-mile route through bogs and along ridge lines in the Ottawa National Forest. This trail, built by the Youth Conservation Corps in 1976, begins on road FR 789 one mile north of Merriweather. The path heads southeast, bends around Pendock Pond, then rises to a beautiful scenic overlook of Lake Gogebic. From there, the trail turns north and crosses rough and rugged country until it intersects with M-64 three miles north of Bergland and eight miles south of White Pine. The trail crosses M-64, then ends a half mile east at the Bergland Section of the North Country Trail.

From the junction of the two trails, hikers have three choices. One: They can retrace their steps back to FR 789.

Two: They can head west on a potential 15-mile backpacking venture to Porcupine Mountains Wilderness State Park. From the North Country/Gogebic Ridge intersection, the trail turns north, crosses the west branch of the Big Iron River, then meanders westerly along the river valley until ending at the South Boundary Road at Porcupine Mountains. Shallow depres-

(Continued on page 182.)

157 BLACK RIVER HARBOR AREA

Seven breathtaking waterfalls along one of Michigan's finest whitewater rivers is the main draw to this picturesque harbor area tucked away in the extreme western Upper Peninsula. In just one 10-mile stretch of County Road 513—which follows the Black River valley for 15 miles from Bessemer north to Black River Harbor on Lake Superior—short .25- to 1.5-mile trails through hardwood and hemlock forests lead to splendid views of six of the falls: Algonquin, Great Conglomerate, Gorge, Potawatomi, Sandstone, and Rainbow. Because of its unusual beauty and unique design, including a series of stairways and observation platforms, the trail to Gorge and Potawatomi falls has been designated a National Recreation Trail.

In this section of the Ottawa National Forest, you can also hike alongside the last 10 miles of the Black River to where it empties into Lake Superior. A 30-mile segment of the yet-to-be-completed North Country Trail that will eventually link the east-coast Appalachian Trail to the Lewis and Clark Trail in North Dakota begins near the Copper Peak Ski Flying Hill on CR

County: Gogebic

City: Bessemer

Fees: None.

Schedule: Trails—No posted hours. Campground—Open June 1-Labor Day.

Directions: From US-2 in Bessemer drive north on County Road 513.

Further Information:
Bessemer Ranger District
500 N. Moore St.
Bessemer MI 49911

513, parallels the river and passes all seven major falls before turning east at Rainbow Falls and heading toward Porcupine Mountains State Park.

Facilities at a 41-site campground at Black River Harbor include flush toilets, a trailer dump station, a picnic area and a children's playground.

GOGEBIC RIDGE
NORTH COUNTRY TRAIL

(Continued from page 181.)

sions and old foundations along the way are the only reminders of the area's rich lumbering and copper mining history.

Three: Hikers can turn east and walk approximately 10 miles to the North Country Trail's end, just beyond Norwich. This section intermittently follows several escarpments offering scenic views of the surrounding area and dips into lowlands to cross several creeks. Approximately six miles east of the Gogebic/North Country intersection, the North Country Trail crosses Forest Road 222. From that point, a side trip south on FR 222 about a mile to a short well-marked trail that leads to picturesque Cascade Falls is well worth the effort. The North Country trail continues from FR 222 another 2.5 miles to its end at Forest Road 219 two miles west of Norwich Road and 10 miles north of Matchwood.

The Gogebic Ridge Trail is open in the winter for cross-country skiing.

—Photo by Craig Date—

Conglomerate Falls (Black River Harbor, page 182)

Upper Peninsula

158

PORCUPINE MOUNTAINS WILDERNESS STATE PARK

Porcupine Mountains' 58,335 acres of untamed rivers, spectacular waterfalls, rapids, gorges, crystal-clear lakes, rugged Lake Superior coastline, and low mountains covered by the world's largest virgin pine/hemlock forest seem to swallow up anyone who ventures very far from its few civilized or developed areas. Peace and solitude, then, are just about guaranteed—actually, almost hard to avoid—in Michigan's largest state park and one of the last large wilderness areas between the Appalachian and Rocky mountains

Easy walks to breathtaking scenery, multi-day rugged backpacks deep into the interior, and just about every kind of experience in between are all available on the 85 miles of trails that network Michigan's premier state park.

A short path from the parking lot at the end of M-107, for example, leads to the rim of a vertical cliff and the park's easiest-to-reach, most-photographed attraction: a view of Lake of the Clouds. From this precipitous cliff on mid-America's highest mountain range, you can see miles of pristine wilderness stretching in three directions. From the viewpoint, easy trails lead for short distances in either direction along the escarpment. Or if you really want to stretch your legs, take the steep trail down to the Lake of the Clouds and back, about an hour's round trip.

Other short, easy trails include the the East and West River trails (on the west end of the park off County Road 519) which border both sides of the Presque Isle River in its final mile to Lake Superior. In a rush of rapids and whitewater, the river in this stretch drops a total of 125 feet through gorges and over three stunning waterfalls. The two trails, however, are easy walking over generally level terrain. On the east end of the park two miles south of M-107 on South Boundary Road, another short trail, the Union Mine Trail, wanders for a mile through the woods, alongside the Little Union River and past the ruins of the Union Copper Mine. Interpretive signs spaced along this easy path highlight and explain the natural and human history of the area.

An elaborate network of interconnecting longer trails—ranging in length from four miles to the 16-mile-long Lake Superior Trail—makes it possible to hike the rugged, wild interior of the park for several days without backtracking. A map of the trail system is absolutely essential in planning and successfully executing a hike on the intricate web of steep climbs, sharp descents and many stream crossings. Access to the interior from the west end of the park comes near the campground. At the east end of the park about three miles from the campground there, several of the trails intersect or begin along M-107. Some hikers set up camp at Union Bay and walk in from there.

Backcountry camping is allowed but not within a quarter mile of any roads, cabins, shelters or designated scenic areas. Backpackers can also use any of nine cabins and several Adirondack shelters, spaced through the interior

(Continued on page 185.)

PORCUPINE MOUNTAINS STATE PARK

(Continued from page 184.)

of the park and reached only by foot. Amenities at each of the cabins, which must be reserved in advance, include a wood stove, a sink, cupboards, a table, chairs, a kitchen, cooking and dining utensils, a saw, an axe and four to six bunks with mattresses. The Adirondack shelters, available on a first-come first-served basis, contain only bunks. All backpackers must register at one of the visitor centers before venturing into the backcountry.

Modern campgrounds are located at both the east and west ends of the park. Ninety-five sites on an open grassy shelf overlooking the rocky Lake Superior shore make up the Union Bay Campground, at the east entrance. Facilities there include electricity, flush toilets and hot showers. Facilities at the 88-site Presque Isle Campground, at the west entrance, include flush toilets and hot showers but no electricity. Picnic areas complement both campgrounds and are also scattered along the road to Lake of the Clouds.

In June and July, black flies greatly outnumber tourists, so bring a good supply of effective insect repellent. Numerous black bears also roam the park, so campers should hang all food at least 10 feet off the ground 100 feet from camp and never cook or keep food in tents.

In addition to black flies and bears, a wide variety of other wildlife and flora thrives in the park. Mergansers and gulls, which inhabit the Lake Superior shoreline, and forest-dwelling warblers and woodpeckers are among the 194 bird species that have been spotted in the park. Countless wildflowers, shrubs and 26 different kinds of trees grow within the park boundaries. The low, thickly forested hills, in fact, are responsible for the park's name—they reminded early Indians of crouching porcupines.

Formation of this slanted, twisted mountain range, one of the world's oldest, began over 1,000 million years ago with geological faults, mammoth warping of the rock, and flows of lava containing copper and traces of silver.

Copper mining was briefly tried here in 1848 but never proved profitable. Indians in the area traded chunks of pure silver, but folk lore tells of only one white man who ever found the source of the nuggets and he supposedly disappeared without a trace. In 1872, silver was discovered near Silver City, at the east entrance to the park. But after a wild stampede to stake claims, only sporadic mining took place and the unprofitable pursuit of that metal there ceased in 1876.

In the 1930s and 1940s, the uniqueness and potential recreational value of the Porcupine Mountains led many people to push for the land to be set aside as either a state or federal park. In 1948, Porcupine Mountains State Park was established.

Porcupine Mountains is also a major winter recreation area. A double chairlift, T-bars and tow ropes lift skiers to the Midwest's highest ski runs, 10 miles of Alpine trails that drop 600 vertical feet. Cross-country skiers can use 25 miles of groomed trails.

County: Ontonagon

City: Ontonagon

Fees: $2.00 daily vehicle permit or $10.00 annual vehicle permit valid in all state parks.

Schedule: Open year round.

Directions: Go 17 miles west of Ontonagon on M-107.

Further Information:
Porcupine Mountains Wilderness State Park
Route 2, M-107
Ontonagon MI 49953

---

159   BARAGA STATE PARK

Located at the tip of Keweenaw Bay, Baraga State Park makes either a good base camp for exploring the wilds and waterfalls of Baraga County or an easily accessible, pleasant stop after a hard day's travel from other Upper Peninsula attractions.

At the back of the park, a .75-mile self-guided nature trail crosses the railroad tracks, then cuts through a typical morainal landscape of aspen, evergreens, hardwoods and deep valleys to the top of a glacial moraine.

But Baraga, though beautiful, is not a place to go for peace and seclusion. The park is relatively small (56 acres), and US-41 cuts directly through it, separating the picnic area and beach on Keweenaw Bay from the 137-site inland campground.

County: Baraga

City: Baraga

Fees: **$2.00 daily vehicle permit or $10.00 annual vehicle permit valid in all state parks.**

Schedule: **Open all summer; Contact park for winter hours.**

Directions: **Go one mile south of Baraga on US-41.**

Further Information:
   Baraga State Park
   Baraga MI 49908

160   TWIN LAKES STATE PARK

One of the warmest inland lakes in the Upper Peninsula plus two scenic overlooks draw more than 25,000 visitors annually to this 175-acre state park on the southwest shore of Lake Ro-land.

Highway M-26 divides the park into two une-

(Continued on page 187.)

County: Houghton

City: Toivola

Fees: **$2.00 daily vehicle permit or $10.00 annual vehicle permit valid in all state parks.**

Schedule: **Open year round.**

Directions: **Go 26 miles south of Houghton on M-26.**

Further Information:
   Twin Lakes State Park
   Route #1, Box 234
   Toivola MI 49965

161 MCLAIN STATE PARK

Located northwest of Hancock, McLain state park stretches for nearly two miles along the edge of Lake Superior not only in the heart of Michigan's picturesque Copper Country but also in the midst of a rock hound's paradise. Outcroppings throughout the area, plus the bedrock that underlies the entire Keweenaw Peninsula is Pre-Cambrian, the oldest rock formations on earth. The serious searcher can also find agates, datolite, pure copper and Isle Royale greenstones. Rock shops, park officers and tourist information services all can give advice on the best places to look.

But there's more to see then just rocks, and there's plenty of room to see it—418 acres to be exact, which includes a long shoreline and extensive pine-, red-oak-, aspen- and birch-covered wooded areas. Among the wildflowers, lucky (and quiet) hikers along the park's two trails might catch a glimpse of deer, beaver, black bear, woodchuck, muskrat, mink, otter and many waterfowl that inhabit the area. The Bear Lake Trail crosses to the south of M-203, which cuts through the park, and borders the shoreline of Bear Lake before circling back to the campground. This trail is open in the winter for cross-country skiing. The Beaver Trail, a one-mile

County: Houghton

City: Hancock

Fees: $2.00 daily vehicle permit or $10.00 annual vehicle permit valid in all state parks.

Schedule: Open year round.

Directions: From Hancock go northwest on M-203 approximately eight miles.

Further Information:
McLain State Park
M-203 Box 82
Hancock MI 49930

fitness trail, starts and ends at the northeast corner of the campground.

Other facilities at McLain include a 90-site (22 on the lakeshore) modern campground and, on the southern edge of the park at the mouth of the Portage Lake Ship Canal, a swimming beach and picnic area. The beach is protected by a seawall and lighthouse that guard the entrance to this canal which links Portage Lake to Lake Superior.

TWIN LAKES STATE PARK
(Continued from page 186.)

qual sections. A 1.5-mile nature trail winds through the majority of the park's acreage, on the northwest side of the pavement, to two scenic overlooks where on a clear day you can see Lake Superior, nearly 10 miles away. Trail mileage in the winter increases to 2.5 miles for cross-country skiers.

Facilities at the day-use area on the southeast side of M-26 include a 62-site campground on the lakeshore, a boat ramp, a picnic area, a bathhouse and a swimming beach.

162 ESTIVANT PINES SANCTUARY

On Michigan's northernmost piece of real estate in 1970, loggers who couldn't see beyond a quick profit were quickly cutting down 500 acres of virgin white pine, the Upper Peninsula's last stand and one of only three or four stands remaining in the entire state. But the Michigan Nature Association stepped in and, with the help of contributions from people throughout the state (but especially the Keweenaw Peninsula), created the Estivant Pines Sanctuary to save a few remaining specimens of Michigan's official state tree.

One of the trees now protected in this 200-acre preserve is the Leaning Giant, at 23 feet in circumference and 120 feet tall, Michigan's largest white pine. This awe-inspiring, alarmingly canted pine, as a matter of fact, is the only one left uncut in a 20-acre parcel on the southern edge of the sanctuary across the Montreal River.

A grove of magnificent cathedral pines located in the center of this quiet, remote land is also impressive and inspiring. Red oak, spruce, tamarack and balsam surround the white pine here, and the sanctuary also shelters several kinds of orchids, rare ferns, beaver, deer, bear and coyote.

A well-marked trail from Burma Road winds through the preserve for a half mile to the cathedral grove and past a beaver pond, then, after another half mile, reaches the Leaning Giant. Several other trails crisscross the area. But because the sanctuary embraces a wild and rugged terrain marked by cliffs, rock outcroppings, abandoned copper mines, dense forest, marshes and swamps, you shouldn't leave the main trail without a compass and topographical map.

County: Keweenaw

City: Copper Harbor

Fees: None.

Schedule: No posted hours.

Directions: On the west side of Copper Harbor, turn south from US-41 onto the road that passes the west end of Lake Fanny Hooe and travel 2.3 miles to Burma Road; turn west (right) and travel .6 miles to the sanctuary entrance; park on the side of the road.

Further Information:
Michigan Nature Association
P.O. Box 102
Avoca MI 48006

163 FORT WILKINS STATE PARK

Wild scenic beauty, rich historical heritage—including the only surviving original wooden fort east of the Mississippi—and its central location for exploring the northern end of the Keweenaw Peninsula are reasons Fort Wilkins is always included on lists of "must-visit" Upper Peninsula state parks. And its setting on a narrow strip of land separating the dark, quiet waters of Lake Fanny Hooe from the rugged rock-tumbled shores of Copper Harbor also ranks it as one of the most beautiful.

Hikers can roam the extensive shoreline on both lakes, bushwhack it into the 199-acre park's large undeveloped areas, or take the Lake Superior Nature Trail. The nature trail, which begins at the picnic area, follows the shore of Lake Fanny Hooe, cuts through the woods, touches the shore of Copper Harbor, then follows the ruggedly beautiful Lake Superior coastline before turning inland along Fanny Hooe Creek back to the park's centerpiece and main attraction, Fort Wilkins.

As men rushed to the Keweenaw Peninsula to make their fortunes mining copper, the U.S. War Department constructed the fort in 1844 to protect the miners from Indians. But instead the fort ended up protecting miners from each other by bringing law and order into the remote area, then crawling with claim jumpers, card sharks and other shady characters drawn to the lure of easy money. The fort was abandoned two short years later when the garrison was sent to fight in the Mexican War and remain unoccupied except for a few years after the Civil War when it was used as a convalescent home.

Of the 16 buildings in the park today, 12 remain from the original construction, and many are completely restored and furnished in period detail. Extensive displays and exhibits on the natural and human history of the fort and peninsula fill other buildings. And interpretive history programs vividly bring to life the northern Michigan frontier of the 1840s.

Facilities at the park stretch along the shore of Lake Fanny Hooe on either side of the fort and include playgrounds, a picnic area and a 165-site campground.

Photographers, especially, will like the scenic views—Lake Superior, a lighthouse on a peninsula, a sheltered bay and several small islands—that come from park property near the harbor. You can visit the lighthouse—built during the 1860s to replace the original structure that had marked the entrance to the harbor since 1848—by taking a tour boat from the Copper Harbor Marina. You can also walk the several acres of shoreline here in relative seclusion.

Because of its central location, the park makes an excellent base for exploring the entire north-

---

County: Keweenaw

City: Copper Harbor

Fees: $2.00 daily vehicle permit or $10.00 annual vehicle permit valid in all state parks.

Schedule: Open daily, 8:00 a.m.-10:00 p.m.; Buildings are closed in the winter.

Directions: Go one mile east of Copper Harbor on US-41.

Further Information:
Fort Wilkins State Park
US-41 East
Copper harbor MI 49918

(Continued on page 190.)

164 BROCKWAY MOUNTAIN DRIVE

The highest above-sea-level roadway anywhere between the Alleghanies and the Rockies is right here in Michigan. It's called Brockway Mountain Drive, and spectacular views come like stop-action movie frames as the pavement twists and turns for 9.5 miles along the edge of precipitous cliffs in the northern Keweenaw Peninsula. An added plus for nature lovers: Two Michigan Nature Association sanctuaries plus some great birdwatching sites are located along the drive.

The volcanic bedrock of Brockway Mountain, which runs like a spine along the northern edge of the peninsula, slopes gently toward Lake Superior to the north, dips below the waters, then thrusts up again miles out in the lake to form Isle

---

County: Keweenaw

City: Copper Harbor

Fees: None.

Schedule: No posted hours.

Directions: To reach the drive, go on M-26 either a half mile south from Copper Harbor or five miles north from Eagle Harbor.

Further Information:
Michigan Nature Association
P.O. Box 102
Avoca MI 48006

Royale. But the south side of the mountain ends abruptly at the edge of a cliff that in many places appears to rise almost vertically from the valley floor 300 feet below. It is along this cliff that Depression-era public-works laborers constructed the road an average of 700 feet above Lake Superior and 1,300 feet above sea level.

At the eastern end, just before the road turns back on itself as it snakes off the mountain, a beautiful panoramic view of Copper Harbor, Lake Superior and Lake Fanny Hooe comes from a scenic overlook with parking facilities. About three miles farther west, spectacular views of the semi-alpine habitat of the surrounding countryside comes from Brockway Mountain Lookout, at 1,337 feet above sea level, the highest point on the drive.

Many of the plants found here are also found on threatened or endangered lists, and Brockway Mountain is the only place in Michigan where a few of those rare species grow. Forty-seven species of trees and shrubs—including shadbush, red-berried elder, buffaloberry, arrowwood, snowberry, and the popular thimbleberry that makes great jams and jellies—grow on the mountain. The list of more than 700 flowers identified here includes trillium, Indian pipe, buttercups, wild strawberry and several kinds of orchids.

(Continued on page 191.)

FORT WILKINS STATE PARK
(Continued from page 189.)

ern part of the Keweenaw Peninsula. Brockway Mountain Drive and Estivant Pines Sanctuary, for example, are both within a couple of miles of the campground. Just a mile south of Copper

Harbor, the city dump, known locally as the "bear pits," attracts carloads of tourists every evening who come to watch bears carefully pick among the refuse looking for new epicurean experiences. Farther south is Lac La Belle and its surrounding waterfalls; farther west is the picturesque village of Eagle Harbor.

165   ISLE ROYALE NATIONAL PARK

If you want to accept the challenge of one of the few true wilderness experiences in the Midwest, or if you just want to enjoy nature about as far away from civilization as you can get without leaving Michigan soil, visit Isle Royale, the most remote national park outside Alaska.

And getting there, as they say, is half the fun. The only way in and out is by boat or plane, which is more than likely why this 134,000-acre island 56 miles northwest of Copper Harbor is also the least-visited national park.

If you come here to hike extensively or backpack, make sure you're experienced and in good shape. Most of the island's rugged wilderness is no place for a novice. And it is important even for experienced hikers to know their limitations. There are no medical facilities on the island, and once you're in the backcountry you are usually hours to several days from food, shelter and even rudimentary first aid. Park officials also advise against leaving the trails to hike cross country because of the extensive undergrowth, bogs and extensive swamp.

But there's really no need to wander from the park's 175 miles of established trails because hikers here have an almost Heinz-57 variety of unique departure points, challenging routes and even unusual endings to choose from. For example, the Greenstone Ridge Trail, the park's longest, follows the spine of the island for 42 miles and requires a minimum of five days to complete. Several other major routes, numerous side trails and short paths and loops—many starting at the island's two main entry points, Rock Harbor and Windigo—web the 44-mile-long by three- to nine-mile-wide island, Lake Superior's largest. You can also arrange to have a seaplane or boat drop you at any of several locations, from which you then trek back to either one of

(Continued on page 192.)

BROCKWAY MOUNTAIN DRIVE

(Continued from page 190.)

To help ensure the preservation of the area's plant life, the Michigan Nature Association, in 1979, acquired the James H. Klipfel Memorial Nature Sanctuary—160 acres within a half mile of the drive's highest point—and the Brockway Mountain Nature Sanctuary, a 78-acre parcel adjacent to the east end. Parking areas at both are good places to leave your car and enjoy some unforgettable scenic vistas plus close-up looks at the flora by walking along the roadway. You can also explore the sanctuaries, but you shouldn't venture into the woods without a compass.

The entire Keweenaw Peninsula is a major spring hawk-migration route. At Brockway Mountain, the drafts created by the cliffs attract numerous hawks that ride the rising air as they effortlessly soar northeast to the end of the peninsula where they strike out across Lake Superior. Since many of the hawks, while using the updrafts, are below the cliff top, observers have the unique opportunity to look down on them. The Klipfel Sanctuary and the adjacent Brockway Mountain Lookout are both excellent locations to watch the spring hawk migration, which reaches its peak in mid-April. At the lookout on one 1976 day, for example, a pair of experienced hawk spotters counted 1,033 birds of prey. Sharp-shinned and Broad-winged hawks were the most plentiful, but also numbered among the day's sightings were Snowy Owls and Bald and Golden eagles.

ISLE ROYALE NATIONAL PARK
(Continued from page 191.)

the information centers. A ferry, too, picks up and drops off passengers as it regularly circles the island.

Backpackers have their choice of 31 campgrounds which are scattered throughout the park. Campfires are not permitted at most sites, so overnighters should bring a backpacking stove. Because tapeworm eggs contaminate all lakes and streams in the park, you must boil all surface water used for washing or cooking for at least two minutes or filter it through a 25-micron water filter. Chemical treatment of the water will not destroy the tapeworm eggs. Neither venomous snakes or spiders nor poison ivy inhabit the park, but in June or July be sure to bring a good supply of insect repellant to repel the regular invasion of black flies and mosquitoes. Groceries, supplies and boat rentals are available at the in-

formation centers at both ends of the island.

For those who don't want to rough it, rooms, housekeeping accommodations and a restaurant are available at the Rock Harbor Information Center. Activities available at this Center include short interpretive trails, daily naturalist programs, slide shows, guided tours by park rangers, day hikes on nature trails and short boat excursions to several nearby islands.

No lodging or meals are available at Windigo, on the island's south end, but like its northern counterpart, this Center, too, has an interpretive trail and similar naturalist programs.

During the summer of 1985, the Isle Royale Natural History Association initiated a new program called Field Seminars. These week-long accredited courses—conducted by professional instructors and available to the public at a an enrollment fee of $50 per person—specialize in the natural setting and history of the island. The Ecology of Isle Royale and Wilderness Photography, for example, were the two seminars conducted in 1985.

The closed environment of Isle Royale has been extensively studied, especially its two most famous inhabitants, moose and wolves. Moose crossed over from the mainland in 1912 when Lake Superior completely froze over. But the herd size fluctuated greatly as it overgrazed the island, died off, then increased again with the reappearance of forage. During the winter of 1948-49, Eastern timber wolves crossed an ice bridge which joined the island to the Canadian shore. Since then the wolves, by preying on the young and sick of the herd, have balanced the cycle of over and under population. Hikers seldom catch a glimpse of the wolves, but sightings of moose are fairly common.

Formed by volcanic eruptions and carved by wind, water and glaciers, Isle Royale is also home to a wide range of flora and wildflowers including 30 varieties of orchid. Beaver and fox also thrive here, but there are no white-tailed deer or bear in the park.

(Continued on page 193.)

ISLE ROYALE NATIONAL PARK

(Continued from page 192.)

Man first came to Isle Royale as early as 2500 B.C. in pursuit of copper. And according to a report by Jean Nicolet, one of the first European visitors, "gold, rubies, and precious stones are found in abundance on the island." Though the Frenchman may have picked up a few pure copper nuggets, pretty agates or Isle Royale Greenstone, no one yet has left the island with gold or rubies in their pockets. Much copper, however, did leave the island and was, in fact, mined until 1899. Isle Royale visitors today can walk beside mines varying in age from a hundred to several thousand years old.

And copper, but not for the mineral's monetary worth, is the reason that the island, though only 15 miles from Canada, ended up in American territory. Benjamin Franklin, a major negotiator of the treaty that ended the American Revolution, made sure the island came into American hands. Why? Franklin, a scientist as well as a politician, wanted to make sure he had a source of copper within national boundaries with which he could continue his experiments with electricity.

Through the years, trappers and fishermen have worked Isle Royale, and until it became a national park in 1940, the island was also an expensive and popular summer resort spot.

County: Keweenaw

City: Houghton

Fees: None.

Schedule: Open April 16 through October 31.

Directions: Although there are no entrance fees to the park, getting there can be expensive. From Houghton, the *Sky Ranger*, a nine-passenger sea plane, makes the daily half-hour flights to the island for $98 round trip per person. The *Ranger III*, a 153-foot ferry, makes the trip twice weekly in six hours. Cost is $48 round trip per person. From Copper Harbor, the *Isle Royale Queen*, a 65-foot 57-passenger vessel takes 4.5 hours to reach Rock Harbor daily at a cost of $44 per person round trip. Advance reservations are required for all methods of transportation.

For schedules and rates write to:
Isle Royale National Park
87 N. Ripley St.
Houghton MI 49931

Isle Royale Seaplane Service
P.O. Box 371
Houghton MI 49931

Isle Royale Ferry Service
Copper Harbor MI 49918

Further Information:
Isle Royale National Park
87 N. Ripley St.
Houghton MI 49931

Appendix I
Alphabetical Listing of Areas

(Continued on page 195)

(Continued on page 196)

Appendix II
Handicapped Access

Many areas included in this book have specifically designed or incorporated special trails and/or other facilities and exhibits for use by the handicapped.

They are:

ALPHABETICAL LISTING
(Continued from page 195)

The Author

Tom Powers, a life-long Michigan resident, divides his time among writing, hiking, birdwatching, reading, traveling and coaching high-school hockey. When not involved in those activities, he can usually be found at the Flint Public Library, where he is the Head of the General Reading Department. Mr. Powers has also welcomed the opportunity to examine, participate in, and perhaps partially solve the cosmic puzzle: Why do authors' biographies in the back of books sound like poorly written advertisements in "Personals" columns?

All of his pursuits are lovingly tolerated by Barbara, his wife of 22 years, and his two children, Chris, 21, and Stephanie, 18.